W9-AFB-829

Stock Investing

for

dummies®

A Wiley Brand

Stock Investing

6th Edition

by Paul Mladjenovic

A Wiley Brand

LONGWOOD PUBLIC LIBRARY

Stock Investing For Dummies®, 6th Edition

Published by: **John Wiley & Sons, Inc.**, 111 River Street, Hoboken, NJ 07030-5774, www.wiley.com

Copyright © 2020 by John Wiley & Sons, Inc., Hoboken, New Jersey

Published simultaneously in Canada

No part of this publication may be reproduced, stored in a retrieval system or transmitted in any form or by any means, electronic, mechanical, photocopying, recording, scanning or otherwise, except as permitted under Sections 107 or 108 of the 1976 United States Copyright Act, without the prior written permission of the Publisher. Requests to the Publisher for permission should be addressed to the Permissions Department, John Wiley & Sons, Inc., 111 River Street, Hoboken, NJ 07030, (201) 748-6011, fax (201) 748-6008, or online at http://www.wiley.com/go/permissions.

Trademarks: Wiley, For Dummies, the Dummies Man logo, Dummies.com, Making Everything Easier, and related trade dress are trademarks or registered trademarks of John Wiley & Sons, Inc., and may not be used without written permission. All other trademarks are the property of their respective owners. John Wiley & Sons, Inc., is not associated with any product or vendor mentioned in this book.

LIMIT OF LIABILITY/DISCLAIMER OF WARRANTY: THE PUBLISHER AND THE AUTHOR MAKE NO REPRESENTATIONS OR WARRANTIES WITH RESPECT TO THE ACCURACY OR COMPLETENESS OF THE CONTENTS OF THIS WORK AND SPECIFICALLY DISCLAIM ALL WARRANTIES, INCLUDING WITHOUT LIMITATION WARRANTIES OF FITNESS FOR A PARTICULAR PURPOSE. NO WARRANTY MAY BE CREATED OR EXTENDED BY SALES OR PROMOTIONAL MATERIALS. THE ADVICE AND STRATEGIES CONTAINED HEREIN MAY NOT BE SUITABLE FOR EVERY SITUATION. THIS WORK IS SOLD WITH THE UNDERSTANDING THAT THE PUBLISHER IS NOT ENGAGED IN RENDERING LEGAL, ACCOUNTING, OR OTHER PROFESSIONAL SERVICES. IF PROFESSIONAL ASSISTANCE IS REQUIRED, THE SERVICES OF A COMPETENT PROFESSIONAL PERSON SHOULD BE SOUGHT. NEITHER THE PUBLISHER NOR THE AUTHOR SHALL BE LIABLE FOR DAMAGES ARISING HEREFROM. THE FACT THAT AN ORGANIZATION OR WEBSITE IS REFERRED TO IN THIS WORK AS A CITATION AND/OR A POTENTIAL SOURCE OF FURTHER INFORMATION DOES NOT MEAN THAT THE AUTHOR OR THE PUBLISHER ENDORSES THE INFORMATION THE ORGANIZATION OR WEBSITE MAY PROVIDE OR RECOMMENDATIONS IT MAY MAKE. FURTHER, READERS SHOULD BE AWARE THAT INTERNET WEBSITES LISTED IN THIS WORK MAY HAVE CHANGED OR DISAPPEARED BETWEEN WHEN THIS WORK WAS WRITTEN AND WHEN IT IS READ.

For general information on our other products and services, please contact our Customer Care Department within the U.S. at 877-762-2974, outside the U.S. at 317-572-3993, or fax 317-572-4002. For technical support, please visit https://hub.wiley.com/community/support/dummies.

Wiley publishes in a variety of print and electronic formats and by print-on-demand. Some material included with standard print versions of this book may not be included in e-books or in print-on-demand. If this book refers to media such as a CD or DVD that is not included in the version you purchased, you may download this material at http://booksupport.wiley.com. For more information about Wiley products, visit www.wiley.com.

Library of Congress Control Number: 2020934807

ISBN 978-1-119-66076-7 (pbk); ISBN 978-1-119-66080-4 (ebk); ISBN 978-1-119-66082-8 (ebk)

Manufactured in the United States of America

SKY10024355_012221

Contents at a Glance

Table of Contents

Introduction

I am thrilled that you have the 6th edition of *Stock Investing For Dummies*, and it is a privilege once again to be the author. I recall finishing the 1st edition literally the night before my son Adam was born in March 2002, and this sixth go-round comes as the stock market enters exciting economic and political territory (2020 is a presidential election year, as you know).

The stock market ended 2019 with the Dow Jones Industrial Average, S&P 500, and Nasdaq all in record territory. As always, no one can tell for sure if 2020–2021 will see new record highs or if a market crash or bear market is near, but if you choose your stocks wisely, you will continue to prosper and make more gains. I think that "choosing wisely" says it all — and it's something this edition strives for. Yes, I do expect bumps and bruises along the way — market pullbacks, crashes, corrections, fabulous up days, and scary down days — but that means that focusing on the stocks of quality companies and exchange-traded funds (ETFs) is more important than ever. Remember that had you bought quality stocks right before the 2008 crash, today you would be sitting on fantastic total returns (capital gains and dividends, too) in spite of that ugly and catastrophic bear market event. So be of good cheer — prudent, long-term investing (versus trading, speculating, or guessing) will have you coming out ahead and beating those investors who didn't read this book!

Successful stock investing takes diligent work and acquired knowledge, like any other meaningful pursuit. This book can definitely help you avoid the mistakes others have made and can point you in the right direction. It gives you a heads-up about trends and conditions that are found in few other stock investing guides. Explore the pages of this book and find the topics that most interest you within the world of stock investing. Let me assure you that I've squeezed more than a quarter-century of experience, education, and expertise between these covers. My track record is as good as (or better than) the track records of many experts who trumpet their successes. More important, I share information to avoid common mistakes (some of which I made myself!). Understanding what not to do can be just as important as figuring out what to do.

In all the years that I've counseled and educated investors, the single difference between success and failure, between gain and loss, has boiled down to two words: applied knowledge. Take this book as your first step in a lifelong learning adventure.

About This Book

The stock market has been a cornerstone of the investor's passive wealth-building program for over a century and continues in this role. Recent years have been one huge roller-coaster ride for stock investors. Fortunes have been made and lost. With all the media attention and all the talking heads on radio and television, the investing public still didn't avoid losing trillions in a historic stock market debacle. Sadly, even the so-called experts who understand stocks didn't see the economic and geopolitical forces that acted like a tsunami on the market. With just a little more knowledge and a few wealth-preserving techniques, more investors could have held onto their hard-earned stock market fortunes. Cheer up, though: This book gives you an early warning on those megatrends and events that will affect your stock portfolio. While other books may tell you about stocks, this book tells you about companies' performance and financial condition and how their stock prices are affected.

This book is designed to give you a realistic approach to making money in stocks. It provides the essence of sound, practical stock investing strategies and insights that have been market-tested and proven from more than 100 years of stock market history. I don't expect you to read it cover to cover, although I'd be delighted if you read every word! Instead, this book is designed as a reference tool. Feel free to read the chapters in whatever order you choose. You can flip to the sections and chapters that interest you or those that include topics that you need to know more about.

Sidebars (boxes of text) in this book give you a more in-depth look at a certain topic. Although they further illuminate a particular point, these sidebars aren't crucial to your understanding of the rest of the book. Feel free to read them or skip them. Of course, I'd love for you to read them all, but my feelings won't be hurt if you decide to skip over them.

The text that accompanies the Technical Stuff icon (see the forthcoming section "Icons Used in This Book") can be passed over as well. The text associated with this icon gives some technical details about stock investing that are certainly interesting and informative, but you can still come away with the information you need without reading this text.

Stock Investing For Dummies, 6th Edition, is also quite different from the "get rich with stocks" titles that have crammed the bookshelves in recent years. It doesn't take a standard approach to the topic; it doesn't assume that stocks are a sure thing and the be-all, end-all of wealth-building. In fact, at times in this book, I tell you *not* to invest in stocks (or even to bet against them!).

This book can help you succeed not only in up markets but also in down markets. Bull markets and bear markets come and go, but the informed investor can keep making money regardless. To give you an extra edge, I've tried to include information about the investing environment for stocks. Whether it's politics or hurricanes (or both), you need to know how the big picture affects your stock investment decisions.

One last note: Within this book, you may note that some web addresses break across two lines of text. If you're reading this book in print and want to visit one of these web pages, simply key in the web address exactly as it's noted in the text, pretending as though the line break doesn't exist. If you're reading this as an e-book, you've got it easy — just click the web address to be taken directly to the web page.

Foolish Assumptions

I figure you've picked up this book for one or more of the following reasons:

» You're a beginner and want a crash course on stock investing that's an easy read.

» You're already a stock investor, and you need a book that allows you to read only those chapters that cover specific stock investing topics of interest to you.

» You need to review your own situation with the information in this book to see whether you missed anything when you invested in that hot stock that your brother-in-law recommended.

» You need a great gift! When Uncle Mo is upset over his poor stock picks, you can give him this book so he can get back on his financial feet. Be sure to get a copy for his broker, too. (Odds are that the broker was the one who made those picks to begin with.)

Icons Used in This Book

Useful icons appear in the margins of this book; here's what they mean.

REMEMBER

When you see this icon, I'm reminding you about some information that you should always keep stashed in your memory, whether you're new to investing or an old pro.

TECHNICAL STUFF

The text attached to this icon may not be crucial to your success as an investor, but it may enable you to talk shop with investing gurus and better understand the financial pages of your favorite business publication or website.

TIP

This icon flags a particular bit of advice that just may give you an edge over other investors.

WARNING

Pay special attention to this icon because the advice can prevent headaches, heart-aches, and financial aches.

Beyond the Book

In addition to the material in the print or digital book you're reading right now, *Stock Investing For Dummies*, 6th Edition, comes with other great content available online. To get the Cheat Sheet, simply go to www.dummies.com and search for "Stock Investing For Dummies Cheat Sheet" in the Search box.

Where to Go from Here

You may not need to read every chapter to make you more confident as a stock investor, so feel free to jump around to suit your personal needs. Because every chapter is designed to be as self-contained as possible, it won't do you any harm to cherry-pick what you really want to read. But if you're like me, you may still want to check out every chapter because you never know when you may come across a new tip or resource that will make a profitable difference in your stock portfolio. I want you to be successful so that I can brag about you in the next edition!

1

The Essentials of Stock Investing

Find out what you should do before you invest your first dollar in stocks. Evaluate your current financial goals and situation.

Know the different approaches to stock investing and which may be right for you.

Figure out the risks of stock investing and discover the best ways around them. Understand the concept of volatility.

Invest in the best stocks with a single exchange-traded fund (ETF) purchase.

Chapter **1**

Surveying the World of Stock Investing

As I write this, the stock market is near an all-time high (circa 29,000), and the economy is rebounding to generational highs in employment and a return to improved prosperity for Main Street America unseen in decades, which bodes well for stock investors in the near term. I think that there are great stock investment opportunities in virtually any time — even for newbies. There are great stocks to help you build your wealth (or provide dividend income) in both up and down markets. In fact, a bear (or down) market can be a great time to buy stocks because they're cheaper (think "sale!"). The key is knowing what to do (and even why), but that's what this book is for!

Today's stock market is a little puzzling, but it can still be rewarding. I can only promise you that if you read this book seriously, you'll do *much* better than the average investor. Note that patience and discipline count now more than ever.

The purpose of this book is not only to tell you about the basics of stock investing but also to let you in on solid strategies that can help you profit from the stock market. Before you invest, you need to understand the fundamentals of stock investing, which I introduce in this chapter. Then I give you an overview of how to put your money where it will count the most.

Understanding the Basics

The basics of stock investing are so elementary that few people recognize them. When you lose track of the basics, you lose track of why you invested to begin with. Part 1 of this book helps you grasp these basics:

>> **Knowing the risk and volatility involved:** Perhaps the most fundamental (and therefore most important) concept to grasp is the risk you face whenever you put your hard-earned money in an investment such as a stock. Related to risk is the concept of volatility. *Volatility* refers to a condition in which there is rapid movement in the price of a particular stock (or other security); investors use this term especially when there's a sudden drop in price in a relatively short period of time. Find out more about risk and volatility in Chapter 4.

>> **Assessing your financial situation:** You need a firm awareness of your starting point and where you want to go. Chapter 2 helps you take stock of your current financial status and your goals.

>> **Understanding approaches to investing:** You want to approach investing in a way that works best for you. Chapter 3 defines the most common approaches to investing.

>> **Seeing what exchange-traded funds have to offer:** Exchange-traded funds (ETFs) are like mutual funds, but they can be traded like stocks. I think that every stock investor should consider ETFs as a positive addition to their portfolio strategies. See Chapter 5 for the lowdown on ETFs.

REMEMBER

The bottom line in stock investing is that you shouldn't immediately send your money to a brokerage account or go to a website and click "buy stock." The first thing you should do is find out as much as you can about what stocks are and how to use them to achieve your wealth–building goals.

Before you continue, I want to clarify exactly what a stock is. *Stock* is a type of security that indicates ownership in a corporation and represents a defined portion (measured in shares) of that corporation's future success. The two primary types of stocks are common and preferred:

>> **Common stock:** This type of stock, which I cover throughout this book, entitles the owner to vote at shareholders' meetings and receive any dividends that the company issues.

>> **Preferred stock:** This type of stock doesn't usually confer voting rights, but it does include some rights that exceed those of common stock. Preferred stockholders, for example, have preferential treatment in certain conditions, such as receiving dividends before common stockholders in the event of a

corporate liquidation or bankruptcy. Additionally, preferred stock seeks to operate similarly to a bond for investors seeking stable income. (In this book I mostly cover common stock.)

In addition to common stock, in this edition, I also cover exchange-traded funds (ETFs) because they can be a valuable part of the stock investor's portfolio.

Preparing to Buy Stocks

Gathering information is critical in your stock-investing pursuits. You should gather information on your stock picks two times: before you invest and after. Obviously, you should become more informed before you invest your first dollar, but you also need to stay informed about what's happening to the company whose stock you buy as well as about the industry and the general economy. To find the best information sources, check out Chapter 6.

When you're ready to invest, you need to open a brokerage account. How do you know which broker to use? Chapter 7 provides some answers and resources to help you choose a broker. After you have opened a brokerage account, it pays to get familiar with the types of orders you can implement inside that account; find out more in Chapter 17.

Knowing How to Pick Winners

When you get past the basics, you can get to the meat of stock-picking. Successful stock-picking isn't mysterious, but it does take some time, effort, and analysis. And the effort is worthwhile because stocks are a convenient and important part of most investors' portfolios. Read the following sections and be sure to leapfrog to the relevant chapters to get the inside scoop on hot stocks.

Recognizing stock value

Imagine that you like eggs, and you're buying them at the grocery store. In this example, the eggs are like companies, and the prices represent the prices that you would pay for the companies' stock. The grocery store is the stock market. What if two brands of eggs are similar, but one costs $2.99 a carton, and the other costs $3.99? Which would you choose? Odds are that you'd look at both brands, judge their quality, and, if they're indeed similar, take the cheaper eggs. The eggs at $3.99 are overpriced. The same is true of stocks. What if you compare two companies that are similar in every respect but have different share prices? All things being equal, the cheaper price represents a better buy for the investor.

But the egg example has another side. What if the quality of the two brands of eggs is significantly different, but their prices are the same? If one brand of eggs is stale, of poor quality, and priced at $2.99 and the other brand is fresh, of superior quality, and also priced at $2.99, which would you get? I'd take the good brand because they're better eggs. Perhaps the lesser eggs are an acceptable purchase at $1.99, but they're overpriced at $2.99. The same example works with stocks. A poorly run company isn't a good choice if you can buy a better company in the marketplace at the same — or a better — price.

REMEMBER

Comparing the value of eggs may seem overly simplistic, but doing so does cut to the heart of stock investing. Eggs and egg prices can be as varied as companies and stock prices. As an investor, you must make it your job to find the best value for your investment dollars. (Otherwise, you get egg on your face. You saw that one coming, right?)

Understanding how market capitalization affects stock value

You can determine a company's value (and thus the value of its stock) in many ways. The most basic way is to look at the company's market value, also known as market capitalization (or market cap). *Market capitalization* is simply the value you get when you multiply all the outstanding shares of a stock by the price of a single share. Calculating the market cap is easy; for example, if a company has 1 million shares outstanding and its share price is $10, the market cap is $10 million.

Small cap, mid cap, and large cap aren't references to headgear; they're references to how large a company is as measured by its market value. Here are the five basic stock categories of market capitalization:

>> **Micro cap (less than $300 million):** These stocks are the smallest, and hence the riskiest, available. (There's even a subsection of micro cap called *nano cap,* which refers to stocks under $50 million, but they're not appropriate for this book.)

>> **Small cap ($300 million to $2 billion):** These stocks fare better than the micro caps and still have plenty of growth potential. The key word here is "potential." Chapter 14 covers small caps and micro caps.

>> **Mid cap ($2 billion to $10 billion):** For many investors, this category offers a good compromise between small caps and large caps. These stocks have some of the safety of large caps while retaining some of the growth potential of small caps.

» **Large cap ($10 billion to $200 billion):** This category is usually best reserved for conservative stock investors who want steady appreciation with greater safety. Stocks in this category are frequently referred to as *blue chips.*

» **Ultra cap or mega cap (more than $200 billion):** These stocks obviously refer to companies that are the biggest of the big. Stocks such as Google and Apple are examples.

REMEMBER

From a safety point of view, a company's size and market value do matter. All things being equal, large cap stocks are considered safer than small cap stocks. However, small cap stocks have greater potential for growth. Compare these stocks to trees: Which tree is sturdier, a giant California redwood or a small oak tree that's just a year old? In a great storm, the redwood holds up well, whereas the smaller tree has a rough time. But you also have to ask yourself which tree has more opportunity for growth. The redwood may not have much growth left, but the small oak tree has plenty of growth to look forward to.

For beginning investors, comparing market cap to trees isn't so far-fetched. You want your money to branch out without becoming a sap.

REMEMBER

Although market capitalization is important to consider, don't invest (or not invest) based solely on it. It's just one measure of value. You need to look at numerous factors that can help you determine whether any given stock is a good investment. Keep reading — this book is full of information to help you decide.

Sharpening your investment skills

Investors who analyze a company can better judge the value of its stock and profit from buying and selling it. Your greatest asset in stock investing is knowledge (and a little common sense). To succeed in the world of stock investing, keep in mind these key success factors:

» **Understand why you want to invest in stocks.** Are you seeking appreciation (capital gains) or income (dividends)? Look at Chapters 8 and 9 for information on these topics.

» **Timing your buys and sells does matter.** Terms like *overbought* and *oversold* can give you an edge when you're deciding whether to purchase or sell a stock. *Technical analysis* is a way to analyze securities through their market activity (past prices and volume) to find patterns that suggest where those investments may be headed in the short term. For more information, see Chapter 10.

- >> **Do some research.** Look at the company whose stock you're considering to see whether it's a profitable business worthy of your investment dollars. Chapters 11 and 12 help you scrutinize companies. If you're considering small cap stocks, then be sure to read Chapter 14.

- >> **Understand and identify what's up with "the Big Picture."** It's a small world after all, and you should be aware of how the world can affect your stock portfolio. Everyone from the bureaucrats in Europe to the politicians in the U.S. Capitol can affect a stock or industry like a match in a dry haystack. Chapters 13 and 15 give you lots of guidance on sector opportunities, megatrends, and, yes, the Big Picture (both economic and political). An excellent way to invest in stocks is through *motifs*, which I cover in Chapter 14.

- >> **Use investing strategies like the pros do.** Chapter 16 gives you the low-down on stock-screening tools that many pros use, which will help you find great stocks very quickly. I'm very big on strategies such as trailing stops and limit orders, and fortunately, today's technology gives you even more tools to help you grow or protect your money so head on over to Chapter 17 for insights on ways to transact stock.

- >> **Look outside the U.S. stock market for opportunities.** It is easier than ever before to profit from stocks offered across the globe! Find out more about investing in international stocks through American Depositary Receipts (ADRs) and international ETFs. Get the details in Chapter 18.

- >> **Consider buying in smaller quantities.** Buying stocks doesn't always mean that you must buy through a broker and that it must be 100 shares. You can buy stock for as little as $25 using programs such as dividend reinvestment plans. Chapter 19 tells you more.

- >> **Do as others do, not as they say.** Sometimes, what people tell you to do with stocks is not as revealing as what people are actually doing. This is why I like to look at company insiders before I buy or sell a particular stock. I even touch on insider trading done by Congress. To find out more about insider buying and selling, read Chapter 20.

- >> **Keep more of the money you earn.** After all your great work in getting the right stocks and making the big bucks, you should know about keeping more of the fruits of your investing. I cover taxes in Chapter 21.

Every chapter in this book offers you valuable guidance on some essential aspect of the fantastic world of stocks. The knowledge you pick up and apply from these pages has been tested over nearly a century of stock-picking. The investment experience of the past — the good, the bad, and some of the ugly — is here for your benefit. Use this information to make a lot of money (and make me proud!). And don't forget to check out the appendixes, where I provide a wide variety of investing resources and financial ratios.

Chapter **2**

Taking Stock of Your Current Financial Situation and Goals

Yes, you want to make the big bucks. Or maybe you just want to get back the big bucks you lost in stocks during the *bear market* (a long period of falling prices) of the infamous global financial crisis of 2008–09. (Investors who followed the guidelines from previous editions of this book did much better than the crowd!) Either way, you want your money to grow so that you can have a better life. But before you make reservations for that Caribbean cruise you're dreaming about, you have to map out your action plan for getting there. Stocks can be a great component of most wealth-building programs, but you must first do some homework on a topic that you should be very familiar with — yourself. That's right. Understanding your current financial situation and clearly defining your financial goals are the first steps in successful investing.

Let me give you an example. I met an investor at one of my seminars who had a million dollars' worth of Procter & Gamble (PG) stock, and he was nearing retirement. He asked me whether he should sell his stock and become more growth-oriented by investing in a batch of *small cap* stocks (stocks of a company worth $250 million to $1 billion; see Chapter 1 for more information). Because he already had enough assets to retire on at that time, I said that he didn't need to get more aggressive. In fact, I told him that he had too much tied to a single stock, even though it was a solid, large company. What would happen to his assets if problems arose at PG? Telling him to shrink his stock portfolio and put that money elsewhere — by paying off debt or adding investment-grade bonds for diversification, for example — seemed obvious.

This chapter is undoubtedly one of the most important chapters in this book. At first, you may think it's a chapter more suitable for some general book on personal finance. Wrong! Unsuccessful investors' greatest weakness is not understanding their financial situations and how stocks fit in. Often, I counsel people to stay out of the stock market if they aren't prepared for the responsibilities of stock investing, such as regularly reviewing the financial statements and progress of the companies they invest in.

REMEMBER

Investing in stocks requires balance. Investors sometimes tie up too much money in stocks, putting themselves at risk of losing a significant portion of their wealth if the market plunges. Then again, other investors place little or no money in stocks and, therefore, miss out on excellent opportunities to grow their wealth. Investors should make stocks a part of their portfolios, but the operative word is *part*. You should let stocks take up only a *portion* of your money. A disciplined investor also has money in bank accounts, investment-grade bonds, precious metals, and other assets that offer growth or income opportunities. Diversification is the key to minimizing risk. (For more on risk, see Chapter 4. I even touch on volatility there.)

Establishing a Starting Point by Preparing a Balance Sheet

Whether you already own stocks or are looking to get into the stock market, you need to find out about how much money you can afford to invest. No matter what you hope to accomplish with your stock investing plan, the first step you should take is to figure out how much you own and how much you owe. To do this, prepare and review your personal balance sheet. A *balance sheet* is simply a list of your assets, your liabilities, and what each item is currently worth so you can arrive at your net worth. Your *net worth* is total assets minus total liabilities. (I know these terms sound like accounting mumbo jumbo, but knowing your net worth is important to your future financial success, so just do it.)

Composing your balance sheet is simple. You can use a spreadsheet program such as Excel, or you can pull out a pencil and a piece of paper. Gather all your financial documents, such as bank and brokerage statements and other such paperwork; you need figures from these documents. Then follow the steps that I outline in the following sections. Update your balance sheet at least once a year to monitor your financial progress (is your net worth going up or down?).

Note: Your personal balance sheet is really no different from balance sheets that giant companies prepare. (The main difference is a few zeros, but you can use my advice in this book to work on changing that.) In fact, the more you find out about your own balance sheet, the easier it is to understand the balance sheet of companies in which you're seeking to invest. See Chapter 11 for details on reviewing company balance sheets.

Step 1: Make sure you have an emergency fund

First, list cash on your balance sheet. Your goal is to have a reserve of at least three to six months' worth of your gross living expenses in cash and cash equivalents. The cash is important because it gives you a cushion. Three to six months' worth is usually enough to get you through the most common forms of financial disruption, such as losing your job.

REMEMBER

If your monthly expenses (or *outgo*) are $2,000, for example, you should have at least $6,000, and probably closer to $12,000, in a secure, FDIC insured, interest-bearing bank account (or another relatively safe, interest-bearing vehicle such as a money market fund). Consider this account an emergency fund, not an investment. Don't use this money to buy stocks.

Too many Americans don't have an emergency fund, meaning that they put themselves at risk. Walking across a busy street while wearing a blindfold is a great example of putting yourself at risk, and in recent years, investors have done the financial equivalent. Investors piled on tremendous debt, put too much into investments (such as stocks) that they didn't understand, and had little or no savings. One of the biggest problems during this past decade was that savings were sinking to record lows while debt levels were reaching new heights. People then sold many stocks because they needed funds for — you guessed it — paying bills and servicing debt.

WARNING

Resist the urge to start thinking of your investment in stocks as a savings account generating more than 20 percent per year. This is dangerous thinking! If your investments tank or if you lose your job, you'll have financial difficulty, and that will affect your stock portfolio; you may have to sell some stocks in your account just to get money to pay the bills. An emergency fund helps you through a temporary cash crunch.

Step 2: List your assets in descending order of liquidity

Liquid assets aren't references to beer or cola (unless you're Anheuser-Busch InBev). Instead, *liquidity* refers to how quickly you can convert a particular *asset* (something you own that has value) into cash. If you know the liquidity of your assets, including investments, you have some options when you need cash to buy some stock (or pay some bills). All too often, people are short on cash and have too much wealth tied up in *illiquid* investments such as real estate. *Illiquid* is just a fancy way of saying that you don't have the immediate cash to meet a pressing need. (Hey, we've all had those moments!) Review your assets and take measures to ensure that enough of them are liquid (along with your illiquid assets).

TIP

Listing your assets in order of liquidity on your balance sheet gives you an immediate picture of which assets you can quickly convert to cash and which ones you can't. If you need money *now*, you can see that cash in hand, your checking account, and your savings account are at the top of the list. The items last in order of liquidity become obvious; they're things like real estate and other assets that can take a long time to convert to cash.

WARNING

Selling real estate, even in a seller's market, can take months. Investors who don't have adequate liquid assets run the risk of having to sell assets quickly and possibly at a loss as they scramble to accumulate the cash for their short-term financial obligations. For stock investors, this scramble may include prematurely selling stocks that they originally intended as long-term investments.

Table 2-1 shows a typical list of assets in order of liquidity. Use it as a guide for making your own asset list.

Here's how to break down the information in Table 2-1:

>> **The first column** describes the asset. You can quickly convert *current assets* to cash — they're more liquid. *Long-term assets* have value, but you can't necessarily convert them to cash quickly — they aren't very liquid.

   Note: I have stocks listed as short-term in the table. The reason is that this balance sheet is meant to list items in order of liquidity. Liquidity is best embodied in the question, "How quickly can I turn this asset into cash?" Because a stock can be sold and converted to cash very quickly, it's a good example of a liquid asset. (However, that's not the main purpose for buying stocks.)

>> **The second column** gives the current market value for that item. Keep in mind that this value isn't the purchase price or original value; it's the amount you'd realistically get if you sold the asset in the current market at that moment.

TABLE 2-1	**Listing Personal Assets in Descending Order of Liquidity**	
Asset Item	Market Value	Annual Growth Rate %
Current assets		
Cash on hand and in checking	$150	
Bank savings accounts and certificates of deposit	$5,000	1%
Stocks	$2,000	11%
Mutual funds	$2,400	9%
Other assets (collectibles and so on)	$240	
Total current assets	**$9,790**	
Long-term assets		
Auto	$1,800	–10%
Residence	$150,000	5%
Real estate investment	$125,000	6%
Personal stuff (such as jewelry)	$4,000	
Total long-term assets	**$280,800**	
Total assets	**$290,590**	

>> **The third column** tells you how well that investment is doing compared to one year ago. If the percentage rate is 5 percent, that item is worth 5 percent more today than it was a year ago. You need to know how well all your assets are doing. Why? So you can adjust your assets for maximum growth or get rid of assets that are losing money. You should keep assets that are doing well (and you should consider increasing your holdings in these assets) and scrutinize assets that are down in value to see whether they're candidates for removal. Perhaps you can sell them and reinvest the money elsewhere. In addition, the realized loss has tax benefits (see Chapter 21).

TIP

Figuring the annual growth rate (in the third column) as a percentage isn't difficult. Say that you buy 100 shares of the stock Gro-A-Lot Corp. (GAL), and its market value on December 31, 2019, is $50 per share for a total market value of $5,000 (100 shares multiplied by $50 per share). When you check its value on December 31, 2020, you find out that the stock is at $60 per share for a total market value of $6,000 (100 shares multiplied by $60). The annual growth rate is 20 percent. You calculate this percentage by taking the amount of the gain ($60 per share – $50 per share = $10 gain per share), which is $1,000 (100 shares times the $10 gain), and dividing it by the value at the beginning of the time period ($5,000). In this case, you get 20 percent ($1,000 divided by $5,000).

TIP

>> What if GAL also generates a dividend of $2 per share during that period — now what? In that case, GAL generates a total return of 24 percent. To calculate the total return, add the appreciation ($10 per share multiplied by 100 shares = $1,000) and the dividend income ($2 per share multiplied by 100 shares = $200) and divide that sum ($1,000 plus $200, or $1,200) by the value at the beginning of the year ($50 per share multiplied by 100 shares, or $5,000). The total return is $1,200 on the $5,000 market value, or 24 percent.

>> **The last line** lists the total for all the assets and their current market value.

Step 3: List your liabilities

Liabilities are simply the bills that you're obligated to pay — your debt. Whether it's a credit card bill or a mortgage payment, a liability is an amount of money you have to pay back eventually (usually with interest). If you don't keep track of your liabilities, you may end up thinking that you have more money than you really do.

Table 2-2 lists some common liabilities. Use it as a model when you list your own. You should list the liabilities according to how soon you need to pay them. Credit card balances tend to be short-term obligations, whereas mortgages are long-term.

TABLE 2-2   **Listing Personal Liabilities**

Liabilities	Amount	Paying Rate %
Credit cards	$4,000	18%
Personal loans	$13,000	10%
Mortgage	$100,000	4%
Total liabilities	$117,000	

Here's a summary of the information in Table 2-2:

REMEMBER

>> **The first column** names the type of debt. Don't forget to include student loans and auto loans if you have them.

Never avoid listing a liability because you're embarrassed to see how much you really owe. Be honest with yourself — doing so helps you improve your financial health.

>> **The second column** shows the current value (or current balance) of your liabilities. List the most current balance to see where you stand with your creditors.

>> **The third column** reflects how much interest you're paying for carrying that debt. This information is an important reminder about how debt can be a wealth zapper. Credit card debt can have an interest rate of 18 percent or more, and to add insult to injury, it isn't even tax-deductible. Using a credit card to make even a small purchase costs you if you don't pay off the balance each month. Within a year, a $50 sweater at 18 percent costs $59 when you add in the annual potential interest on the $50 you paid.

TIP

If you compare your liabilities in Table 2-2 and your personal assets in Table 2-1, you may find opportunities to reduce the amount you pay for interest. Say, for example, that you pay 18 percent on a credit card balance of $4,000 but also have a personal asset of $5,000 in a bank savings account that's earning 2 percent in interest. In that case, you may want to consider taking $4,000 out of the savings account to pay off the credit card balance. Doing so saves you $640; the $4,000 in the bank was earning only $80 (2 percent of $4,000), while you were paying $720 on the credit card balance (18 percent of $4,000). Paying off your debt as soon as possible should always be your first consideration.

If you can't pay off high-interest debt, at least look for ways to minimize the cost of carrying the debt. The most obvious ways include the following:

>> **Replace high-interest cards with low-interest cards.** Many companies offer incentives to consumers, including signing up for cards with favorable rates (recently under 10 percent) that can be used to pay off high-interest cards (typically 12 to 18 percent or higher).

>> **Replace unsecured debt with secured debt.** Credit cards and personal loans are *unsecured* (you haven't put up any collateral or other asset to secure the debt); therefore, they have higher interest rates because this type of debt is considered riskier for the creditor. Sources of *secured debt* (such as home equity line accounts and brokerage accounts) provide you with a means to replace your high-interest debt with lower-interest debt. You get lower interest rates with secured debt because it's less risky for the creditor — the debt is backed up by collateral (your home or your stocks).

>> **Replace variable-interest debt with fixed-interest debt.** Think about how homeowners got blindsided when their monthly payments on adjustable-rate mortgages went up drastically in the wake of the housing bubble that popped during 2005–2008. If you can't lower your debt, at least make it fixed and predictable.

I OWE, I OWE, SO OFF TO WORK I GO

Of course, getting a handle on debt is important in our personal financial situations, but debt could affect you and your financial well-being indirectly. If you're employed by a company that is losing money and subsequently is overly indebted, it can affect your employment. But additionally, it can affect your investments, which in turn can have an adverse effect on your long-term wealth-building plans.

Excessive debt played a huge role in the stock market's painful plunge in 2008 and 2009. The general economy and financial markets are still very vulnerable to debt-related dangers for 2020 and beyond. If individuals and companies managed their liabilities more responsibly, the general economy would be much better off.

According to Bloomberg.com, worldwide debt was a staggering $244 trillion in early 2019. For comparison's sake, the world's GDP during that time frame (according to WorldBank.org) was about $850 trillion (give or take a billion). The greatest portion of that debt comes from the public sector. In the United States, federal, state, and municipal debt are at all-time highs. Everyone has to deal with this debt indirectly because it's incurred by politicians and government bureaucrats but must be addressed by us. The pressure is on for higher income taxes, real estate taxes, and other taxes. Yikes! (Now I know why some people become cave-dwelling hermits.) And yes . . . the stock market (and the stocks in your portfolio) will be affected! A good way to track the "big picture of debt" for the United States is the website www.usdebtclock.org.

WARNING

In 2019, many categories of debt hit all-time highs. Personal, corporate, and especially government debt is at nosebleed heights, while interest rates hit historic lows in 2019. I guess those with burdensome debt should be grateful at the (temporarily!) low levels of interest rates . . . but what if conditions change? What happens when one can't continue to carry his debt? I believe that the massive and pervasive levels of debt will have an ominous impact on both the economy and the stock market; all of us must be diligent in reducing our personal debt loads so we reduce our financial vulnerability. I offer specifics about debt challenges to stock investors in Chapter 25.

Make a diligent effort to control and reduce your debt; otherwise, the debt can become too burdensome. If you don't control it, you may have to sell your stocks just to stay liquid. Remember, Murphy's Law states that you *will* sell your stock at the worst possible moment! Don't go there.

Step 4: Calculate your net worth

Your *net worth* is an indication of your total wealth. You can calculate your net worth with this basic equation: total assets (Table 2-1) minus total liabilities (Table 2-2) equal net worth (net assets or net equity).

Table 2-3 shows this equation in action with a net worth of $173,590 — a very respectable number. For many investors, just being in a position where assets exceed liabilities (a positive net worth) is great news. Use Table 2-3 as a model to analyze your own financial situation. Your mission (if you choose to accept it — and you should) is to ensure that your net worth increases from year to year as you progress toward your financial goals (I discuss financial goals later in this chapter).

TABLE 2-3

Figuring Your Personal Net Worth

Totals	Amounts ($)	Increase from Year Before
Total assets (from Table 2-1)	$290,590	+5%
Total liabilities (from Table 2-2)	($117,000)	–2%
Net worth (total assets less total liabilities)	$173,590	+3%

Step 5: Analyze your balance sheet

After you create a balance sheet (based on the steps in the preceding sections) to illustrate your current finances, take a close look at it, and try to identify any changes you can make to increase your wealth. Sometimes, reaching your financial goals can be as simple as refocusing the items on your balance sheet (use Table 2-3 as a general guideline). Here are some brief points to consider:

>> **Is the money in your emergency (or rainy day) fund sitting in an ultrasafe account and earning the highest interest available?** Bank money market accounts or money market funds are recommended. The safest type of account is a U.S. Treasury money market fund. Banks are backed by the Federal Deposit Insurance Corporation (FDIC), while U.S. treasury securities are backed by the "full faith and credit" of the federal government. Shop around for the best rates at sites such as www.bankrate.com, www.lendingtree.com, and www.lowermybills.com.

>> **Can you replace depreciating assets with appreciating assets?** Say that you have two stereo systems. Why not sell one and invest the proceeds? You may say, "But I bought that unit two years ago for $500, and if I sell it now, I'll get only $300." That's your choice. You need to decide what helps

your financial situation more — a $500 item that keeps shrinking in value (a *depreciating asset*) or $300 that can grow in value when invested (an *appreciating asset*).

» **Can you replace low-yield investments with high-yield investments?** Maybe you have $5,000 in a bank certificate of deposit (CD) earning 3 percent. You can certainly shop around for a better rate at another bank, but you can also seek alternatives that can offer a higher yield, such as U.S. savings bonds or short-term bond funds. Just keep in mind that if you already have a CD and you withdraw the funds before it matures, you may face a penalty (such as losing some interest).

» **Can you pay off any high-interest debt with funds from low-interest assets?** If, for example, you have $5,000 earning 2 percent in a taxable bank account and you have $2,500 on a credit card charging 18 percent (which is not tax-deductible), you may as well pay off the credit card balance and save on the interest.

» **If you're carrying debt, are you using that money for an investment return that's greater than the interest you're paying?** Carrying a loan with an interest rate of 8 percent is acceptable if that borrowed money is yielding more than 8 percent elsewhere. Suppose that you have $6,000 in cash in a brokerage account. If you qualify, you can actually make a stock purchase greater than $6,000 by using *margin* (essentially a loan from the broker). You can buy $12,000 of stock using your $6,000 in cash, with the remainder financed by the broker. Of course, you pay interest on that margin loan. But what if the interest rate is 6 percent and the stock you're about to invest in has a dividend that yields 9 percent? In that case, the dividend can help you pay off the margin loan, and you keep the additional income. (For more on buying on margin, see Chapter 17.)

» **Can you sell any personal stuff for cash?** You can replace unproductive assets with cash from garage sales and auction websites.

» **Can you use your home equity to pay off consumer debt?** Borrowing against your home has more favorable interest rates, and this interest is still tax-deductible.

WARNING

Paying off consumer debt by using funds borrowed against your home is a great way to wipe the slate clean. What a relief to get rid of your credit card balances! Just don't turn around and run up the consumer debt again. You can get overburdened and experience financial ruin (not to mention homelessness). Not a pretty picture.

The important point to remember is that you can take control of your finances with discipline (and with the advice I offer in this book).

Funding Your Stock Program

If you're going to invest money in stocks, the first thing you need is . . . money! Where can you get that money? If you're waiting for an inheritance to come through, you may have to wait a long time, considering all the advances being made in healthcare lately. (What's that? You were going to invest in healthcare stocks? How ironic.) Yet the challenge still comes down to how to fund your stock program.

Many investors can reallocate their investments and assets to do the trick. *Reallocating* simply means selling some investments or other assets and reinvesting that money into something else (such as stocks). It boils down to deciding what investment or asset you can sell or liquidate. Generally, you want to consider those investments and assets that give you a low return on your money (or no return at all). If you have a complicated mix of investments and assets, you may want to consider reviewing your options with a financial planner. Reallocation is just part of the answer; your cash flow is the other part.

Ever wonder why there's so much month left at the end of the money? Consider your cash flow. Your *cash flow* refers to what money is coming in (income) and what money is being spent (outgo). The net result is either a positive cash flow or a negative cash flow, depending on your cash management skills. Maintaining a positive cash flow (more money coming in than going out) helps you increase your net worth. A negative cash flow ultimately depletes your wealth and wipes out your net worth if you don't turn it around immediately.

The following sections show you how to calculate and analyze your cash flow. The first step is to do a cash flow statement. With a cash flow statement, you ask yourself three questions:

>> **What money is coming in?** In your cash flow statement, jot down all sources of income. Calculate income for the month and then for the year. Include everything: salary, wages, interest, dividends, and so on. Add them all up and get your grand total for income.

>> **What is your outgo?** Write down all the things that you spend money on. List all your expenses. If possible, categorize them as essential and nonessential. You can get an idea of all the expenses that you can reduce without affecting your lifestyle. But before you do that, make as complete a list as possible of what you spend your money on.

DOT-COM-AND-GO

If you were publishing a book about negative cash flow, you could look for the employees of any one of 100 dot-com companies to write it. Their qualifications include working for a company that flew sky-high in 1999 and crashed in 2000 and 2001. Companies such as eToys.com, Pets.com, and DrKoop.com were given millions, yet they couldn't turn a profit and eventually closed for business. You may as well call them "dot-com-and-go." You can learn from their mistakes. (Actually, they could have learned from you.) In the same way that profit is the most essential single element in a business, a positive cash flow is important for your finances in general and for funding your stock investment program in particular.

>> **What's left?** If your income is greater than your outgo, you have money ready and available for stock investing. No matter how small the amount seems, it definitely helps. I've seen fortunes built when people started to diligently invest as little as $25 to $50 per week or per month. If your outgo is greater than your income, you better sharpen your pencil. Cut down on nonessential spending and/or increase your income. If your budget is a little tight, hold off on your stock investing until your cash flow improves.

REMEMBER

Don't confuse a cash flow statement with an income statement (also called a *profit and loss statement* or an *income and expense statement*). A cash flow statement is simple to calculate because you can easily track what goes in and what goes out. Income statements are a little different (especially for businesses) because they take into account things that aren't technically cash flow (such as depreciation or amortization). Find out more about income statements in Chapter 11.

TIP

Consider treating regular, small stock investments as an expense in your budget. Many investors have made it a habit of paying $25, $50, or more per month into a dividend reinvestment plan so that they can conveniently build up a stock portfolio with relatively small amounts of money, and they do so with a disciplined approach. For more information on dividend reinvestment plans, head over to Chapter 19.

Step 1: Tally up your income

Using Table 2-4 as a worksheet, list and calculate the money you have coming in. The first column describes the source of the money, the second column indicates the monthly amount from each respective source, and the last column indicates the amount projected for a full year. Include all income, such as wages, business income, dividends, interest income, and so on. Then project these amounts for a year (multiply by 12) and enter those amounts in the third column.

TABLE 2-4

Listing Your Income

Item	Monthly $ Amount	Yearly $ Amount
Salary and wages		
Interest income and dividends		
Business net (after taxes) income		
Other income		
Total income		

REMEMBER

Your total income is the amount of money you have to work with. To ensure your financial health, don't spend more than this amount. Always be aware of and carefully manage your income.

Step 2: Add up your outgo

Using Table 2-5 as a worksheet, list and calculate the money that's going out. How much are you spending and on what? The first column describes the source of the expense, the second column indicates the monthly amount, and the third column shows the amount projected for a full year. Include all the money you spend: credit card and other debt payments; household expenses, such as food, utility bills, and medical expenses; and nonessential expenses such as video games and elephant-foot umbrella stands.

TIP

Payroll taxes is just a category in which to lump all the various taxes that the government takes out of your paycheck. Feel free to put each individual tax on its own line if you prefer. The important thing is creating a comprehensive list that's meaningful to you.

REMEMBER

You may notice that the outgo doesn't include items such as payments to a 401(k) plan and other savings vehicles. Yes, these items do impact your cash flow, but they're not expenses; the amounts that you invest (or your employer invests for you) are essentially assets that benefit your financial situation versus expenses that don't help you build wealth. To account for the 401(k), simply deduct it from the gross pay before you calculate the preceding worksheet (Table 2-5). If, for example, your gross pay is $2,000 and your 401(k) contribution is $300, then use $1,700 as your income figure.

TABLE 2-5 **Listing Your Expenses (Outgo)**

Item	Monthly $ Amount	Yearly $ Amount
Payroll taxes		
Rent or mortgage		
Utilities		
Food		
Clothing		
Insurance (medical, auto, homeowners, and so on)		
Telephone/Internet		
Real estate taxes		
Auto expenses		
Charity		
Recreation		
Credit card payments		
Loan payments		
Other		
Total outgo		

Step 3: Create a cash flow statement

Okay, you're almost to the end. The next step is creating a cash flow statement so that you can see (all in one place) how your money moves — how much comes in and how much goes out and where it goes.

Plug the amount of your total income (from Table 2-4) and the amount of your total expenses (from Table 2-5) into the Table 2-6 worksheet to see your cash flow. Do you have positive cash flow — more coming in than going out — so that you can start investing in stocks (or other investments), or are expenses over-powering your income? Doing a cash flow statement isn't just about finding money in your financial situation to fund your stock program. First and fore-most, it's about your financial well-being. Are you managing your finances well or not?

TABLE 2-6

Looking at Your Cash Flow

Item	Monthly $ Amount	Yearly $ Amount
Total income (from Table 2-4)		
Total outgo (from Table 2-5)		
Net inflow/outflow		

REMEMBER

At the time of this writing, 2019 was shaping up to be yet another record year for personal, government, and business debt. Personal debt and expenses far exceeded whatever income they generated. That announcement is another reminder to watch your cash flow; keep your income growing and your expenses and debt as low as possible.

Step 4: Analyze your cash flow

Use your cash flow statement in Table 2-6 to identify sources of funds for your investment program. The more you can increase your income and decrease your outgo, the better. Scrutinize your data. Where can you improve the results? Here are some questions to ask yourself:

>> How can you increase your income? Do you have hobbies, interests, or skills that can generate extra cash for you?

>> Can you get more paid overtime at work? How about a promotion or a job change?

>> Where can you cut expenses?

>> Have you categorized your expenses as either "necessary" or "nonessential"?

>> Can you lower your debt payments by refinancing or consolidating loans and credit card balances?

>> Have you shopped around for lower insurance or telephone rates?

>> Have you analyzed your tax withholdings in your paycheck to make sure that you're not overpaying your taxes (just to get your overpayment back next year as a refund)?

Another option: Finding investment money in tax savings

According to the Tax Foundation (www.taxfoundation.org), the average U.S. citizen pays more in taxes than for food, clothing, and shelter combined. Sit down with your tax advisor and try to find ways to reduce your taxes. A home-based business, for example, is a great way to gain new income and increase your tax deductions, resulting in a lower tax burden. Your tax advisor can make recommendations that work for you.

TIP

One tax strategy to consider is doing your stock investing in a tax-sheltered account such as a traditional Individual Retirement Account (IRA) or a Roth Individual Retirement Account (Roth IRA). Again, check with your tax advisor for deductions and strategies available to you. For more on the tax implications of stock investing, see Chapter 21.

Setting Your Sights on Your Financial Goals

Consider stocks as tools for living, just like any other investment — no more, no less. Stocks are among the many tools you use to accomplish something — to achieve a goal. Yes, successfully investing in stocks is the goal that you're probably shooting for if you're reading this book. However, you must complete the following sentence: "I want to be successful in my stock investing program to accomplish _____." You must consider stock investing as a means to an end. When people buy a computer, they don't (or shouldn't) think of buying a computer just to have a computer. People buy a computer because doing so helps them achieve a particular result, such as being more efficient in business, playing fun games, or having a nifty paperweight (tsk, tsk).

REMEMBER

Know the difference between long-term, intermediate-term, and short-term goals, and then set some of each (see Chapter 3 for more information):

>> **Long-term goals** refer to projects or financial goals that need funding five or more years from now.

>> **Intermediate-term goals** refer to financial goals that need funding two to five years from now.

>> **Short-term goals** need funding less than two years from now.

REMEMBER

Stocks, in general, are best suited for long-term goals such as these:

>> Achieving financial independence (think retirement funding)

>> Paying for future college costs

>> Paying for any long-term expenditure or project

Some categories of stock (such as conservative or large cap) may be suitable for intermediate-term financial goals. If, for example, you'll retire four years from now, conservative stocks can be appropriate. If you're optimistic (or *bullish*) about the stock market and confident that stock prices will rise, go ahead and invest. However, if you're negative about the market (you're *bearish*, or you believe that stock prices will decline), you may want to wait until the economy starts to forge a clear path.

WARNING

Stocks generally aren't suitable for short-term investing goals because stock prices can behave irrationally in a short period of time. Stocks fluctuate from day to day, so you don't know what the stock will be worth in the near future. You may end up with less money than you expected. For investors seeking to reliably accrue money for short-term needs, short-term bank certificates of deposit or money market funds are more appropriate.

REMEMBER

In recent years, investors have sought quick, short-term profits by trading and speculating in stocks. Lured by the fantastic returns generated by the stock market during 2009–2019, investors saw stocks as a get-rich-quick scheme. It's very important for you to understand the differences among *investing, saving,* and *speculating*. Which one do you want to do? Knowing the answer to this question is crucial to your goals and aspirations. Investors who don't know the difference tend to get burned. Here's some information to help you distinguish among these three actions:

>> ***Investing* is the act of putting your current funds into securities or tangible assets for the purpose of gaining future appreciation, income, or both.** You need time, knowledge, and discipline to invest. The investment can fluctuate in price, but you've chosen it for long-term potential.

>> ***Saving* is the safe accumulation of funds for a future use.** Savings don't fluctuate and are generally free of financial risk. The emphasis is on safety and liquidity.

>> *Speculating* **is the financial world's equivalent of gambling.** An investor who speculates is seeking quick profits gained from short-term price movements in a particular asset or investment. In recent years, many folks have been trading stocks (buying and selling in the short term with frequency), which is in the realm of short-term speculating.

These distinctly different concepts are often confused, even among so-called financial experts. I know of one financial advisor who actually put a child's college fund money into an internet stock fund, only to lose more than $17,000 in less than ten months! For more on the topic of risk, go to Chapter 4.

Chapter 3

Defining Common Approaches to Stock Investing

"Investing for the long term" isn't just some perfunctory investment slogan from a bygone era; it's just as valid today as it was long ago. It's a culmination of proven stock market experience that goes back many decades. Unfortunately, investor buying and selling habits have deteriorated in recent years due to impatience. Today's investors think that short term is measured in days, intermediate term is measured in weeks, and long term is measured in months. Yeesh! No wonder so many folks are complaining about lousy investment returns. Investors have lost the profitable art of patience!

What should you do? Become an investor with a time horizon greater than one year (the emphasis is on "greater"). Give your investments time to grow. Everybody dreams about emulating the success of someone like Warren Buffett, but few emulate his patience (a huge part of his investment success).

Stocks are tools you can use to build your wealth. When used wisely, for the right purpose and in the right environment, they do a great job. But when improperly applied, they can lead to disaster. In this chapter, I show you how to choose the right types of investments based on your short-term, intermediate-term, and long-term financial goals. I also show you how to decide on your purpose for investing (growth or income investing) and your style of investing (conservative or aggressive).

Matching Stocks and Strategies with Your Goals

Various stocks are out there, as well as various investment approaches. The key to success in the stock market is matching the right kind of stock with the right kind of investment situation. You have to choose the stock and the approach that match your goals. (Chapter 2 has more on defining your financial goals.)

REMEMBER

Before investing in a stock, ask yourself, "When do I want to reach my financial goal?" Stocks are a means to an end. Your job is to figure out what that end is — or, more important, when it is. Do you want to retire in ten years or next year? Must you pay for your kid's college education next year or 18 years from now? The length of time you have before you need the money you hope to earn from stock investing determines what stocks you should buy. Table 3-1 gives you some guidelines for choosing the kind of stock best suited for the type of investor you are and the goals you have.

TABLE 3-1   Investor Types, Financial Goals, and Stock Types

Type of Investor	Time Frame for Financial Goals	Type of Stock Most Suitable
Conservative (worries about risk)	Long term (more than 5 years)	Large cap stocks and mid cap stocks
Aggressive (high tolerance to risk)	Long term (more than 5 years)	Small cap stocks and mid cap stocks
Conservative (worries about risk)	Intermediate term (2 to 5 years)	Large cap stocks, preferably with dividends
Aggressive (high tolerance to risk)	Intermediate term (2 to 5 years)	Small cap stocks and mid cap stocks
Short term	1 to 2 years	Stocks are not suitable for the short term. Instead, look at vehicles such as savings accounts and money market funds.
Very short term	Less than 1 year	Stocks? Don't even think about it! Well . . . you *can* invest in stocks for less than a year, but seriously, you're not really investing — you're either trading or short-term speculating. Instead, use savings accounts and money market funds.

TIP

Dividends are payments made to a stock owner (unlike *interest*, which is payment to a creditor). Dividends are a great form of income, and companies that issue dividends tend to have more stable stock prices as well. For more information on dividend-paying stocks, see the later section "Steadily making money: Income investing" as well as Chapter 9.

REMEMBER

Table 3-1 gives you general guidelines, but not everyone fits into a particular profile. Every investor has a unique situation, set of goals, and level of risk tolerance. The terms *large cap, mid cap,* and *small cap* refer to the size (or *market capitalization,* also known as *market cap*) of the company. All factors being equal, large companies are safer (less risky) than small companies. For more on market caps, see the later section "Investing for Your Personal Style" as well as Chapter 1.

Investing for the Future

Are your goals long-term or short-term? Individual stocks can be either great or horrible choices, depending on the time period you want to focus on. Generally, the length of time you plan to invest in stocks can be short-term, intermediate-term, or long-term. The following sections outline what kinds of stocks are most appropriate for each term length.

REMEMBER

Investing in quality stocks becomes less risky as the time frame lengthens. Stock prices tend to fluctuate daily but have a tendency to trend up or down over an extended period of time. Even if you invest in a stock that goes down in the short term, you're likely to see it rise and possibly exceed your investment if you have the patience to wait it out and let the stock price appreciate.

Focusing on the short term

Short term generally means one year or less, although some people extend the period to two years or less. Short-term investing isn't about making a quick buck on your stock choices — it refers to when you may need the money.

Every person has short-term goals. Some are modest, such as setting aside money for a vacation next month or paying for medical bills. Other short-term goals are more ambitious, such as accruing funds for a down payment to purchase a new home within six months. Whatever the expense or purchase, you need a predictable accumulation of cash soon. If this sounds like your situation, stay away from the stock market!

SHORT-TERM INVESTING = SPECULATING

My case files are littered with examples of long-term stock investors who morphed into short-term speculators. I know of one fellow who had $80,000 and was set to get married within 12 months and then put a down payment on a new home for him and his bride. He wanted to surprise her by growing his nest egg quickly so they could have a glitzier wedding and a larger down payment. What happened? The money instead shrank to $11,000 as his stock choices pulled back sharply. Ouch! How does that go again? For better or for worse . . . uh . . . for richer or for poorer? I'm sure they had to adjust their plans accordingly. I recall some of the stocks he chose, and now, years later, those stocks have recovered and gone on to new highs.

The bottom line is that investing in stocks for the short term is nothing more than speculating. Your only possible strategy is luck.

WARNING

Because stocks can be so unpredictable in the short term, they're a bad choice for short-term considerations. I get a kick out of market analysts on TV saying things such as, "At $25 a share, XYZ is a solid investment, and we feel that its stock should hit our target price of $40 within six to nine months." You know an eager investor hears that and says, "Gee, why bother with 1 percent at the bank when this stock will rise by more than 50 percent? I better call my broker." It may hit that target amount (or surpass it), or it may not. Most of the time, the stock doesn't reach the target price, and the investor is disappointed. The stock can even go down!

The reason that target prices are frequently missed is that it's difficult to figure out what millions of investors will do in the short term. The short term can be irrational because so many investors have so many reasons for buying and selling that it can be difficult to analyze. If you invest for an important short-term need, you can lose very important cash quicker than you think.

TECHNICAL STUFF

During the raging bull market of 2002–2007, investors watched as some high-profile stocks went up 20 to 50 percent in a matter of months. Hey, who needs a savings account earning a measly interest rate when stocks grow like that! Of course, when the 2008–2009 bear market hit and those same stocks fell 50 to 85 percent, a savings account earning a measly interest rate suddenly didn't seem so bad. The Dow Jones Industrial Average hit 29,000 in January 2020, but the message and points in this chapter are just as valid.

REMEMBER

Short-term stock investing is very unpredictable. Stocks — even the best ones — fluctuate in the short term. In a negative environment, they can be very volatile. No one can accurately predict the price movement (unless he has some inside information), so stocks are definitely inappropriate for any financial goal you need to reach within one year. You can better serve your short-term goals with stable, interest-bearing investments like certificates of deposit at your local bank. Refer to Table 3-1 for suggestions about your short-term strategies.

Considering intermediate-term goals

Intermediate term refers to the financial goals you plan to reach in two to five years. For example, if you want to accumulate funds to put money down for investment in real estate four years from now, some growth-oriented investments may be suitable. (I discuss growth investing in more detail later in this chapter.)

Although some stocks *may* be appropriate for a two- or three-year period, not all stocks are good intermediate-term investments. Some stocks are fairly stable and hold their value well, such as the stock of large or established dividend-paying companies. Other stocks have prices that jump all over the place, such as those of untested companies that haven't been in existence long enough to develop a consistent track record.

TIP

If you plan to invest in the stock market to meet intermediate-term goals, consider large, established companies or dividend-paying companies in industries that provide the necessities of life (like the food and beverage industry or electric utilities). In today's economic environment, I strongly believe that stocks attached to companies that serve basic human needs should have a major presence in most stock portfolios. They're especially well-suited for intermediate investment goals.

REMEMBER

Just because a particular stock is labeled as being appropriate for the intermediate term doesn't mean you should get rid of it by the stroke of midnight five years from now. After all, if the company is doing well and going strong, you can continue holding the stock indefinitely. The more time you give a well-positioned, profitable company's stock to grow, the better you'll do.

Preparing for the long term

Stock investing is best suited for making money over a long period of time. Usually, when you measure stocks against other investments in terms of five to (preferably) ten or more years, they excel. Even investors who bought stocks during the depths of the Great Depression saw profitable growth in their stock portfolios over a ten-year period. In fact, if you examine any 10-year period over the past 50 years, you see that stocks beat out other financial investments (such as bonds or bank investments) in almost every period when measured by total return (taking into account reinvesting and compounding of capital gains and dividends)!

Of course, your work doesn't stop at deciding on a long-term investment. You still have to do your homework and choose stocks wisely, because even in good times, you can lose money if you invest in companies that go out of business. Part 3 of this book shows you how to evaluate specific companies and industries and alerts you to factors in the general economy that can affect stock behavior. Appendix A provides plenty of resources you can turn to.

REMEMBER

Because so many different types and categories of stocks are available, virtually any investor with a long-term perspective should add stocks to his investment portfolio. Whether you want to save for a young child's college fund or for future retirement goals, carefully selected stocks have proven to be a superior long-term investment.

Investing for a Purpose

When someone asked the lady why she bungee jumped off the bridge that spanned a massive ravine, she answered, "Because it's fun!" When someone asked the fellow why he dove into a pool chock-full of alligators and snakes, he responded, "Because someone pushed me." You shouldn't invest in stocks unless you have a purpose that you understand, like investing for growth or income. Keep in mind that stocks are just a means to an end — figure out your desired end and then match the means. The following sections can help.

TIP

Even if an advisor pushes you to invest, be sure that advisor gives you an explanation of how each stock choice fits your purpose. I know of a very nice, elderly lady who had a portfolio brimming with aggressive-growth stocks because she had an overbearing broker. Her purpose should've been conservative, and she should've chosen investments that would preserve her wealth rather than grow it. Obviously, the broker's agenda got in the way. (To find out more about dealing with brokers, go to Chapter 7.)

Making loads of money quickly: Growth investing

When investors want their money to grow (versus just trying to preserve it), they look for investments that appreciate in value. *Appreciate* is just another way of saying *grow*. If you bought a stock for $8 per share and now its value is $30 per share, your investment has grown by $22 per share — that's appreciation. I know I would appreciate it.

Appreciation is also known as capital gain (*capital gain* is most commonly used when it comes to taxes) and is probably the number-one reason people invest in stocks. Few investments have the potential to grow your wealth as conveniently as stocks. If you want the stock market to make you loads of money (and you can assume some risk), head to Chapter 8, which takes an in-depth look at investing for growth.

WARNING

Stocks are a great way to grow your wealth, but they're not the only way. Many investors seek alternative ways to make money, but many of these alternative ways are more aggressive than stocks and carry significantly more risk. You may have heard about people who made quick fortunes in areas such as commodities (like wheat, pork bellies, or precious metals), options, and other more-sophisticated investment vehicles. Keep in mind that you should limit these riskier investments to only a small portion of your portfolio, such as 5 or 10 percent of your investable funds. Experienced investors can go higher.

Steadily making money: Income investing

Not all investors want to take on the risk that comes with making a killing. (Hey . . . no guts, no glory!) Some people just want to invest in the stock market as a means of providing a steady income. They don't need stock values to go through the ceiling. Instead, they need stocks that perform well consistently.

If your purpose for investing in stocks is to create income, you need to choose stocks that pay dividends. Dividends are typically paid quarterly to stockholders on record as of specific dates. How do you know if the dividend you're being paid is higher (or lower) than other vehicles (such as bonds)? The following sections help you figure it out.

Distinguishing between dividends and interest

Don't confuse dividends with interest. Most people are familiar with interest because that's how you grow your money over the years in the bank. The important difference is that *interest* is paid to creditors, and *dividends* are paid to owners (meaning *shareholders* — and if you own stock, you're a shareholder because shares of stock represent ownership in a publicly traded company).

REMEMBER

When you buy stock, you buy a piece of that company. When you put money in a bank (or when you buy bonds), you basically loan your money. You become a creditor, and the bank or bond issuer is the debtor; as such, it must eventually pay your money back to you with interest.

Recognizing the importance of an income stock's yield

When you invest for income, you have to consider your investment's yield and compare it with the alternatives. The *yield* is an investment's payout expressed as a percentage of the investment amount. Looking at the yield is a way to compare the income you expect to receive from one investment with the expected income from others. Table 3-2 shows some comparative yields.

TABLE 3-2   **Comparing the Yields of Various Investments**

Investment	Type	Amount	Pay Type	Payout	Yield
Smith Co.	Stock	$50/share	Dividend	$2.50	5.0%
Jones Co.	Stock	$100/share	Dividend	$4.00	4.0%
Acme Bank	Bank CD	$500	Interest	$5.00	1.0%
Acme Bank	Bank CD	$2,500	Interest	$31.25	1.25%
Acme Bank	Bank CD	$5,000	Interest	$75.00	1.50%
Brown Co.	Bond	$5,000	Interest	$300.00	6.0%

REMEMBER

To calculate yield, use the following formula:

yield = payout ÷ investment amount

For the sake of simplicity, the following exercise is based on an annual percentage yield basis (compounding would increase the yield).

Jones Co. and Smith Co. are typical dividend-paying stocks. Looking at Table 3-2 and presuming that both companies are similar in most respects except for their differing dividends, how can you tell whether the $50 stock with a $2.50 annual dividend is better (or worse) than the $100 stock with a $4.00 dividend? The yield tells you. Even though Jones Co. pays a higher dividend ($4.00), Smith Co. has a higher yield (5 percent). Therefore, if you have to choose between those two stocks as an income investor, you should choose Smith Co. Of course, if you truly want to maximize your income and don't really need your investment to appreciate a lot, you should probably choose Brown Co.'s bond because it offers a yield of 6 percent.

REMEMBER

Dividend-paying stocks do have the ability to increase in value. They may not have the same growth potential as growth stocks, but at the very least, they have a greater potential for capital gain than CDs or bonds. I cover dividend-paying stocks (good for investing for income) in Chapter 9.

Investing for Your Personal Style

Your investing style isn't a blue-jeans-versus-three-piece-suit debate. It refers to your approach to stock investing. Do you want to be conservative or aggressive? Would you rather be the tortoise or the hare? Your investment personality greatly depends on your purpose and the term over which you're planning to invest (see the previous two sections). The following sections outline the two most general investment styles.

Conservative investing

Conservative investing means that you put your money in something proven, tried, and true. You invest your money in safe and secure places, such as banks and government-backed securities. But how does that apply to stocks? (Table 3-1 gives you suggestions.)

TIP

If you're a conservative stock investor, you want to place your money in companies that exhibit some of the following qualities:

>> **Proven performance:** You want companies that have shown increasing sales and earnings year after year. You don't demand anything spectacular — just a strong and steady performance.

>> **Large market size:** You want to invest in *large cap* companies (short for *large capitalization*). In other words, they should have a market value exceeding $5–$25 billion. Conservative investors surmise that bigger is safer.

>> **Proven market leadership:** Look for companies that are leaders in their industries.

>> **Perceived staying power:** You want companies with the financial clout and market position to weather uncertain market and economic conditions. What happens in the economy or who gets elected shouldn't matter.

REMEMBER

As a conservative investor, you don't mind if the companies' share prices jump (who would?), but you're more concerned with steady growth over the long term.

Aggressive investing

Aggressive investors can plan long term or look over only the intermediate term, but in any case, they want stocks that resemble jackrabbits — those that show the potential to break out of the pack.

TIP

If you're an aggressive stock investor, you want to invest your money in companies that exhibit some of the following qualities:

>> **Great potential:** Choose companies that have superior goods, services, ideas, or ways of doing business compared to the competition.

>> **Capital gains possibility:** Don't even consider dividends. If anything, you dislike dividends. You feel that the money dispensed in dividend form is better reinvested in the company. This, in turn, can spur greater growth.

>> **Innovation:** Find companies that have innovative or disruptive technologies, ideas, or methods that make them stand apart from other companies.

REMEMBER

Aggressive investors usually seek out small capitalization stocks, known as *small caps*, because they can have plenty of potential for growth. Take the tree example, for instance: A giant redwood may be strong, but it may not grow much more, whereas a brand-new sapling has plenty of growth to look forward to. Why invest in big, stodgy companies when you can invest in smaller enterprises that may become the leaders of tomorrow? Aggressive investors have no problem buying stock in obscure businesses because they hope that such companies will become another Apple or McDonald's. Find out more about growth investing in Chapter 8, and check out small cap stocks in Chapter 14.

Chapter **4**

Recognizing Risk and Volatility

I nvestors face many risks, most of which I cover in this chapter. The simplest definition of *risk* for investors is "the possibility that your investment will lose some (or all) of its value." Yet you don't have to fear risk if you understand it and plan for it. You must understand the oldest equation in the world of investing — risk versus return. This equation states the following:

> If you want a greater return on your money, you need to tolerate more risk. If you don't want to tolerate more risk, you must tolerate a lower rate of return.

This point about risk is best illustrated from a moment in one of my investment seminars. One of the attendees told me that he had his money in the bank but was dissatisfied with the rate of return. He lamented, "The yield on my money in the bank is pitiful! I want to put my money somewhere where it can grow." I asked him, "How about investing in common stocks? Or what about growth mutual funds? They have a solid, long-term growth track record." He responded, "Stocks? I don't want to put my money there. It's too risky!" Okay, then. If you don't want to tolerate more risk, don't complain about earning less on your money. Risk (in all its forms) has a bearing on all your money concerns and goals. That's why understanding risk before you invest is so important.

This man — as well as the rest of us — needs to remember that risk is not a four-letter word. (Well, it is a four-letter word, but you know what I mean.) Risk is present no matter what you do with your money. Even if you simply stick your money in your mattress, risk is involved — several kinds of risk, in fact. You have the risk of fire. What if your house burns down? You have the risk of theft. What if burglars find your stash of cash? You also have relative risk. (In other words, what if your relatives find your money?)

Be aware of the different kinds of risk that I describe in this chapter, so you can easily plan around them to keep your money growing. And don't forget risk's kid brother — volatility! Volatility is about the rapid movement in a short time frame (such as a single day of trading) of buying or selling, which, in turn, causes stock prices to rise or fall rapidly. Technically, volatility is considered a "neutral" condition, but it's usually associated with rapid downward movement of stock because that means sudden loss for investors and causes anxiety.

Exploring Different Kinds of Risk

Think about all the ways that an investment can lose money. You can list all sorts of possibilities — so many that you may think, "Holy cow! Why invest at all?"

Don't let risk frighten you. After all, life itself is risky. Just make sure that you understand the different kinds of risk in the following sections before you start navigating the investment world. Be mindful of risk and find out about the effects of risk on your investments and personal financial goals.

Financial risk

The financial risk of stock investing is that you can lose your money if the company whose stock you purchase loses money or goes belly up. This type of risk is the most obvious because companies do go bankrupt.

REMEMBER

You can greatly enhance the chances of your financial risk paying off by doing an adequate amount of research and choosing your stocks carefully (which this book helps you do — see Part 3 for details). Financial risk is a real concern even when the economy is doing well. Some diligent research, a little planning, and a dose of common sense help you reduce your financial risk.

In the stock investing mania of the late 1990s, millions of investors (along with many well-known investment gurus) ignored some obvious financial risks of many then-popular stocks. Investors blindly plunked their money into stocks that were bad choices. Consider investors who put their money in DrKoop.com, a health information website, in 1999 and held on during 2000. This company had no profit and was over-indebted. DrKoop.com went into cardiac arrest as it collapsed from $45 per share to $2 per share by mid-2000. By the time the stock was DOA, investors lost millions. RIP (risky investment play!).

Internet and tech stocks littered the graveyard of stock market catastrophes during 2000–2001 because investors didn't see (or didn't want to see?) the risks involved with companies that didn't offer a solid record of results (profits, sales, and so on). When you invest in companies that don't have a proven track record, you're not investing, you're speculating.

Fast forward to 2008. New risks abounded as the headlines railed on about the credit crisis on Wall Street and the subprime fiasco in the wake of the housing bubble popping. Think about how this crisis impacted investors as the market went through its stomach-churning roller-coaster ride. A good example of a casualty you didn't want to be a part of was Bear Stearns (BSC), which was caught in the subprime buzz saw. Bear Stearns was sky-high at $170 a share in early 2007, yet it crashed to $2 a share by March 2008. Yikes! Its problems arose from massive overexposure to bad debt, and investors could have done some research (the public data was revealing!) and avoided the stock entirely.

Investors who did their homework regarding the financial conditions of companies such as the internet stocks (and Bear Stearns, among others) discovered that these companies had the hallmarks of financial risk — high debt, low (or no) earnings, and plenty of competition. They steered clear, avoiding tremendous financial loss. Investors who didn't do their homework were lured by the status of these companies and lost their shirts.

Of course, the individual investors who lost money by investing in these trendy, high-profile companies don't deserve all the responsibility for their tremendous financial losses; some high-profile analysts and media sources also should have known better. The late 1990s may someday be a case study of how euphoria and the herd mentality (rather than good, old-fashioned research and common sense) ruled the day (temporarily). The excitement of making potential fortunes gets the best of people sometimes, and they throw caution to the wind. Historians may look back at those days and say, "What *were* they thinking?" Achieving true wealth takes diligent work and careful analysis.

REMEMBER

In terms of financial risk, the bottom line is . . . well . . . the bottom line! A healthy bottom line means that a company is making money. And if a company is making money, then you can make money by investing in its stock. However, if a company isn't making money, you won't make money if you invest in it. Profit is the lifeblood of any company. See Chapter 11 for the scoop on determining whether a company's bottom line is healthy.

Interest rate risk

You can lose money in an apparently sound investment because of something that sounds as harmless as "interest rates have changed." Interest rate risk may sound like an odd type of risk, but in fact, it's a common consideration for investors. Be aware that interest rates change on a regular basis, causing some challenging moments. Banks set interest rates, and the primary institution to watch closely is the Federal Reserve (the Fed), which is, in effect, the country's central bank. The Fed raises or lowers its interest rates, actions that, in turn, cause banks to raise or lower their interest rates accordingly. Interest rate changes affect consumers, businesses, and, of course, investors.

Here's a generic introduction to the way fluctuating interest rate risk can affect investors in general: Suppose you buy a long-term, high-quality corporate bond and get a yield of 6 percent. Your money is safe, and your return is locked in at 6 percent. Whew! That's 6 percent. Not bad, huh? But what happens if, after you commit your money, interest rates increase to 8 percent? You lose the opportunity to get that extra 2-percent interest. The only way to get out of your 6-percent bond is to sell it at current market values and use the money to reinvest at the higher rate.

The only problem with this scenario is that the 6-percent bond is likely to drop in value because interest rates rose. Why? Say that the investor is Bob and the bond yielding 6 percent is a corporate bond issued by Lucin-Muny (LM). According to the bond agreement, LM must pay 6 percent (called the *face rate* or *nominal rate*) during the life of the bond and then, upon maturity, pay the principal. If Bob buys $10,000 of LM bonds on the day they're issued, he gets $600 (of interest) every year for as long as he holds the bonds. If he holds on until maturity, he gets back his $10,000 (the principal). So far so good, right? The plot thickens, however.

Say that he decides to sell the bonds long before maturity and that, at the time of the sale, interest rates in the market have risen to 8 percent. Now what? The reality is that no one is going to want his 6-percent bonds if the market is offering bonds at 8 percent. What's Bob to do? He can't change the face rate of 6 percent, and he can't change the fact that only $600 is paid each year for the life of the bonds. What has to change so that current investors get the *equivalent* yield of 8 percent? If you said, "The bonds' value has to go down," bingo! In this example, the bonds' market value needs to drop to $7,500 so that investors buying the bonds get an equivalent yield of 8 percent. (For simplicity's sake, I left out the time it takes for the bonds to mature.) Here's how that figures.

New investors still get $600 annually. However, $600 is equal to 8 percent of $7,500. Therefore, even though investors get the face rate of 6 percent, they get a yield of 8 percent because the actual investment amount is $7,500. In this example, little, if any, financial risk is present, but you see how interest rate risk presents itself. Bob finds out that you can have a good company with a good bond yet still lose $2,500 because of the change in the interest rate. Of course, if Bob doesn't sell, he doesn't realize that loss.

REMEMBER

Historically, rising interest rates have had an adverse effect on stock prices. I outline several reasons why in the following sections. Because our country is top-heavy in debt, rising interest rates are an obvious risk that threatens both stocks and fixed-income securities (such as bonds).

Hurting a company's financial condition

Rising interest rates have a negative impact on companies that carry a large current debt load or that need to take on more debt, because when interest rates rise, the cost of borrowing money rises, too. Ultimately, the company's profitability and ability to grow are reduced. When a company's profits (or earnings) drop, its stock becomes less desirable, and its stock price falls.

Affecting a company's customers

A company's success comes from selling its products or services. But what happens if increased interest rates negatively impact its customers (specifically, other companies that buy from it)? The financial health of its customers directly affects the company's ability to grow sales and earnings.

For a good example, consider Home Depot (HD) during 2005–2008. The company had soaring sales and earnings during 2005 and into early 2006 as the housing boom hit its high point (record sales, construction, and so on). As the housing bubble popped and the housing and construction industries went into an agonizing decline, the fortunes of Home Depot followed suit because its success is directly tied to home building, repair, and improvement. By late 2006, HD's sales were slipping, and earnings were dropping as the housing industry sunk deeper into its depression. This was bad news for stock investors. HD's stock went from more than $44 in 2005 to $21 by October 2008 (a drop of about 52 percent). Ouch! No "home improvement" there.

The point to keep in mind is that because Home Depot's fortunes are tied to the housing industry, and this industry is very sensitive and vulnerable to rising interest rates, in an indirect — but significant — way, Home Depot is also vulnerable. In 2015, HD was one of the few retail stocks that went up due to the rebounding real estate market.

In the years leading up to 2020, interest rates declined. As I write this, there is scuttlebutt about "negative interest rates," which is a hazardous concept. In any case, lower interest rates bode well for stocks and real estate (which means lower interest rates are positive for companies such as HD).

Impacting investors' decision-making considerations

When interest rates rise, investors start to rethink their investment strategies, resulting in one of two outcomes:

>> Investors may sell any shares in interest-sensitive stocks that they hold. Interest-sensitive industries include electric utilities, real estate, and the financial sector. Although increased interest rates can hurt these sectors, the reverse is also generally true: Falling interest rates boost the same industries. Keep in mind that interest rate changes affect some industries more than others.

>> Investors who favor increased current income (versus waiting for the investment to grow in value to sell for a gain later on) are definitely attracted to investment vehicles that offer a higher yield. Higher interest rates can cause investors to switch from stocks to bonds or bank certificates of deposit.

Hurting stock prices indirectly

High or rising interest rates can have a negative impact on any investor's total financial picture. What happens when an investor struggles with burdensome debt, such as a second mortgage, credit card debt, or *margin debt* (debt from borrowing against stock in a brokerage account)? He may sell some stock to pay off some of his high-interest debt. Selling stock to service debt is a common practice that, when taken collectively, can hurt stock prices.

As I write this in 2019, the U.S. economy seems solid, the market indexes (such as the Dow Jones Industrial Average) are at historic highs, and interest rates are at record lows, but storm clouds are gathering. In terms of gross domestic product (GDP), the size of the economy is about $20 trillion (give or take $100 billion), but the debt level is more than $80 trillion (this amount includes personal, corporate, mortgage, college, and government debt). This already enormous amount doesn't include more than $120 trillion of liabilities such as Social Security and Medicare. Additionally (Yikes! There's more?), some U.S. financial institutions hold more than 1.1 quadrillion dollars' worth of derivatives. These can be very complicated and risky investment vehicles that can backfire. Derivatives have, in fact, sunk some large organizations (such as Enron in 2001, Bear Stearns in 2008, and the trading firm Glencore in 2015), and investors should be aware of them. Just check out the company's financial reports. (Find out more in Chapter 12.)

REMEMBER

Because of the effects of interest rates on stock portfolios, both direct and indirect, successful investors regularly monitor interest rates in both the general economy and in their personal situations. Although stocks have proven to be a superior long-term investment (the longer the term, the better), every investor should maintain a balanced portfolio that includes other investment vehicles. A diversified investor has some money in vehicles that do well when interest rates rise. These vehicles include money market funds, U.S. savings bonds (series I), and other variable-rate investments whose interest rates rise when market rates rise. These types of investments add a measure of safety from interest rate risk to your stock portfolio. (I discuss diversification in more detail later in this chapter.)

Market risk

People talk about *the market* and how it goes up or down, making it sound like a monolithic entity instead of what it really is — a group of millions of individuals making daily decisions to buy or sell stock. No matter how modern our society and economic system, you can't escape the laws of supply and demand. When masses of people want to buy a particular stock, it becomes in demand, and its price rises. That price rises higher since the supply of stock is limited. Conversely, if no one's interested in buying a stock (and there are folks selling their stock), its price falls. Supply and demand is the nature of market risk. The price of the stock you purchase can rise and fall on the fickle whim of market demand.

Millions of investors buying and selling each minute of every trading day affect the share price of your stock. This fact makes it impossible to judge which way your stock will move tomorrow or next week. This unpredictability and seeming irrationality is why stocks aren't appropriate for short-term financial growth.

Markets are volatile by nature; they go up and down, and investments need time to grow. Market volatility is an increasingly common condition that everyone has to live with (see the later section "Getting the Scoop on Volatility"). Investors should be aware of the fact that stocks in general, especially in today's marketplace, aren't suitable for short-term (one year or less) goals (see Chapters 2 and 3 for more on short-term goals). Despite the fact that companies you're invested in may be fundamentally sound, all stock prices are subject to the gyrations of the marketplace and need time to trend upward.

WARNING

Investing requires diligent work and research before putting your money in quality investments with a long-term perspective. Speculating is attempting to make a relatively quick profit by monitoring the short-term price movements of a particular investment. Investors seek to minimize risk, whereas speculators don't mind risk because it can also magnify profits. Speculating and investing have clear differences, but investors frequently become speculators and ultimately put themselves and their wealth at risk. Don't go there!

Consider the married couple nearing retirement who decided to play with their money in an attempt to make their pending retirement more comfortable. They borrowed a sizable sum by tapping into their home equity to invest in the stock market. (Their home, which they had paid off, had enough equity to qualify for this loan.) What did they do with these funds? You guessed it; they invested in the high-flying stocks of the day, which were high-tech and internet stocks. Within eight months, they lost almost all their money.

WARNING

Understanding market risk is especially important for people who are tempted to put their nest eggs or emergency funds into volatile investments such as growth stocks (or mutual funds that invest in growth stocks or similar aggressive invest-ment vehicles). Remember, you can lose everything.

Inflation risk

Inflation is the artificial expansion of the quantity of money so that too much money is used in exchange for goods and services. To consumers, inflation shows up in the form of higher prices for goods and services. Inflation risk is also referred to as *purchasing power risk*. This term just means that your money doesn't buy as much as it used to. For example, a dollar that bought you a sandwich in 1980 barely bought you a candy bar a few years later. For you, the investor, this risk means that the value of your investment (a stock that doesn't appreciate much, for example) may not keep up with inflation.

Say that you have money in a bank savings account currently earning 4 percent (in 2019, the bank interest rate is much lower). This account has flexibility — if the market interest rate goes up, the rate you earn in your account goes up. Your account is safe from both financial risk and interest rate risk. But what if inflation is running at 5 percent? At that point you're losing money. I touch on inflation in Chapter 15.

Tax risk

Taxes (such as income tax or capital gains tax) don't affect your stock investment directly, but taxes can obviously affect how much of your money (what portion of your gain) you get to keep. Because the entire point of stock investing is to build wealth, you need to understand that taxes take away a portion of the wealth that you're trying to build. Taxes can be risky because if you make the wrong move with your stocks (selling them at the wrong time, for example), you can end up paying higher taxes than you need to. Because tax laws change so frequently, tax risk is part of the risk-versus-return equation, as well.

It pays to gain knowledge about how taxes can impact your wealth-building pro-gram before you make your investment decisions. Chapter 21 covers the impact of taxes in greater detail, and I also touch on the latest tax law changes that may affect you.

Political and governmental risk

If companies were fish, politics and government policies (such as taxes, laws, and regulations) would be the pond. In the same way that fish die in a toxic or polluted pond, politics and government policies can kill companies. Of course, if you own stock in a company exposed to political and governmental risks, you need to be aware of these risks. For some companies, a single new regulation or law is enough to send them into bankruptcy. For other companies, a new law can help them increase sales and profits.

What if you invest in companies or industries that become political targets? You may want to consider selling them (you can always buy them back later) or consider putting in stop-loss orders on the stock (see Chapter 17). For example, tobacco companies were the targets of political firestorms that battered their stock prices. Whether you agree or disagree with the political machinations of today is not the issue. As an investor, you have to ask yourself, "How do politics affect the market value and the current and future prospects of my chosen investment?" (Chapter 15 gives some insights on how politics can affect the stock market.)

Keep in mind that political risk doesn't just mean in the good ol' US of A; it can also mean geopolitical risk. Many companies have operations across many countries, and geopolitical events can have a major impact on those companies exposed to risks ranging from governmental risks (such as in Venezuela in 2019) to war and unrest (as in the Middle East) to recessions and economic downturns in friendly countries (such as in Western Europe). Appendix A has resources to help with international investing.

TIP

If international investing interests you, and you see it as a good way to be more diversified (beyond the U.S. stock market), then consider exchange-traded funds (ETFs) as a convenient way to do it. Find out more about international ETFs in Chapter 5.

Personal risk

Frequently, the risk involved with investing in the stock market isn't directly related to the investment; rather, the risk is associated with the investor's circumstances.

Suppose that investor Ralph puts $15,000 into a portfolio of common stocks. Imagine that the market experiences a drop in prices that week, and Ralph's stocks drop to a market value of $14,000. Because stocks are good for the long term, this type of decrease usually isn't an alarming incident. Odds are that this dip is temporary, especially if Ralph carefully chose high-quality companies.

Incidentally, if a portfolio of high-quality stocks *does* experience a temporary drop in price, it can be a great opportunity to get more shares at a good price. (Chapter 17 covers orders you can place with your broker to help you do that.)

Over the long term, Ralph will probably see the value of his investment grow substantially. But what if Ralph experiences financial difficulty and needs quick cash during a period when his stocks are declining? He may have to sell his stock to get some money.

This problem occurs frequently for investors who don't have an emergency fund to handle large, sudden expenses. You never know when your company may lay you off or when your basement may flood, leaving you with a huge repair bill. Car accidents, medical emergencies, and other unforeseen events are part of life's bag of surprises — for anyone.

REMEMBER

You probably won't get much comfort from knowing that stock losses are tax-deductible — a loss is a loss (see Chapter 21 for more on taxes). However, you can avoid the kind of loss that results from prematurely having to sell your stocks if you maintain an emergency cash fund. A good place for your emergency cash fund is in either a bank savings account or a money market fund. Then you aren't forced to prematurely liquidate your stock investments to pay emergency bills. (Chapter 2 provides more guidance on having liquid assets for emergencies.)

Emotional risk

What does emotional risk have to do with stocks? Emotions are important risk considerations because investors are human beings. Logic and discipline are critical factors in investment success, but even the best investor can let emotions take over the reins of money management and cause loss. For stock investing, you're likely to be sidetracked by three main emotions: greed, fear, and love. You need to understand your emotions and what kinds of risk they can expose you to. If you get too attached to a sinking stock, you don't need a stock investing book — you need a therapist!

Paying the price for greed

In 1998–2000, millions of investors threw caution to the wind and chased highly dubious, risky dot-com stocks. The dollar signs popped up in their eyes (just like slot machines) when they saw that Easy Street was lined with dot-com stocks that were doubling and tripling in a very short time. Who cares about price/earnings (P/E) ratios when you can just buy stock, make a fortune, and get out with millions? (Of course, *you* care about making money with stocks, so you can flip to Chapter 11 and Appendix B to find out more about P/E ratios.)

WARNING

Unfortunately, the lure of the easy buck can easily turn healthy attitudes about growing wealth into unhealthy greed that blinds investors and discards common sense. Avoid the temptation to invest for short-term gains in dubious hot stocks instead of doing your homework and buying stocks of solid companies with strong fundamentals and a long-term focus, as I explain in Part 3.

Recognizing the role of fear

Greed can be a problem, but fear is the other extreme. People who are fearful of loss frequently avoid suitable investments and end up settling for a low rate of return. If you have to succumb to one of these emotions, at least fear exposes you to less loss.

Also, keep in mind that fear is frequently a symptom of lack of knowledge about what's going on. If you see your stocks falling and don't understand why, fear will take over, and you may act irrationally. When stock investors are affected by fear, they tend to sell their stocks and head for the exits and the lifeboats. When an investor sees his stock go down 20 percent, what goes through his head? Experienced, knowledgeable investors realize that no bull market goes straight up. Even the strongest bull goes up in a zigzag fashion. Conversely, even bear markets don't go straight down; they zigzag down. Out of fear, inexperienced investors sell good stocks when they see them go down temporarily (the *correction*), whereas experienced investors see that temporary downward move as a good buying opportunity to add to their positions.

Looking for love in all the wrong places

Stocks are dispassionate, inanimate vehicles, but people can look for love in the strangest places. Emotional risk occurs when investors fall in love with a stock and refuse to sell it, even when the stock is plummeting and shows all the symptoms of getting worse. Emotional risk also occurs when investors are drawn to bad investment choices just because they sound good, are popular, or are pushed by family or friends. Love and attachment are great in relationships with people but can be horrible with investments. To deal with this emotion, investors have to deploy techniques that take the emotion out. For example, you can use brokerage orders (such as trailing stops and limit orders; see Chapter 17), which can automatically trigger buy and sell transactions and leave out some of the agonizing. Hey, disciplined investing may just become your new passion!

INVESTMENT LESSONS FROM SEPTEMBER 11

September 11, 2001, was a horrific day that is burned in our minds and won't be forgotten in our lifetime. The acts of terrorism that day took more than 3,000 lives and caused untold pain and grief. A much less important aftereffect was the hard lessons that investors learned that day. Terrorism reminds us that risk is more real than ever and that we should never let our guard down. What lessons can investors learn from the worst acts of terrorism to ever happen on U.S. soil? Here are a few pointers:

- **Diversify your portfolio.** Of course, the events of September 11 were certainly surreal and unexpected. But before the events occurred, investors should have made it a habit to assess their situations and see whether they had any vulnerability. Stock investors with no money outside the stock market are always more at risk. Keeping your portfolio diversified is a time-tested strategy that's more relevant than ever before. (I discuss diversification later in this chapter.)

- **Review and reallocate.** September 11 triggered declines in the overall market, but specific industries, such as airlines and hotels, were hit particularly hard. In addition, some industries, such as defense and food, saw stock prices rise. Monitor your portfolio and ask yourself whether it's overly reliant on or exposed to events in specific sectors. If so, reallocate your investments to decrease your risk exposure.

- **Check for signs of trouble.** Techniques such as trailing stops (which I explain in Chapter 17) come in very handy when your stocks plummet because of unexpected events. Even if you don't use these techniques, you can make it a regular habit to check your stocks for signs of trouble, such as debts or P/E ratios that are too high. If you see signs of trouble, consider selling.

Getting the Scoop on Volatility

How often have you heard a financial guy on TV say, "Well, it looks like a volatile day as the markets plunge 700 points. . . ." Oh dear . . . pass me the antacid! Volatility has garnered a bad reputation because roller coasters and weak stomachs don't mix — especially when your financial future seems to be acting like a kite in a tornado.

People may think of volatility as "risk on steroids," but you need to understand what volatility actually is. Technically, it isn't really good or bad (although it's usually associated with bad movements in the marketplace). *Volatility* is the movement of an asset (or the entire market) very quickly down (or up) in price due to large selling (or buying) in a very short period of time.

WHY MORE VOLATILITY?

People will always gasp at the occasional big up or down day, but volatility is more prevalent overall today than, say, 10 or 20 years ago. Why is that? There are several contributing factors:

- First of all, today's investor has the advantages of cheaper commissions and faster technology. Years ago, if an investor wanted to sell, she had to call the broker — usually during business hours. On top of that, the commission was usually $30 or higher. That discouraged a lot of rapid-fire trading. Today, trading is not only cheaper (with web-based discount brokers), but anyone can do it from home with a few clicks of a mouse on a website literally 24 hours a day, 7 days a week.

- In addition, large organizations — ranging from financial institutions to government-sponsored entities such as sovereign wealth funds — can make large trades or huge amounts of money either nationally or globally within split seconds. The rapid movement of large amounts of money both in and out of a stock or an entire market means that volatility is high and likely to be with us for a long time to come.

- Lastly, the world is now more of a global marketplace, and our markets react more to international events than in the past. With new technology and the internet, news travels farther and faster than ever before.

Volatility tends to be more associated with the negative because of crowd psychology. People are more likely to act quickly (sell!) because of fear than because of other motivators (such as greed; see the earlier section "Emotional risk" for more info). More people are apt to run for the exits than they are to run to the entrance, so to speak.

Not all stocks are equal with regard to volatility. Some can be very volatile, whereas others can be quite stable. A good way to determine a stock's volatility is to look at the beta of the stock. *Beta* is a statistical measure that attempts to give the investor a clue as to how volatile a stock may be. It's determined by comparing the potential volatility of a particular stock to the market in general. The market (as represented by, say, the Standard & Poor's 500) is assigned a beta of 1. Any stock with a beta greater than 1 is considered more volatile than the general stock market, whereas any stock with a beta of less than 1 is considered less volatile. If a stock has a beta of 1.5, for example, it's considered 50 percent more volatile than the general market. Meanwhile, a stock with a beta of 0.85 is considered 15 percent less volatile than the general stock market. In other words, this stock would decline 8.5 percent if the market were to decline 10 percent.

TIP

Therefore, if you don't want to keep gulping down more antacid, consider stocks that have a beta of less than 1. You can easily find the beta in the stock report pages that are usually provided by major financial websites such as Yahoo! Finance (finance.yahoo.com) and MarketWatch (www.marketwatch.com). (See Appendix A for more financial websites.)

Minimizing Your Risk

Now, before you go crazy thinking that stock investing carries so much risk that you may as well not get out of bed, take a breath. Minimizing your risk in stock investing is easier than you think. Although wealth-building through the stock market doesn't take place without some amount of risk, you can practice the following tips to maximize your profits and still keep your money secure.

Gaining knowledge

REMEMBER

Some people spend more time analyzing a restaurant menu to choose a $20 entrée than analyzing where to put their next $5,000. Lack of knowledge constitutes the greatest risk for new investors, so diminishing that risk starts with gaining knowledge. The more familiar you are with the stock market — how it works, factors that affect stock value, and so on — the better you can navigate around its pitfalls and maximize your profits. The same knowledge that enables you to grow your wealth also enables you to minimize your risk. Before you put your money anywhere, you want to know as much as you can. This book is a great place to start — check out Chapter 6 for a rundown of the kinds of information you want to know before you buy stocks, as well as the resources that can give you the information you need to invest successfully.

Staying out until you get a little practice

If you don't understand stocks, don't invest! Yeah, I know this book is about stock investing, and I think that some measure of stock investing is a good idea for most people. But that doesn't mean you should be 100 percent invested 100 percent of the time. If you don't understand a particular stock (or don't understand stocks, period), stay away until you do. Instead, give yourself an imaginary sum of money, such as $100,000, give yourself reasons to invest, and just make believe (a practice called *simulated stock investing*). Pick a few stocks that you think will increase in value, track them for a while, and see how they perform. Begin to understand how the price of a stock goes up and down, and watch what happens to the stocks you choose when various events take place. As you find out more about stock investing, you get better at picking individual stocks, without risking — or losing — any money during your learning period.

TIP

A good place to do your imaginary investing is at websites such as How the Market Works (www.howthemarketworks.com). You can design a stock portfolio and track its performance with thousands of other investors to see how well you do.

Putting your financial house in order

Advice on what to do before you invest could be a whole book all by itself. The bottom line is that you want to make sure that you are, first and foremost, financially secure before you take the plunge into the stock market. If you're not sure about your financial security, look over your situation with a financial planner. (You can find more on financial planners in Appendix A.)

REMEMBER

Before you buy your first stock, here are a few things you can do to get your finances in order:

>> **Have a cushion of money.** Set aside three to six months' worth of your gross living expenses somewhere safe, such as in a bank account or treasury money market fund, in case you suddenly need cash for an emergency (see Chapter 2 for details).

>> **Reduce your debt.** Overindulging in debt was the worst personal economic problem for many Americans in the late 1990s, and this practice has continued in recent years. As of 2019, debt across the board has climbed to new all-time highs. Ideally, you should strive to have zero credit card debt; interest rates on credit cards are very high, so getting to zero as soon as possible is a sure wealth-building strategy!

>> **Make sure that your job is as secure as you can make it.** Are you keeping your skills up to date? Is the company you work for strong and growing? Is the industry that you work in strong and growing?

>> **Make sure that you have adequate insurance.** You need enough insurance to cover your needs and those of your family in case of illness, death, disability, and so on.

Diversifying your investments

Diversification is a strategy for reducing risk by spreading your money across different investments. It's a fancy way of saying, "Don't put all your eggs in one basket." But how do you go about divvying up your money and distributing it among different investments?

The easiest way to understand proper diversification may be to look at what you *shouldn't* do:

>> **Don't put all your money in one stock.** Sure, if you choose wisely and select a hot stock, you may make a bundle, but the odds are tremendously against you. Unless you're a real expert on a particular company, it's a good idea to have small portions of your money in several different stocks. As a general rule, the money you tie up in a single stock should be money you can do without.

>> **Don't put all your money in one industry.** I know people who own several stocks, but the stocks are all in the same industry. Again, if you're an expert in that particular industry, it can work out. But just understand that you're not properly diversified. If a problem hits an entire industry, you may get hurt.

>> **Don't put all your money in one type of investment.** Stocks may be a great investment, but you need to have money elsewhere. Bonds, bank accounts, treasury securities, real estate, and precious metals are perennial alternatives to complement your stock portfolio. Some of these alternatives can be found in mutual funds or exchange-traded funds (ETFs). An *exchange-traded fund* is a fund with a fixed portfolio of stocks or other securities that tracks a particular index but is traded like a stock. By the way, I love ETFs, and I think that every serious investor should consider them; see Chapter 5 for more information.

Okay, now that you know what you *shouldn't* do, what *should* you do? Until you become more knowledgeable, follow this advice:

>> **Keep only 5 to 10 percent (or less) of your investment money in a single stock.** Because you want adequate diversification, you don't want overexposure to a single stock. Aggressive investors can certainly go for 10 percent or even higher, but conservative investors are better off at 5 percent or less.

>> **Invest in four or five (and no more than ten) different stocks that are in different industries.** Which industries? Choose industries that offer products and services that have shown strong, growing demand. To make this decision, use your common sense (which isn't as common as it used to be). Think about the industries that people need no matter what happens in the general economy, such as food, energy, and other consumer necessities. See Chapter 13 for more information about analyzing sectors and industries.

BETTER LUCK NEXT TIME!

A little knowledge can be very risky. Consider the true story of one "lucky" fellow who played the California lottery in 1987. He discovered that he had a winning ticket, with the first prize of $412,000. He immediately ordered a Porsche, booked a lavish trip to Hawaii for his family, and treated his wife and friends to a champagne dinner at a posh Hollywood restaurant. When he finally went to collect his prize, he found out that he had to share first prize with more than 9,000 other lottery players who also had the same winning numbers. His share of the prize was actually only $45! Hopefully, he invested that tidy sum based on his increased knowledge about risk. (That story always cracks me up.)

Weighing Risk against Return

How much risk is appropriate for you, and how do you handle it? Before you try to figure out what risks accompany your investment choices, analyze yourself. Here are some points to keep in mind when weighing risk versus return in your situation:

>> **Your financial goal:** In five minutes with a financial calculator, you can easily see how much money you're going to need to become financially independent (presuming financial independence is your goal). Say that you need $500,000 in ten years for a worry-free retirement and that your financial assets (such as stocks, bonds, and so on) are currently worth $400,000. In this scenario, your assets need to grow by only 2.25 percent to hit your target. Getting investments that grow by 2.25 percent safely is easy to do because that's a relatively low rate of return.

REMEMBER

The important point is that you don't have to knock yourself out trying to double your money with risky, high-flying investments; some run-of-the-mill bank investments will do just fine. All too often, investors take on more risk than is necessary. Figure out what your financial goal is so that you know what kind of return you realistically need. Flip to Chapters 2 and 3 for details on determining your financial goals.

>> **Your investor profile:** Are you nearing retirement, or are you fresh out of college? Your life situation matters when it comes to looking at risk versus return:

• If you're just beginning your working years, you can certainly tolerate greater risk than someone facing retirement. Even if you lose big time, you still have a long time to recoup your money and get back on track.

- However, if you're within five years of retirement, risky or aggressive investments can do much more harm than good. If you lose money, you don't have as much time to recoup your investment, and odds are that you'll need the investment money (and its income-generating capacity) to cover your living expenses after you're no longer employed.

>> **Asset allocation:** I never tell retirees to put a large portion of their retirement money into a high-tech stock or other volatile investment. But if they still want to speculate, I don't see a problem as long as they limit such investments to 5 percent of their total assets. As long as the bulk of their money is safe and sound in secure investments (such as U.S. Treasury bonds), I know I can sleep well (knowing that *they* can sleep well!).

REMEMBER

Asset allocation beckons back to diversification, which I discuss earlier in this chapter. For people in their 20s and 30s, having 75 percent of their money in a diversified portfolio of growth stocks (such as mid cap and small cap stocks; see Chapter 1) is acceptable. For people in their 60s and 70s, it's not acceptable. They may, instead, consider investing no more than 20 percent of their money in stocks (mid caps and large caps are preferable). Check with your financial advisor to find the right mix for your particular situation.

Chapter **5**

Stock Investing through Exchange-Traded Funds

When it comes to stock investing, there's more than one way to do it. Buying stocks directly is good; sometimes, buying stocks indirectly is equally good (or even better) — especially if you're risk-averse. Buying a great stock is every stock investor's dream, but sometimes you face investing environments that make finding a winning stock a hazardous pursuit. For 2020–2021, prudent stock investors should definitely consider adding exchange-traded funds to their wealth-building arsenal.

An *exchange-traded fund* (ETF) is basically a mutual fund that invests in a fixed basket of securities but with a few twists. In this chapter, I show you how ETFs are similar to (and different from) mutual funds (MFs), I provide some pointers on picking ETFs, and I note the fundamentals of stock indexes (which are connected to ETFs).

Comparing Exchange-Traded Funds and Mutual Funds

For many folks and for many years, the only choice besides investing directly in stocks was to invest indirectly through mutual funds (MFs). After all, why buy a single stock for roughly the same few thousand dollars that you can buy a mutual fund for and get benefits such as professional management and diversification?

For small investors, mutual fund investing isn't a bad way to go. Investors participate by pooling their money with others and get professional money management in an affordable manner. But MFs have their downsides too. Mutual fund fees, which include management fees and sales charges (referred to as *loads*), eat into gains, and investors have no choice about investments after they're in a mutual fund. Whatever the fund manager buys, sells, or holds onto is pretty much what the investors in the fund have to tolerate. Investment choice is limited to either being in the fund . . . or out.

But now, with the advent of ETFs, investors have greater choices than ever, a scenario that sets the stage for the inevitable comparison between MFs and ETFs. The following sections go over the differences and similarities between ETFs and MFs.

The differences

Simply stated, in a mutual fund, securities such as stocks and bonds are constantly bought, sold, and held (in other words, the fund is *actively managed*). An ETF holds similar securities, but the portfolio typically isn't actively managed. Instead, an ETF usually holds a fixed basket of securities that may reflect an index or a particular industry or sector (see Chapter 13). An *index* is a method of measuring the value of a segment of the general stock market. It's a tool used by money managers and investors to compare the performance of a particular stock to a widely accepted standard; see the later section "Taking Note of Indexes" for more details.

For example, an ETF that tries to reflect the S&P 500 will attempt to hold a securities portfolio that mirrors the composition of the S&P 500 as closely as possible. Here's another example: A water utilities ETF may hold the top 35 or 40 publicly held water companies. (You get the picture.)

REMEMBER

Where ETFs are markedly different from MFs (and where they're really advantageous, in my opinion) is that they can be bought and sold like stocks. In addition, you can do with ETFs what you can generally do with stocks (but can't usually do with MFs): You can buy in share allotments, such as 1, 50, or 100 shares or more. MFs, on the other hand, are usually bought in dollar amounts, such as 1,000 or 5,000 dollars' worth. The dollar amount you can initially invest is set by the manager of the individual mutual fund.

Here are some other advantages: You can put various buy/sell brokerage orders on ETFs (see Chapter 17), and many ETFs are *optionable* (meaning you may be able to buy/sell put and call options on them; I discuss some strategies with options in Chapters 23 and 24). MFs typically aren't optionable. I cover put and call options extensively in my book *High-Level Investing For Dummies* (Wiley).

WARNING

Keep in mind that put and call options are typically very speculative, so use them sparingly, and find out as much as possible about their pros and cons before you decide to use them in your stock investing account. Keep in mind that most option strategies are usually not allowed in stock/ETF portfolios within retirement accounts.

In addition, many ETFs are *marginable* (meaning that you can borrow against them with some limitations in your brokerage account). MFs usually aren't marginable when purchased directly (although it is possible if they're within the confines of a stock brokerage account). To find out more about margin, check out Chapter 17.

REMEMBER

Sometimes an investor can readily see the great potential of a given industry or sector but is hard-pressed to get that single really good stock that can take advantage of the profit possibilities of that particular segment of the market. The great thing about an ETF is that you can make that investment very easily, knowing that if you're unsure about it, you can put in place strategies that protect you from the downside (such as stop-loss orders or trailing stops). That way, you can sleep easier!

The similarities

Even though ETFs and mutual funds have some major differences, they do share a few similarities:

>> First and foremost, ETFs and MFs are similar in that they aren't direct investments; they're "conduits" of investing, which means that they act like a connection between the investor and the investments.

>> Both ETFs and MFs basically pool the money of investors and the pool becomes the "fund," which in turn invests in a portfolio of investments.

>> Both ETFs and MFs offer the great advantage of diversification (although they accomplish it in different ways).

>> Investors don't have any choice about what makes up the portfolio of either the ETF or the MF. The ETF has a fixed basket of securities (the money manager overseeing the portfolio makes those choices), and, of course, investors can't control the choices made in a mutual fund.

TIP

For those investors who want more active assistance in making choices and running a portfolio, the MF may very well be the way to go. For those who are more comfortable making their own choices in terms of the particular index or industry/sector they want to invest in, the ETF may be a better venue.

Choosing an Exchange-Traded Fund

Buying a stock is an investment in a particular company, but an ETF is an opportunity to invest in a block of stocks. In the same way a few mouse clicks can buy you a stock at a stock brokerage website, those same clicks can buy you virtually an entire industry or sector (or at least the top-tier stocks anyway).

For investors who are comfortable with their own choices and do their due diligence, a winning stock is a better (albeit more aggressive) way to go. For those investors who want to make their own choices but aren't that confident about picking winning stocks, an ETF is definitely a better way to go.

You had to figure that choosing an ETF wasn't going to be a coin flip. There are considerations that you should be aware of, some of which are tied more to your personal outlook and preferences than to the underlying portfolio of the ETF. I give you the info you need on bullish and bearish ETFs in the following sections.

TIP

Picking a winning industry or sector is easier than finding a great company to invest in. Therefore, ETF investing goes hand in hand with the guidance offered in Chapter 13.

Bullish ETFs

You may wake up one day and say, "I think that the stock market will do very well going forward from today," and that's just fine if you think so. Maybe your research on the general economy, financial outlook, and political considerations makes you feel happier than a starving man on a cruise ship. But you just don't know (or don't care to research) which stocks would best benefit from the good market moves yet to come. No problem!

In the following sections, I cover ETF strategies for bullish scenarios, but fortunately, ETF strategies for bearish scenarios exist too. I cover those later in this chapter.

Major market index ETFs

Why not invest in ETFs that mirror a general major market index such as the S&P 500? ETFs such as SPY construct their portfolios to track the composition of the S&P 500 as closely as possible. As they say, why try to beat the market when you can match it? It's a great way to go when the market is having a good rally. (See the later section "Taking Note of Indexes" for the basics on indexes.)

When the S&P 500 was battered in late 2008 and early 2009, the ETF for the S&P 500, of course, mirrored that performance and hit the bottom in March 2009. But from that moment on and into 2015, the S&P 500 (and the ETFs that tracked it) did extraordinarily well. It paid to buck the bearish sentiment of early 2009. Of course, it did take some contrarian gumption to do so, but at least you had the benefit of the full S&P 500 stock portfolio, which at least had more diversification than a single stock or a single subsection of the market. Of course, as the S&P 500 entered the bull market of 2009–2015, bullish ETFs that mirrored the S&P 500 did very well while the ETFs that were inverse to the S&P 500 (betting on a bearish move) declined in the same period.

ETFs related to human need

Some ETFs cover industries such as food and beverage, water, energy, and other things that people will keep buying no matter how good or bad the economy is. Without needing a crystal ball or having an iron-will contrarian attitude, a stock investor can simply put money into stocks — or in this case, ETFs — tied to human need. Such ETFs may even do better than ETFs tied to major market indexes (see the preceding section).

Here's an example: At the end of 2007 (mere months before the great 2008–2009 market crash), what would have happened if you had invested 50 percent of your money in an ETF that represented the S&P 500 and 50 percent in an ETF that was in consumer staples (such as food and beverage stocks)? I did such a comparison, and it was quite revealing to note that by the end of 2015, the consumer staples ETF (for the record I used one with the securities symbol PBJ) actually beat out the S&P 500 ETF by more than 45 percent (not including dividends). Very interesting!

ETFs that include dividend-paying stocks

ETFs don't necessarily have to be tied to a specific industry or sector; they can be tied to a specific type or subcategory of stock. All things being equal, what basic categories of stocks do you think would better weather bad times: stocks with no dividends or stocks that pay dividends? (I guess the question answers itself, pretty much like, "What tastes better: apple pie or barbed wire?") Although some sectors are known for being good dividend payers, such as utilities (and there are some good ETFs that cover this industry), some ETFs cover stocks that meet specific criteria.

You can find ETFs that include high-dividend income stocks (typically 3.5 percent or higher) as well as ETFs that include stocks of companies that don't necessarily pay high dividends but do have a long track record of dividend increases that meet or exceed the rate of inflation.

TIP

Given these types of dividend-paying ETFs, it becomes clear which is good for what type of stock investor:

>> If I were a stock investor who was currently retired, I'd choose the high-dividend stock ETF. Dividend-paying stock ETFs are generally more stable than those stock ETFs that don't pay dividends, and dividends are important for retirement income.

>> If I were in "pre-retirement" (some years away from retirement but clearly planning for it), I'd choose the ETF with the stocks that had a strong record of growing the dividend payout. That way, those same dividend-paying stocks would grow in the short term and provide better income down the road during retirement.

For more information on dividend investing strategies (and other income ideas), head over to Chapter 9.

REMEMBER

Keep in mind that dividend-paying stocks generally fall within the criteria of human need investing because those companies tend to be large and stable, with good cash flows, giving them the ongoing wherewithal to pay good dividends.

TIP

To find out more about ETFs in general and to get more details on the ETFs I mention in this chapter (SPY, PBJ, and SH), go to websites such as www.etfdb.com and www.etfguide.com. Many of the resources in Appendix A also cover ETFs.

Bearish ETFs

Most ETFs are bullish in nature because they invest in a portfolio of securities that they expect to go up in due course. But some ETFs have a bearish focus. Bearish ETFs (also called *short ETFs*) maintain a portfolio of securities and strategies that are designed to go the opposite way of the underlying or targeted securities. In other words, this type of ETF goes up when the underlying securities go down (and vice versa). Bearish ETFs employ securities such as *put options* (and similar derivatives) and/or employ strategies such as "going short" (see Chapter 17).

Take the S&P 500, for example. If you were bullish on that index, you might choose an ETF such as SPY. However, if you were bearish on that index and wanted to seek gains by betting that it would go down, you could choose an ETF such as SH.

You can take two approaches on bearish ETFs:

>> **Hoping for a downfall:** If you're speculating on a pending market crash, a bearish ETF is a good consideration. In this approach, you're actually seeking to make a profit based on your expectations. Those folks who aggressively

went into bearish ETFs during early or mid-2008 made some spectacular profits during the tumultuous downfall during late 2008 and early 2009.

>> **Hedging against a downfall:** A more conservative approach is to use bearish ETFs to a more moderate extent, primarily as a form of hedging, whereby the bearish ETF acts like a form of insurance in the unwelcome event of a significant market pullback or crash. I say "unwelcome" because you're not really hoping for a crash; you're just trying to protect yourself with a modest form of diversification. In this context, diversification means that you have a mix of both bullish positions and, to a smaller extent, bearish positions.

Taking Note of Indexes

For stock investors, ETFs that are bullish or bearish are ultimately tied to major market indexes. You should take a quick look at indexes to better understand them (and the ETFs tied to them).

Whenever you hear the media commentary or the scuttlebutt at the local watering hole about "how the market is doing," it typically refers to a market proxy such as an index. You'll usually hear them mention "the Dow" or perhaps "the S&P 500." There are certainly other major market indexes, and there are many lesser, yet popular, measurements, such as the Dow Jones Transportation Average. Indexes and averages tend to be used interchangeably, but they're distinctly different entities of measurement.

Most people use these indexes basically as standards of market performance to see whether they're doing better or worse than a yardstick for comparison purposes. They want to know continuously whether their stocks, ETFs, MFs, or overall portfolios are performing well.

TIP

Appendix A gives you resources to help you gain a fuller understanding of indexes. You can also find great resources online, such as www.dowjones.com, www.spindices.com, and www.investopedia.com, that give you the history and composition of indexes. For your purposes, these are the main ones to keep an eye on:

>> **Dow Jones Industrial Average (DJIA):** This is the most widely watched index (technically it's not an index, but it's utilized as one). It tracks 30 widely owned, large cap stocks, and it's occasionally re-balanced to drop (and replace) a stock that's not keeping up.

- **Nasdaq Composite:** This covers a cross section of stocks from Nasdaq. It's generally considered a mix of stocks that are high-growth (riskier) companies with an over-representation of technology stocks.

- **S&P 500 index:** This index tracks 500 leading, publicly traded companies considered to be widely held. The publishing firm Standard & Poor's created this index (I bet you could've guessed that).

- **Wilshire 5000:** This index is considered the widest sampling of stocks across the general stock market and, therefore, a more accurate measure of stock market movement.

TIP

If you don't want to go nuts trying to "beat the market," consider an ETF that closely correlates to any of the indexes mentioned in the preceding list. Sometimes it's better to join 'em than to beat 'em. The resources in Appendix A can help you find an index you believe is suitable for you. You can find ETFs that track or mirror the preceding indexes at sites such as www.etfdb.com.

INTERNATIONAL INVESTING MADE EASY

Interested in investing in stocks on the international scene? Does Europe, China, or India interest you? Perhaps Singapore or Australia appeal to you, but finding a good stock seems a little daunting. Why not do it in a safer way through ETFs? (By the way, international investing is covered in Chapter 18.) Many ETFs invest in a cross section of the major stocks in a given country. So why buy an individual stock when you can get the top 40 or 50 stocks in that country's stock market?

In this chapter, you discover the advantages of ETFs, so including a batch of international stocks in your portfolio is easier than ever. To find major international ETFs, go to www.etfdb.com, and use the country's name in your keyword search. Just remember to do your homework on that country (geopolitical risks and so on) with the help of CIA World Fact Book (www.ciaworldfactbook.us) and the *Financial Times* (www.ft.com). You can find other resources in Appendix A. Of course, if you get skittish about holding such ETFs, you can minimize the risks with techniques such as with stop-loss orders, which I cover in Chapter 17.

2 Before You Start Buying

Know the best information sources for finding great stocks.

Discover how to find and choose a good stock brokerage firm.

Investigate the key elements of a great growth stock.

Find out how to gain cash flow by choosing a solid dividend-income stock and understanding how to write covered calls.

Familiarize yourself with basic technical indicators for short-term stock moves.

IN THIS CHAPTER

» Using stock exchanges to get investment information

» Applying accounting and economic know-how to your investments

» Keeping abreast of financial news

» Deciphering stock tables

» Understanding dividend dates

» Recognizing good (and bad) investing advice

Chapter 6

Gathering Information

Knowledge and information are two critical success factors in stock investing. (Isn't that true about most things in life?) People who plunge headlong into stocks without sufficient knowledge of the stock market in general, and current information in particular, quickly learn the lesson of the eager diver who didn't find out ahead of time that the pool was only an inch deep (ouch!). In their haste to avoid missing so-called golden investment opportunities, investors too often end up losing money.

REMEMBER

Opportunities to *make* money in the stock market will always be there, no matter how well or how poorly the economy and the market are performing in general. There's no such thing as a single (and fleeting) magical moment, so don't feel that if you let an opportunity pass you by, you'll always regret that you missed your one big chance.

For the best approach to stock investing, build your knowledge and find quality information first so you can make your fortunes more assuredly. Before you buy, you need to know that the company you're investing in is

>> Financially sound and growing

>> Offering products and/or services that are in demand by consumers

>> In a strong and growing industry (and general economy)

Where do you start, and what kind of information do you want to acquire? Keep reading.

Looking to Stock Exchanges for Answers

Before you invest in stocks, you need to be completely familiar with the basics of stock investing. At its most fundamental, stock investing is about using your money to buy a piece of a company that will give you value in the form of appreciation or income (or both). Fortunately, many resources are available to help you find out about stock investing. Some of my favorite places are the stock exchanges themselves.

Stock exchanges are organized marketplaces for the buying and selling of stocks (and other securities). The New York Stock Exchange (NYSE; also referred to as the *Big Board*), the premier stock exchange, provides a framework for stock buyers and sellers to make their transactions. The NYSE makes money not only from a cut of every transaction but also from fees (such as listing fees) charged to companies and brokers that are members of its exchanges. In 2007, the NYSE merged with Euronext, a major European exchange, but no material differences exist for stock investors. In 2008, the American Stock Exchange (Amex) was taken over by (and completely merged into) the NYSE. The new name is NYSE American.

The main exchanges for most stock investors are the NYSE and Nasdaq. Technically, Nasdaq isn't an exchange, but it's a formal market that effectively acts as an exchange. Because the NYSE and Nasdaq benefit from increased popularity of stock investing and continued demand for stocks, they offer a wealth of free (or low-cost) resources and information for stock investors. Go to their websites to find useful resources such as the following:

>> Tutorials on how to invest in stocks, common investment strategies, and so on

>> Glossaries and free information to help you understand the language, practice, and purpose of stock investing

» A wealth of news, press releases, financial data, and other information about companies listed on the exchange or market, usually accessed through an on-site search engine

» Industry analysis and news

» Stock quotes and other market information related to the daily market movements of stocks, including data such as volume, new highs, new lows, and so on

» Free tracking of your stock selections (you can input a sample portfolio or the stocks you're following to see how well you're doing)

TIP

What each exchange/market offers keeps changing and is often updated, so explore them periodically at their respective websites:

» New York Stock Exchange: www.nyse.com

» Nasdaq: www.nasdaq.com

Grasping the Basics of Accounting and Economics

Stocks represent ownership in companies. Before you buy individual stocks, you want to understand the companies whose stock you're considering and find out about their operations. It may sound like a daunting task, but you'll digest the point more easily when you realize that companies work very similarly to the way you work. They make decisions on a daily basis just as you do.

Think about how you grow and prosper as an individual or as a family, and you see the same issues with businesses and how they grow and prosper. Low earnings and high debt are examples of financial difficulties that affect both people and companies. You can better understand companies' finances by taking the time to pick up some information in two basic disciplines: accounting and economics. These two disciplines, which I discuss in the following sections, play a significant role in understanding the performance of a firm's stock.

Accounting for taste and a whole lot more

REMEMBER

Accounting. Ugh! But face it: Accounting is the language of business, and believe it or not, you're already familiar with the most important accounting concepts! Just look at the following three essential principles:

» **Assets minus liabilities equals net worth.** In other words, take what you own (your *assets*), subtract what you owe (your *liabilities*), and the rest is yours (your *net worth*)! Your own personal finances work the same way as Microsoft's (except yours have fewer zeros at the end). See Chapter 2 to figure out how to calculate your own net worth.

A company's *balance sheet* shows you its net worth at a specific point in time (such as December 31). The net worth of a company is the bottom line of its asset and liability picture, and it tells you whether the company is *solvent* (has the ability to pay its debts without going out of business). The net worth of a successful company grows regularly. To see whether your company is successful, compare its net worth with the net worth from the same point a year earlier. A firm that has a $4 million net worth on December 31, 2018, and a $5 million net worth on December 31, 2019, is doing well; its net worth has gone up 25 percent ($1 million) in one year.

» **Income minus expenses equals net income.** In other words, take what you make (your *income*), subtract what you spend (your *expenses*), and the remainder is your *net income* (or *net profit* or *net earnings* — your gain).

A company's profitability is the whole point of investing in its stock. As it profits, the business becomes more valuable, and in turn, its stock price becomes more valuable. To discover a firm's net income, look at its income statement. Try to determine whether the company uses its gains wisely, either by reinvesting them for continued growth or by paying down debt.

» **Do a comparative financial analysis.** That's a mouthful, but it's just a fancy way of saying how a company is doing now compared with something else (like a prior period or a similar company).

If you know that the company you're looking at had a net income of $50,000 for the year, you may ask, "Is that good or bad?" Obviously, making a net profit is good, but you also need to know whether it's good compared to something else. If the company had a net profit of $40,000 the year before, you know that the company's profitability is improving. But if a similar company had a net profit of $100,000 the year before and in the current year is making $50,000, then you may want to either avoid the company making the lesser profit or see what (if anything) went wrong with the company making less.

Accounting can be this simple. If you understand these three basic points, you're ahead of the curve (in stock investing as well as in your personal finances). For more information on how to use a company's financial statements to pick good stocks, see Chapters 11 and 12.

Understanding how economics affects stocks

Economics. Double ugh! No, you aren't required to understand "the inelasticity of demand aggregates" (thank heavens!) or "marginal utility" (say what?). But a working knowledge of basic economics is crucial (and I mean crucial) to your success and proficiency as a stock investor. The stock market and the economy are joined at the hip. The good (or bad) things that happen to one have a direct effect on the other. The following sections give you the lowdown.

Getting the hang of the basic concepts

REMEMBER

Alas, many investors get lost on basic economic concepts (as do some so-called experts you see on TV). I owe my personal investing success to my status as a student of economics. Understanding basic economics helps me (and will help you) filter the financial news to separate relevant information from the irrelevant in order to make better investment decisions. Be aware of these important economic concepts:

>> **Supply and demand:** How can anyone possibly think about economics without thinking of the ageless concept of supply and demand? *Supply and demand* can be simply stated as the relationship between what's available (the supply) and what people want and are willing to pay for (the demand). This equation is the main engine of economic activity and is extremely important for your stock investing analysis and decision-making process. I mean, do you really want to buy stock in a company that makes elephant-foot umbrella stands if you find out that the company has an oversupply and nobody wants to buy them anyway?

>> **Cause and effect:** If you pick up a prominent news report and read, "Companies in the table industry are expecting plummeting sales," do you rush out and invest in companies that sell chairs or manufacture tablecloths? Considering cause and effect is an exercise in logical thinking, and believe you me, logic is a major component of sound economic thought.

When you read business news, play it out in your mind. What good (or bad) can logically be expected given a certain event or situation? If you're looking for an effect ("I want a stock price that keeps increasing"), you also want to understand the cause. Here are some typical events that can cause a stock's price to rise:

- **Positive news reports about a company:** The news may report that the company is enjoying success with increased sales or a new product.

- **Positive news reports about a company's industry:** The media may be highlighting that the industry is poised to do well.

- **Positive news reports about a company's customers:** Maybe your company is in industry A, but its customers are in industry B. If you see good news about industry B, that may be good news for your stock.

- **Negative news reports about a company's competitors:** If the competitors are in trouble, their customers may seek alternatives to buy from, including your company.

>> **Economic effects from government actions:** Political and governmental actions have economic consequences. As a matter of fact, nothing (and I mean nothing!) has a greater effect on investing and economics than government. Government actions usually manifest themselves as taxes, laws, or regulations. They also can take on a more ominous appearance, such as war or the threat of war. Government can willfully (or even accidentally) cause a company to go bankrupt, disrupt an entire industry, or even cause a depression. Government controls the money supply, credit, and all public securities markets. For more information on political effects, see Chapter 15.

Gaining insight from past mistakes

Because most investors ignored some basic observations about economics in the late 1990s, they subsequently lost trillions in their stock portfolios during 2000–2002. During 2000–2008, the United States experienced the greatest expansion of total debt in history, coupled with a record expansion of the money supply. The Federal Reserve (or "the Fed"), the U.S. government's central bank, controls both. This growth of debt and money supply resulted in more consumer (and corporate) borrowing, spending, and investing. The debt and spending that hyperstimulated the stock market during the late 1990s (stocks rose 25 percent per year for five straight years during that time period) came back with a vengeance afterwards.

When the stock market bubble popped during 2000–2002, it was soon replaced with the housing bubble, which popped during 2005–2006. And during the writing of this book, February 2020 witnessed a major correction (the Dow Jones industrials, for example, fell over 11 percent during the five trading days ending February 28) over fears due to the coronavirus originating in China and causing a worldwide panic.

Of course, you should always be happy to earn 25 percent per year with your investments, but such a return can't be sustained and encourages speculation. This artificial stimulation by the Fed resulted in the following:

>> More and more people depleted their savings. After all, why settle for less than 1 percent in the bank when you can get so much more in the stock market?

>> More and more people bought on credit (such as auto loans, brokerage margin loans, and so on). If the economy is booming, why not buy now and pay later? Consumer credit hit record highs.

>> More and more people borrowed against their homes. Why not borrow and get rich now? "I can pay off my debt later" was at the forefront of these folks' minds at the time.

>> More and more companies sold more goods as consumers took more vacations and bought SUVs, electronics, and so on. Companies then borrowed to finance expansion, open new stores, and so on.

>> More and more companies went public and offered stock to take advantage of the increase in money that was flowing to the markets from banks and other financial institutions.

In the end, spending started to slow down because consumers and businesses became too indebted. This slowdown in turn caused the sales of goods and services to taper off. Companies were left with too much overhead, capacity, and debt because they had expanded too eagerly. At this point, businesses were caught in a financial bind. Too much debt and too many expenses in a slowing economy mean one thing: Profits shrink or disappear. To stay in business, companies had to do the logical thing — cut expenses. What's usually the biggest expense for companies? People! Many companies started laying off employees. As a result, consumer spending dropped further because more people were either laid off or had second thoughts about their own job security.

As people had little in the way of savings and too much in the way of debt, they had to sell their stock to pay their bills. This trend was a major reason that stocks started to fall in 2000. Earnings started to drop because of shrinking sales from a sputtering economy. As earnings fell, stock prices also fell.

With some hiccups along the way, the stock market has solidly zigzagged upward since the early 2000s, and the Dow Jones breached the 29,000 level in early 2020, but investors should be just as wary when the market is at nosebleed levels as they are when bear markets hit because market highs tend to be followed by the next bear market or downward move. Stock markets in February 2020 did correct painfully (a fall of 10 percent or more is a correction; a bear market is 20 percent or more), and they offered a buying opportunity for value-oriented investors.

KNOW THYSELF BEFORE YOU INVEST IN STOCKS

If you're reading this book, you're probably doing so because you want to become a successful investor. Granted, to be a successful investor, you have to select great stocks, but having a realistic understanding of your own financial situation and goals is equally important. I recall one investor who lost $10,000 in a speculative stock. The loss wasn't that bad because he had most of his money safely tucked away elsewhere. He also understood that his overall financial situation was secure and that the money he lost was "play" money — the loss wouldn't have a drastic effect on his life. But many investors often lose even more money, and the loss does have a major, negative effect on their lives. You may not be like the investor who can afford to lose $10,000. Take time to understand yourself, your own financial picture, and your personal investment goals before you decide to buy stocks. See Chapter 2 for guidance.

REMEMBER

The lessons from the 1990s and the 2000–2020 time frame are important ones for investors today:

>> Stocks are not a replacement for savings accounts. Always have some money in the bank.

>> Stocks should never occupy 100 percent of your investment funds.

>> When anyone (including an expert) tells you that the economy will keep growing indefinitely, be skeptical and read diverse sources of information.

>> If stocks do well in your portfolio, consider protecting your stocks (both your original investment and any gains) with stop-loss orders. See Chapter 17 for more on these strategies.

>> Keep debt and expenses to a minimum.

>> If the economy is booming, a decline is sure to follow as the ebb and flow of the economy's business cycle continues.

Staying on Top of Financial News

Reading the financial news can help you decide where or where not to invest. Many newspapers, magazines, and websites offer great coverage of the financial world. Obviously, the more informed you are, the better, but you don't have to read everything that's written. The information explosion in recent years has gone beyond overload, and you can easily spend so much time reading that you have little time left for investing. In the following sections, I describe the types of information you need to get from the financial news.

TIP

Appendix A of this book provides more information on the following resources, along with a treasure trove of some of the best publications, resources, and websites to assist you:

>> The most obvious publications of interest to stock investors are *The Wall Street Journal* (www.wsj.com) and *Investor's Business Daily* (www.investors.com). These excellent publications report the news and stock data as of the prior trading day.

>> Some of the more obvious websites are MarketWatch (www.marketwatch.com), Yahoo! Finance (http://finance.yahoo.com), Bloomberg (www.bloomberg.com), and Investing.com (www.investing.com). These websites can actually give you news and stock data within minutes after an event occurs.

>> Don't forget the exchanges' websites that I list in the earlier section "Looking to Stock Exchanges for Answers."

Figuring out what a company's up to

Before you invest, you need to know what's going on with the company. When you read about the company, either from the firm's literature (its annual report, for example) or from media sources, be sure to get answers to some pertinent questions:

>> **Is the company making more net income than it did last year?** You want to invest in a company that's growing.

>> **Are the company's sales greater than they were the year before?** Keep in mind that you won't make money if the company isn't making money.

>> **Is the company issuing press releases on new products, services, inventions, or business deals?** All these achievements indicate a strong, vital company.

Knowing how the company is doing, no matter what's happening with the general economy, is obviously important. To better understand how companies tick, see Chapters 11 and 12.

Discovering what's new with an industry

As you consider investing in a stock, make a point of knowing what's going on in that company's industry. If the industry is doing well, your stock is likely to do well, too. But then again, the reverse is also true.

Yes, I've seen investors pick successful stocks in a failing industry, but those cases are exceptional. By and large, it's easier to succeed with a stock when the entire industry is doing well. As you're watching the news, reading the financial pages, or viewing financial websites, check out the industry to ensure that it's strong and dynamic. See Chapter 13 for information on analyzing sectors and megatrends.

Knowing what's happening with the economy

No matter how well or how poorly the overall economy is performing, you want to stay informed about its general progress. It's easier for the value of stock to keep going up when the economy is stable or growing. The reverse is also true: If the economy is contracting or declining, the stock has a tougher time keeping its value. Some basic items to keep tabs on include the following:

>> **Gross domestic product (GDP):** The GDP is roughly the total value of output for a particular nation, measured in the dollar amount of goods and services. It's reported quarterly, and a rising GDP bodes well for your stock. When the GDP is rising 3 percent or more on an annual basis, that's solid growth. If it rises but is less than 3 percent, that's generally considered less than stellar (or mediocre). A GDP under zero (a negative number) means that the economy is shrinking (heading into recession).

>> **The index of leading economic indicators (LEI):** The LEI is a snapshot of a set of economic statistics covering activity that precedes what's happening in the economy. Each statistic helps you understand the economy in much the same way that barometers (and windows!) help you understand what's happening with the weather. Economists don't just look at an individual statistic; they look at a set of statistics to get a more complete picture of what's happening with the economy.

Chapter 15 goes into greater detail on economics and its effect on stock prices.

Seeing what politicians and government bureaucrats are doing

Being informed about what public officials are doing is vital to your success as a stock investor. Because federal, state, and local governments pass literally thousands of laws, rules, and regulations every year, monitoring the political landscape is critical to your success. The news media report what the president and Congress are doing, so always ask yourself, "How does a new law, tax, or regulation affect my stock investment?"

TIP

You can find laws being proposed or enacted by the federal government through Congress's search page (www.congress.gov). Also, some great organizations inform the public about tax laws and their impact, such as the National Taxpayers Union (www.ntu.org) and the Tax Foundation (www.taxfoundation.org). Chapter 15 gives you more insights into politics and its effect on the stock market.

Checking for trends in society, culture, and entertainment

As odd as it sounds, trends in society, popular culture, and entertainment affect your investments, directly or indirectly. For example, when you see a headline such as "There are now more millennials than Baby Boomers," you should find out what their buying habits are, what products and services they favor, and so on. Understanding the basics of demographic shifts can give you some important insights that can help you make wiser long-term choices in your stock portfolio. With that particular headline, you know that companies that are well positioned to cater to that growing market's wants and needs will do well — meaning a successful stock pick for you.

Keep your eyes open to emerging trends in society at large by reading and viewing the media that cover such matters (*Time* magazine, CNN, and so on; other media are in Appendix A). What trends are evident now? Can you anticipate the wants and needs of tomorrow's society? Being alert, staying a step ahead of the public, and choosing stocks appropriately gives you a profitable edge over other investors. If you own stock in a solid company with growing sales and earnings, other investors eventually notice. As more investors buy up your company's stock, you're rewarded as the stock price increases.

Reading (And Understanding) Stock Tables

The stock tables in major business publications such as *The Wall Street Journal* and *Investor's Business Daily* are loaded with information that can help you become a savvy investor — *if* you know how to interpret them. You need the information in the stock tables for more than selecting promising investment opportunities. You also need to consult the tables after you invest to monitor how your stocks are doing.

Looking at the stock tables without knowing what you're looking for or why you're looking is the equivalent of reading *War and Peace* backwards through a kaleidoscope — nothing makes sense. But I can help you make sense of it all (well, at least the stock tables!). Table 6-1 shows a sample stock table. Each item gives you some clues about the current state of affairs for that particular company. The sections that follow describe each column to help you understand what you're looking at.

TABLE 6-1   A Sample Stock Table

52-Wk High	52-Wk Low	Name (Symbol)	Div	Vol	Yld	P/E	Day Last	Net Chg
21.50	8.00	SkyHighCorp (SHC)		3,143		76	21.25	+.25
47.00	31.75	LowDownInc (LDI)	2.35	2,735	5.9	18	41.00	−.50
25.00	21.00	ValueNowInc (VNI)	1.00	1,894	4.5	12	22.00	+.10
83.00	33.00	DoinBadlyCorp (DBC)		7,601			33.50	−.75

REMEMBER

Every newspaper's financial tables are a little different, but they give you basically the same information. Updated daily, these tables aren't the place to start your search for a good stock; they're usually where your search ends. The stock tables are the place to look when you own a stock or know what you want to buy, and you're just checking to see the most recent price.

52-week high

The column in Table 6-1 labeled "52-Wk High" gives you the highest price that particular stock has reached in the most recent 52-week period. Knowing this price lets you gauge where the stock is now versus where it has been recently. SkyHigh-Corp's (SHC) stock has been as high as $21.50, whereas its last (most recent) price is $21.25, the number listed in the "Day Last" column. (Flip to the later section

"Day last" for more on understanding this information.) SkyHighCorp's stock is trading very high right now because it's hovering right near its overall 52-week high figure.

Now, take a look at DoinBadlyCorp's (DBC) stock price. It seems to have tumbled big time. Its stock price has had a high in the past 52 weeks of $83, but it's currently trading at $33.50. Something just doesn't seem right here. During the past 52 weeks, DBC's stock price has fallen dramatically. If you're thinking about investing in DBC, find out why the stock price has fallen. If the company is strong, it may be a good opportunity to buy stock at a lower price. If the company is having tough times, avoid it. In any case, research the firm and find out why its stock has declined. (Chapters 11 and 12 provide the basics of researching companies.)

52-week low

The column labeled "52-Wk Low" gives you the lowest price that particular stock reached in the most recent 52-week period. Again, this information is crucial to your ability to analyze stock over a period of time. Look at DBC in Table 6-1, and you can see that its current trading price of $33.50 in the "Day Last" column is close to its 52-week low of $33.

REMEMBER

Keep in mind that the high and low prices just give you a range of how far that particular stock's price has moved within the past 52 weeks. They can alert you that a stock has problems or tell you that a stock's price has fallen enough to make it a bargain. Simply reading the "52-Wk High" and "52-Wk Low" columns isn't enough to determine which of those two scenarios is happening. They basically tell you to get more information before you commit your money.

Name and symbol

The "Name (Symbol)" column is the simplest in Table 6-1. It tells you the company name (usually abbreviated) and the stock symbol assigned to the company.

TIP

When you have your eye on a stock for potential purchase, get familiar with its symbol. Knowing the symbol makes it easier for you to find your stock in the financial tables, which lists stocks in alphabetical order by the company's name (or symbol depending on the source). Stock symbols are the language of stock investing, and you need to use them in all stock communications, from getting a stock quote at your broker's office to buying stock over the internet.

Dividend

Dividends (shown under the "Div" column in Table 6-1) are basically payments to owners (stockholders). If a company pays a dividend, it's shown in the dividend column. The amount you see is the annual dividend quoted for one share of that stock. If you look at LowDownInc (LDI) in Table 6-1, you can see that you get $2.35 as an annual dividend for each share of stock that you own. Companies usually pay the dividend in quarterly amounts. If I own 100 shares of LDI, the company pays me a quarterly dividend of $58.75 ($235 total per year). A healthy company strives to maintain or upgrade the dividend for stockholders from year to year. (I discuss additional dividend details later in this chapter.)

The dividend is very important to investors seeking income from their stock investments. For more about investing for income, see Chapter 9. Investors buy stocks in companies that don't pay dividends primarily for growth. For more information on growth stocks, see Chapter 8.

Volume

Normally, when you hear the word "volume" on the news, it refers to how much stock is bought and sold for the entire market: "Well, stocks were very active today. Trading volume at the New York Stock Exchange hit 2 billion shares." Volume is certainly important to watch because the stocks that you're investing in are somewhere in that activity. For the "Vol" column in Table 6-1, though, the volume refers to the individual stock.

Volume tells you how many shares of that particular stock were traded that day. If only 100 shares are traded in a day, then the trading volume is 100. SHC had 3,143 shares change hands on the trading day represented in Table 6-1. Is that good or bad? Neither, really. Usually the business news media mention volume for a particular stock only when it's unusually large. If a stock normally has volume in the 5,000 to 10,000 range and all of a sudden has a trading volume of 87,000, then it's time to sit up and take notice.

REMEMBER

Keep in mind that a low trading volume for one stock may be a high trading volume for another stock. You can't necessarily compare one stock's volume against that of any other company. The large cap stocks like IBM or Microsoft typically have trading volumes in the millions of shares almost every day, whereas less active, smaller stocks may have average trading volumes in far, far smaller numbers.

The main point to remember is that trading volume that is far in excess of that stock's normal range is a sign that something is going on with that company. It may be negative or positive, but something newsworthy is happening with that company. If the news is positive, the increased volume is a result of more people buying the stock. If the news is negative, the increased volume is probably a result of more people selling the stock. What are typical events that cause increased trading volume? Some positive reasons include the following:

>> **Good earnings reports:** The company announces good (or better-than-expected) earnings.

>> **A new business deal:** The firm announces a favorable business deal, such as a joint venture, or lands a big client.

>> **A new product or service:** The company's research and development department creates a potentially profitable new product.

>> **Indirect benefits:** The business may benefit from a new development in the economy or from a new law passed by Congress.

Some negative reasons for an unusually large fluctuation in trading volume for a particular stock include the following:

>> **Bad earnings reports:** Profit is the lifeblood of a company. When its profits fall or disappear, you see more volume.

>> **Governmental problems:** The stock is being targeted by government action, such as a lawsuit or a Securities and Exchange Commission (SEC) probe.

>> **Liability issues:** The media report that the company has a defective product or similar problem.

>> **Financial problems:** Independent analysts report that the company's financial health is deteriorating.

REMEMBER

Check out what's happening when you hear about heavier-than-usual volume (especially if you already own the stock).

Yield

In general, yield is a return on the money you invest. However, in the stock tables, *yield* ("Yld" in Table 6-1) is a reference to what percentage that particular dividend is of the stock price. Yield is most important to income investors. It's calculated by dividing the annual dividend by the current stock price. In Table 6-1, you can see that the yield du jour of ValueNowInc (VNI) is 4.5 percent (a dividend of $1 divided by the company's stock price of $22). Notice that many companies report no yield; because they have no dividends, their yield is zero.

REMEMBER

Keep in mind that the yield reported on the financial sites changes daily as the stock price changes. Yield is always reported as if you're buying the stock that day. If you buy VNI on the day represented in Table 6-1, your yield is 4.5 percent. But what if VNI's stock price rises to $30 the following day? Investors who buy stock at $30 per share obtain a yield of just 3.3 percent (the dividend of $1 divided by the new stock price, $30). Of course, because you bought the stock at $22, you essentially locked in the prior yield of 4.5 percent. Lucky you. Pat yourself on the back.

P/E

REMEMBER

The *P/E ratio* is the relationship between the price of a stock and the company's earnings. P/E ratios are widely followed and are important barometers of value in the world of stock investing. The P/E ratio (also called the *earnings multiple* or just *multiple*) is frequently used to determine whether a stock is expensive (a good value). Value investors (such as yours truly) find P/E ratios to be essential to analyzing a stock as a potential investment. As a general rule, the P/E should be 10 to 20 for large cap or income stocks. For growth stocks, a P/E no greater than 30 to 40 is preferable. (See Chapter 11 and Appendix B for full details on P/E ratios.)

In the P/E ratios reported in stock tables, *price* refers to the cost of a single share of stock. *Earnings* refers to the company's reported earnings per share as of the most recent four quarters. The P/E ratio is the price divided by the earnings. In Table 6-1, VNI has a reported P/E of 12, which is considered a low P/E. Notice how SHC has a relatively high P/E (76). This stock is considered too pricey because you're paying a price equivalent to 76 times earnings. Also notice that DBC has no available P/E ratio. Usually this lack of a P/E ratio indicates that the company reported a loss in the most recent four quarters.

Day last

The "Day Last" column tells you how trading ended for a particular stock on the day represented by the table. In Table 6-1, LDI ended the most recent day of trading at $41. Some newspapers report the high and low for that day in addition to the stock's ending price for the day.

Net change

The information in the "Net Chg" column answers the question, "How did the stock price end today compared with its price at the end of the prior trading day?" Table 6-1 shows that SHC stock ended the trading day up 25 cents (at $21.25). This column tells you that SHC ended the prior day at $21. VNI ended the day at $22 (up 10 cents), so you can tell that the prior trading day it ended at $21.90.

Using News about Dividends

Reading and understanding the news about dividends is essential if you're an *income investor* (someone who invests in stocks as a means of generating regular income; see Chapter 9 for details). The following sections explain some basics you should know about dividends.

TIP

You can find news and information on dividends in newspapers such as *The Wall Street Journal, Investor's Business Daily,* and *Barron's.* You can find their websites online with your favorite search engine or just check out Appendix A.

Looking at important dates

REMEMBER

To understand how buying stocks that pay dividends can benefit you as an investor, you need to know how companies report and pay dividends. Some important dates in the life of a dividend are as follows:

>> **Date of declaration:** This is the date when a company reports a quarterly dividend and the subsequent payment dates. On January 15, for example, a company may report that it "is pleased to announce a quarterly dividend of 50 cents per share to shareholders of record as of February 10." That was easy. The date of declaration is really just the announcement date. Whether you buy the stock before, on, or after the date of declaration doesn't matter in regard to receiving the stock's quarterly dividend. The date that matters is the date of record (see that bullet later in this list).

>> **Date of execution:** This is the day you actually initiate the stock transaction (buying or selling). If you call up a broker (or contact her online) today to buy (or sell) a particular stock, then today is the date of execution, or the date on which you execute the trade. You don't own the stock on the date of execution; it's just the day you put in the order. For an example, skip to the following section.

>> **Closing date (settlement date):** This is the date on which the trade is finalized, which usually happens one business day after the date of execution. The closing date for stock is similar in concept to a real estate closing. On the closing date, you're officially the proud new owner (or happy seller) of the stock.

>> **Ex-dividend date:** *Ex-dividend* means *without dividend.* Because it takes one day to process a stock purchase before you become an official owner of the stock, you have to qualify (that is, you have to own or buy the stock) *before* the one-day period. That one-day period is referred to as the "ex-dividend period." When you buy stock during this short time frame, you aren't on the books of record, because the closing (or settlement) date falls after the date of record.

However, you will be able to buy the stock for a slighter lower price to offset the amount of the dividend. See the next section to see the effect that the ex-dividend date can have on an investor.

» **Date of record:** This is used to identify which stockholders qualify to receive the declared dividend. Because stock is bought and sold every day, how does the company know which investors to pay? The company establishes a cut-off date by declaring a date of record. All investors who are official stockholders as of the declared date of record receive the dividend on the payment date, even if they plan to sell the stock any time between the date of declaration and the date of record.

» **Payment date:** The date on which a company issues and mails its dividend checks to shareholders. Finally!

For typical dividends, the events in Table 6-2 happen four times per year.

TABLE 6-2   **The Life of the Quarterly Dividend**

Event	Sample Date	Comments
Date of declaration	January 15	The date that the company declares the quarterly dividend
Ex-dividend date	February 9	Starts the one-day period during which, if you buy the stock, you don't qualify for the dividend
Date of record	February 10	The date by which you must be on the books of record to qualify for the dividend
Payment date	February 27	The date that payment is made (a dividend check is issued and mailed to stockholders who were on the books of record as of February 10)

Understanding why certain dates matter

REMEMBER

One business day passes between the date of execution and the closing date. One business day passes between the ex-dividend date and the date of record. This information is important to know if you want to qualify to receive an upcoming dividend. Timing is important, and if you understand these dates, you know when to purchase stock and whether you qualify for a dividend.

As an example, say that you want to buy ValueNowInc (VNI) in time to qualify for the quarterly dividend of 25 cents per share. Assume that the date of record (the date by which you have to be an official owner of the stock) is February 10. You have to execute the trade (buy the stock) no later than February 8 to be assured of the dividend. If you execute the trade right on February 9 (the ex-dividend date), you will not qualify for the dividend because settlement will occur after the date of record.

But what if you execute the trade on February 10, a day later? Well, the trade's closing date is February 11, which occurs *after* the date of record. Because you aren't on the books as an official stockholder on the date of record, you aren't getting that quarterly dividend. In this example, the February 9–10 period is called the *ex-dividend period*.

TIP

Fortunately, for those people who buy the stock during this brief ex-dividend period, the stock actually trades at a slightly lower price to reflect the amount of the dividend. If you can't get the dividend, you may as well save on the stock purchase. How's that for a silver lining?

Evaluating Investment Tips

Psssst. Have I got a stock tip for you! Come closer. You know what it is? Research! What I'm trying to tell you is to never automatically invest just because you get a hot tip from someone. Good investment selection means looking at several sources before you decide on a stock. No shortcut exists. That said, getting opinions from others never hurts — just be sure to carefully analyze the information you get. Here are some important points to bear in mind as you evaluate tips and advice from others:

>> **Consider the source.** Frequently, people buy stock based on the views of some market strategist or market analyst. People may see an analyst being interviewed on a television financial show and take that person's opinions and advice as valid and good. The danger here is that the analyst may be biased because of some relationship that isn't disclosed on the show. Analysts are required to disclose conflicts of interest on business channels.

WARNING

It happens on TV all too often. The show's host interviews analyst U.R. Kiddingme from the investment firm Foollum & Sellum. The analyst says, "Implosion Corp. is a good buy with solid, long-term upside potential." You later find out that the analyst's employer gets investment banking fees from Implosion Corp. Do you really think that analyst would ever issue a negative report on a company that's helping to pay the bills? It's not likely.

>> **Get multiple views.** Don't base your investment decisions on just one source unless you have the best reasons in the world for thinking that a particular, single source is outstanding and reliable. A better approach is to scour current issues of independent financial publications, such as *Barron's* or *Money* magazine, and other publications and websites listed in Appendix A.

>> **Gather data from the SEC.** When you want to get more objective information about a company, why not take a look at the reports that firms must file with the SEC? These reports are the same reports that the pundits and financial reporters read. Arguably, the most valuable report you can look at is the 10K. The 10K is a report that all publicly traded companies must file with the SEC. It provides valuable information on the company's operations and financial data for the most recent year, and it's likely to be less biased than the information a company includes in other corporate reports, such as an annual report. The next most important document from the SEC is the 10Q, which gives the investor similar detailed information but for a single quarter. (See Chapter 12 for more information about these documents.)

TIP

To access 10K and 10Q reports, go to the SEC's website (www.sec.gov). From there, you can find the SEC's extensive database of public filings called EDGAR (the Electronic Data Gathering, Analysis, and Retrieval system). By searching EDGAR, you can find companies' balance sheets, income statements, and other related information so that you can verify what others say and get a fuller picture of what a business is doing and what its financial condition is.

IN THIS CHAPTER

» **Finding out what brokers do**

» **Comparing full-service and discount brokers**

» **Selecting a broker**

» **Exploring the types of brokerage accounts**

» **Evaluating the recommendations of brokers**

Chapter **7**

Going for Brokers

When you're ready to dive in and start investing in stocks, you first have to choose a broker. It's kind of like buying a car: You can do all the research in the world and know exactly what kind of car you want, but you still need a venue to conduct the actual transaction. Similarly, when you want to buy stock, your task is to do all the research you can to select the company you want to invest in. Still, you need a broker to actually buy the stock, whether you buy over the phone or online. In this chapter, I introduce you to the intricacies of the investor/broker relationship.

TIP

For information on various types of orders you can place with a broker, such as market orders, stop-loss orders, and so on, flip to Chapter 17.

Defining the Broker's Role

The broker's primary role is to serve as the vehicle through which you either buy or sell stock. When I talk about brokers, I'm referring to companies such as Charles Schwab, TD Ameritrade, E*TRADE, and many other organizations that can buy stock on your behalf. Brokers can also be individuals who work for such firms. Although you can buy some stocks directly from the company that issues them (I discuss direct purchase plans in Chapter 19), to purchase most stocks, you still need a brokerage account with a stockbroker.

REMEMBER

The distinction between institutional stockbrokers and personal stockbrokers is important:

>> **Institutional stockbrokers** make money from institutions and companies through investment banking and securities placement fees (such as initial public offerings and secondary offerings), advisory services, and other broker services.

>> **Personal stockbrokers** generally offer the same services to individuals and small businesses.

Although the primary task of brokers is the buying and selling of securities (the word *securities* refers to the world of financial or paper investments, and stocks are only a small part of that world), they can perform other tasks for you, including the following:

>> **Providing advisory services:** Investors pay brokers a fee for investment advice. Customers also get access to the firm's research.

>> **Offering limited banking services:** Brokers can offer features such as interest-bearing accounts, check-writing, electronic deposits and withdrawals, and credit/debit cards.

>> **Brokering other securities:** In addition to stocks, brokers can buy bonds, mutual funds, options, exchange-traded funds (ETFs; see Chapter 5), and other investments on your behalf.

Personal stockbrokers make their money from individual investors like you and me through various fees, including the following:

>> **Brokerage commissions:** This fee is for buying and/or selling stocks and other securities.

>> **Margin interest charges:** This interest is charged to investors for borrowing against their brokerage account for investment purposes. (I discuss margin accounts in more detail later in this chapter.)

>> **Service charges:** These charges are for performing administrative tasks and other functions. Brokers charge fees to investors for Individual Retirement Accounts (IRAs) and for mailing stocks in certificate form.

REMEMBER

Any broker (some brokers are now called *financial advisors*) you deal with should be registered with the Financial Industry Regulatory Authority (FINRA) and the Securities and Exchange Commission (SEC). In addition, to protect your money after you deposit it into a brokerage account, that broker should be a member of the Securities Investor Protection Corporation (SIPC). SIPC doesn't protect you from market losses; it protects your money in case the brokerage firm goes out of business or if your losses are due to brokerage fraud. To find out whether the broker is registered with these organizations, contact FINRA (www.finra.org), SEC (www.sec.gov), or SIPC (www.sipc.org). See Appendix A for more information on these organizations.

Distinguishing between Full-Service and Discount Brokers

Stockbrokers fall into two basic categories, which I discuss in the following sections: full-service and discount. The type you choose really depends on what type of investor you are. Here are the differences in a nutshell:

>> **Full-service brokers** are suitable for investors who need some guidance and personal attention.

>> **Discount brokers** are better for those investors who are sufficiently confident and knowledgeable about stock investing to manage with minimal help (usually through the broker's website).

TIP

Before you deal with any broker (either full-service or discount), get a free report on the broker from FINRA by calling 800-289-9999 or through its website at www.finra.org. Through its service called BrokerCheck, you can get a report on either a brokerage firm or an individual broker. You can find more details on this and other services (such as investor education and so forth) at www.finra.org. FINRA can tell you in its report whether any complaints or penalties have been filed against a brokerage firm or an individual rep.

At your disposal: Full-service brokers

Full-service brokers are just what the name indicates. They try to provide as many services as possible for investors who open accounts with them. When you open an account at a brokerage firm, a representative is assigned to your account. This representative is usually called an *account executive*, a *registered rep*, or a *financial advisor* by the brokerage firm. This person usually has a securities license (meaning that she's registered with the FINRA and the SEC) and is knowledgeable about stocks in particular and investing in general.

Examples of full-service brokers are Goldman Sachs and Morgan Stanley. Of course, all brokers now have full-featured websites to give you further information about their services. Get as informed as possible before you open your account. A full-service broker is there to help you build wealth, not make you . . . uh . . . broker.

What they can do for you

Your account executive is responsible for assisting you, answering questions about your account and the securities in your portfolio, and transacting your buy and sell orders. Here are some things that full-service brokers can do for you:

>> **Offer guidance and advice:** The greatest distinction between full-service brokers and discount brokers is the personal attention you receive from your account rep. You get to be on a first-name basis with a full-service broker, and you disclose much information about your finances and financial goals. The rep is there to make recommendations about stocks and funds that are hopefully suitable for you.

>> **Provide access to research:** Full-service brokers can give you access to their investment research department, which can give you in-depth information and analysis on a particular company. This information can be very valuable, but be aware of the pitfalls. (See the later section "Judging Brokers' Recommendations.")

>> **Help you achieve your investment objectives:** A good rep gets to know you and your investment goals and *then* offers advice and answers your questions about how specific investments and strategies can help you accomplish your wealth-building goals.

>> **Make investment decisions on your behalf:** Many investors don't want to be bothered when it comes to investment decisions. Full-service brokers can actually make decisions for your account with your authorization (this is also referred to as a *discretionary* account, although many brokers have scaled back the use of discretion for ordinary brokerage accounts). This service is fine, but be sure to require brokers to explain their choices to you.

What to watch out for

Although full-service brokers, with their seemingly limitless assistance, can make life easy for an investor, you need to remember some important points to avoid problems:

>> Brokers and account reps are salespeople. No matter how well they treat you, they're still compensated based on their ability to produce revenue for the brokerage firm. They generate commissions and fees from you on behalf of the company. (In other words, they're paid to sell you things.)

REMEMBER

>> Whenever your rep makes a suggestion or recommendation, be sure to ask why and request a complete answer that includes the reasoning behind the recommendation. A good advisor is able to clearly explain the reasoning behind every suggestion. If you don't fully understand and agree with the advice, don't take it.

>> Working with a full-service broker costs more than working with a discount broker. Discount brokers are paid for simply buying or selling stocks for you. Full-service brokers do that and much more, like provide advice and guidance. Because of that, full-service brokers are more expensive (through higher brokerage commissions and advisory fees). Also, most full-service brokers expect you to invest at least $5,000 to $10,000 just to open an account, although many require higher minimums.

>> Handing over decision-making authority to your rep can be a possible negative because letting others make financial decisions for you is always dicey — especially when they're using *your* money. If they make poor investment choices that lose you money, you may not have any recourse because you authorized them to act on your behalf.

WARNING

>> Some brokers engage in an activity called churning. *Churning* is basically buying and selling stocks for the sole purpose of generating commissions. Churning is great for brokers but bad for customers. If your account shows a lot of activity, ask for justification. Commissions, especially by full-service brokers, can take a big bite out of your wealth, so don't tolerate churning or other suspicious activity.

Just the basics: Discount brokers

Perhaps you don't need any hand-holding from a broker (that'd be kinda weird anyway). You know what you want, and you can make your own investment decisions. All you need is a convenient way to transact your buy/sell orders. In that case, go with a discount broker. They don't offer advice or premium services — just the basics required to perform your stock transactions.

Discount brokers, as the name implies, are cheaper to engage than full-service brokers. Because you're advising yourself (or getting advice and information from third parties such as newsletters, hotlines, or independent advisors), you can save on costs that you'd incur if you used a full-service broker.

REMEMBER

If you choose to work with a discount broker, you must know as much as possible about your personal goals and needs. You have a greater responsibility for conducting adequate research to make good stock selections, and you must be prepared to accept the outcome, whatever that may be. (See the rest of Part 2 for information you need before you get started and Part 3 for details on researching stock selections.)

For a while, the regular investor had two types of discount brokers to choose from: conventional discount brokers and internet discount brokers. But the two are basically synonymous now, so the differences are hardly worth mentioning. Through industry consolidation, most of the conventional discount brokers today have full-featured websites, while internet discount brokers have adapted by adding more telephone and face-to-face services.

Charles Schwab and TD Ameritrade are examples of conventional discount brokers that have adapted well to the internet era. Internet brokers such as E*TRADE (us.etrade.com), Ally (www.ally.com), TradeStation (www.tradestation.com), and Fidelity (www.fidelity.com) have added more conventional services.

What they can do for you

Discount brokers offer some significant advantages over full-service brokers, such as the following:

>> **Lower cost:** This lower cost is usually the result of lower commissions, and it's the primary benefit of using discount brokers.

>> **Unbiased service:** Because they don't offer advice, discount brokers have no vested interest in trying to sell you any particular stock.

>> **Access to information:** Established discount brokers offer extensive educational materials at their offices or on their websites.

What to watch out for

Of course, doing business with discount brokers also has its downsides, including the following:

>> **No guidance:** Because you've chosen a discount broker, you *know* not to expect guidance, but the broker should make this fact clear to you anyway. If you're a knowledgeable investor, the lack of advice is considered a positive thing — no interference.

>> **Hidden fees:** Discount brokers may shout about their lower commissions, but commissions aren't their only way of making money. Many discount brokers charge extra for services that you may think are included, such as issuing a stock certificate (rarely if ever done anymore) or mailing a statement. Ask whether they assess fees for maintaining IRAs or for transferring stocks and other securities (like bonds) in or out of your account, and find out what interest rates they charge for borrowing through brokerage accounts.

WARNING

> » **Minimal customer service:** If you deal with an internet brokerage firm, find out about its customer service capability. If you can't transact business on its website, find out where you can call for assistance with your order.

Choosing a Broker

Before you choose a broker, you need to analyze your personal investing style (as I explain in Chapter 3), and then you can proceed to finding the kind of broker that fits your needs. It's almost like choosing shoes; if you don't know your size, you can't get a proper fit (and you can be in for a really uncomfortable future).

REMEMBER

When it's time to choose a broker, keep the following points in mind:

» Match your investment style with a brokerage firm that charges the least amount of money for the services you're likely to use most frequently.

» Compare all the costs of buying, selling, and holding stocks and other securities through a broker. Don't compare only commissions; compare other costs, too, like margin interest and other service charges (see the earlier section "Defining the Broker's Role" for more about these costs).

» Use broker comparison services available in financial publications such as *Kiplinger's Personal Finance* and *Barron's* (and, of course, their websites) as well as online sources.

TIP

Finding brokers is easy. They're listed in the Yellow Pages (or on directory sites like www.superpages.com), in many investment publications, and on many financial websites. Start your search by using the sources in Appendix A, which includes a list of the major brokerage firms.

Discovering Various Types of Brokerage Accounts

When you start investing in the stock market, you have to somehow actually *pay* for the stocks you buy. Most brokerage firms offer investors several types of accounts, each serving a different purpose. I present three of the most common types in the following sections. The basic difference boils down to how particular brokers view your creditworthiness when it comes to buying and selling securities. If your credit isn't great, your only choice is a cash account. If your credit is good, you can open either a cash account or a margin account. After you qualify for a margin account, you can (with additional approval) upgrade it to do options trades.

REMEMBER

To open an account, you have to fill out an application and submit a check or money order for at least the minimum amount required to establish an account.

Cash accounts

A *cash account* (also referred to as a *Type 1 account*) means just what you'd think. You must deposit a sum of money along with the new account application to begin trading. The amount of your initial deposit varies from broker to broker. Some brokers have a minimum of $10,000; others let you open an account for as little as $500. Once in a while you may see a broker offering cash accounts with no minimum deposit, usually as part of a promotion. Use the resources in Appendix A to help you shop around. Qualifying for a cash account is usually easy, as long as you have cash and a pulse.

With a cash account, your money has to be deposited in the account before the closing (or settlement) date for any trade you make. The closing occurs two business days after the date you make the trade (the *date of execution*). You may be required to have the money in the account even before the date of execution. See Chapter 6 for details on these and other important dates.

In other words, if you call your broker on Monday, October 10, and order 50 shares of CashLess Corp. at $20 per share, then on Wednesday, October 12, you better have $1,000 in cash sitting in your account (plus commission).

WARNING

In addition, ask the broker how long it takes deposited cash (such as a check) to be available for investing. Some brokers put a hold on checks for up to ten business days (or longer, depending on the broker), regardless of how soon that check clears your account (that would drive me crazy!).

TIP

See whether your broker will pay you interest on the uninvested cash in your brokerage account. Some brokers offer a service in which uninvested money earns money market rates, and you can even choose between a regular money market account and a tax-free municipal money market account.

Margin accounts

A *margin account* (also called a *Type 2 account*) allows you to borrow money against the securities in the account to buy more stock. Because you can borrow in a margin account, you have to be qualified and approved by the broker. After you're approved, this newfound credit gives you more leverage so you can buy more stock or do short selling. (You can read more about buying on margin and short selling in Chapter 17.)

For stock trading, the margin limit is 50 percent. For example, if you plan to buy $10,000 worth of stock on margin, you need at least $5,000 in cash (or securities owned) sitting in your account. The interest rate you pay varies depending on the broker, but most brokers generally charge a rate that's several points higher than their own borrowing rate.

Why use margin? Margin is to stocks what mortgage is to buying real estate. You can buy real estate with all cash, but using borrowed funds often makes sense because you may not have enough money to make a 100-percent cash purchase, or you may just prefer not to pay all cash. With margin, you can, for example, buy $10,000 worth of stock with as little as $5,000. The balance of the stock purchase is acquired using a loan (margin) from the brokerage firm.

WARNING

Personally, I'm not a big fan of margin, and I use it sparingly. Margin is a form of leverage that can work out fine if you're correct but can be very dangerous if the market moves against you. It's best applied with stocks that are generally stable and dividend-paying. That way, the dividends help pay off the margin interest.

Options accounts

An *options account* (also referred to as a *Type 3 account*) gives you all the capabilities of a margin account (which in turn also gives you the capabilities of a cash account) plus the ability to trade options on stocks and stock indexes. To upgrade your margin account to an options account, the broker usually asks you to sign a statement that you're knowledgeable about options and familiar with the risks associated with them.

TIP

Options can be a very effective addition to a stock investor's array of wealth-building investment tools. A more comprehensive review of options is available in the book *Trading Options For Dummies*, 3rd Edition, by Joe Duarte (Wiley). I personally love to use options (as do my clients and students), and I think they can be a great tool in your wealth-building arsenal. That's why I provide extensive coverage of put and call options in my book *High-Level Investing For Dummies* (published by Wiley).

Judging Brokers' Recommendations

In recent years, Americans have become enamored with a new sport: the rating of stocks by brokers on TV financial shows. Frequently, these shows feature a dapper market strategist talking up a particular stock. Some stocks have been known to jump significantly right after an influential analyst issues a buy recommendation. Analysts' speculation and opinions make for great fun, and many people take their views very seriously. However, most investors should be very wary when analysts, especially the glib ones on TV, make a recommendation. It's often just showbiz. In the following sections, I define basic broker recommendations and list a few important considerations for evaluating them.

Understanding basic recommendations

Brokers issue their recommendations (advice) as a general idea of how much regard they have for a particular stock. The following list presents the basic recommendations (or ratings) and what they mean to you:

>> *Strong buy* and *buy:* Hot diggity dog! These ratings are the ones to get. The analyst loves this pick, and you would be very wise to get a bunch of shares. The thing to keep in mind, however, is that *buy* recommendations are probably the most common because (let's face it) brokers sell stocks.

>> *Accumulate* and *market perform:* An analyst who issues these types of recommendations is positive, yet unexcited, about the pick. This rating is akin to asking a friend whether he likes your new suit and getting the response "It's nice" in a monotone voice. It's a polite reply, but you wish his opinion had been more definitive. For some brokers, *accumulate* is considered a *buy* recommendation.

>> *Hold* or *neutral:* Analysts use this language when their backs are to the wall, but they still don't want to say, "Sell that loser!" This recommendation reminds me of my mother telling me to be nice and either say something positive or keep my mouth shut. In this case, the rating is the analyst's way of keeping his mouth shut.

>> *Sell:* Many analysts should have issued this recommendation during the bear markets of 2000–2002 and 2008 but didn't. What a shame. So many investors lost money because some analysts were too nice (or biased?) or just afraid to be honest, sound the alarm, and urge people to sell.

>> *Avoid like the plague:* I'm just kidding about this one, but I wish this recommendation was available. I've seen plenty of stocks that I thought were dreadful investments — stocks of companies that made no money, were in terrible financial condition, and should never have been considered at all. Yet investors gobble up billions of dollars' worth of stocks that eventually become worthless.

Asking a few important questions

Don't get me wrong. An analyst's recommendation is certainly a better tip than what you'd get from your barber or your sister-in-law's neighbor, but you want to view recommendations from analysts with a healthy dose of reality. Analysts have biases because their employment depends on the very companies that are being presented. What investors need to listen to when a broker talks up a stock is the reasoning behind the recommendation. In other words, why is the broker making this recommendation?

Keep in mind that analysts' recommendations can play a useful role in your personal stock investing research. If you find a great stock and *then* you hear analysts give glowing reports on the same stock, you're on the right track! Here are some questions and points to keep in mind:

>> **How does the analyst arrive at a rating?** The analyst's approach to evaluating a stock can help you round out your research as you consult other sources such as newsletters and independent advisory services.

>> **What analytical approach is the analyst using?** Some analysts use *fundamental analysis* (see Chapters 8 and 11) — looking at the company's financial condition and factors related to its success, such as its standing within the industry and the overall market. Other analysts use *technical analysis* — looking at the company's stock price history and judging past stock price movements to derive some insight regarding the stock's future price movement (see Chapter 10 for more about technical analysis). Many analysts use a combination of the two. Is this analyst's approach similar to your approach or to those of sources that you respect or admire?

>> **What is the analyst's track record?** Has the analyst had a consistently good record through both bull and bear markets? Major financial publications, such as *Barron's* and *Hulbert Financial Digest,* and websites, such as MarketWatch.com, regularly track recommendations from well-known analysts and stock pickers. You can find some resources for getting this type of info in Appendix A.

>> **How does the analyst treat important aspects of the company's performance, such as sales and earnings?** How about the company's balance sheet? The essence of a healthy company is growing sales and earnings coupled with strong assets and low debt. (See Chapter 11 for more details on these topics.)

>> **Is the industry that the company's in doing well?** Do the analysts give you insight on this important information? A strong company in a weak industry can't stay strong for long. The right industry is a critical part of the stock selection process (for more information, see Chapter 13).

>> **What research sources does the analyst cite?** Does the analyst quote the federal government or industry trade groups to support her thesis? These sources are important because they help give a more complete picture regarding the company's prospects for success. Imagine that you decide on the stock of a strong company. What if the federal government (through agencies like the SEC) is penalizing the company for fraudulent activity? Or what if the company's industry is shrinking or has ceased to grow (making it tougher for the company to continue growing)? The astute investor looks at a variety of sources before buying stock.

>> **Is the analyst rational when citing a target price for a stock?** When he says, "We think this $40 stock will hit $100 per share within 12 months," is he presenting a rational model, such as basing the share price on a projected price/earnings ratio (see Chapter 11)? The analyst must be able to provide a logical scenario explaining why the stock has a good chance of achieving the cited target price within the time frame mentioned. You may not necessarily agree with the analyst's conclusion, but the explanation can help you decide whether the stock choice is well thought out.

WARNING

>> **Does the company that's being recommended have any ties to the analyst or the analyst's firm?** During 2000–2002, the financial industry got bad publicity because many analysts gave positive recommendations on stocks of companies that were doing business with the very firms that employed those analysts. This conflict of interest is probably the biggest reason that analysts were so wrong in their recommendations during that period. Ask your broker to disclose any conflict of interest. Additionally, brokers are required to disclose whether their firm is involved with a particular stock as a "market maker" or in another capacity (such as being its investment banker).

>> **What school of economic thought does the analyst adhere to?** This may sound like an odd question, and it may not be readily answered, but it's a good thing to know. If I had to choose between two analysts that were very similar except that Analyst A adhered to the Keynesian school of economic thought, and Analyst B adhered to the Austrian school, guess what? I'd choose Analyst B because those who embrace the Austrian school have a much better grasp of real-world economics (which means better stock investment choices).

REMEMBER

The bottom line with brokerage recommendations is that you shouldn't use them to buy or sell a stock. Instead, use them to confirm your own research. I know that if I buy a stock based on my own research and later discover the same stock being talked up on the financial shows, that's just the icing on the cake. The experts may be great to listen to, and their recommendations can augment your own opinions, but they're no substitute for your own careful research. I devote Part 3 to researching and picking winning stocks. But for starters, Part 2 (including this chapter) helps you lay the groundwork for your stock investing strategy.

Chapter **8**

Investing for Long-Term Growth

What's the number-one reason people invest in stocks? To grow their wealth (also referred to as *capital appreciation*). Yes, some people invest for income (in the form of dividends), but that's a different matter (I discuss investing for income in Chapter 9). Investors seeking growth would rather see the money that could have been distributed as dividends be reinvested in the company so that (hopefully) a greater gain is achieved when the stock's price rises or appreciates. People interested in growing their wealth see stocks as one of the convenient ways to do it. Growth stocks tend to be riskier than other categories of stocks, but they offer excellent long-term prospects for making the big bucks. If you don't believe me, just ask Warren Buffett, Peter Lynch, and other successful, long-term investors.

Although someone like Buffett is not considered a growth investor, his long-term, value-oriented approach has been a successful growth strategy. If you're the type of investor who has enough time to let somewhat risky stocks trend upward or who has enough money so that a loss won't devastate you financially, then growth stocks are definitely for you. As they say, no guts, no glory. The challenge is to figure out which stocks make you richer quicker; I give you tips on how to do so in this chapter.

REMEMBER

Short of starting your own business, stock investing is the best way to profit from a business venture. I want to emphasize that to make money in stocks consistently over the long haul, you must remember that you're investing in a *company*; buying the stock is just a means for you to participate in the company's success (or failure). Why does it matter that you think of stock investing as buying a *company* versus buying a *stock*? Invest in a stock only if you're just as excited about it as you would be if you were the CEO in charge of running the company. If you're the sole owner of the company, do you act differently than one of a legion of obscure stockholders? Of course you do. As the firm's owner, you have a greater interest in the company. You have a strong desire to know how the enterprise is doing. As you invest in stocks, make believe that you're the owner, and take an active interest in the company's products, services, sales, earnings, and so on. This attitude and discipline can enhance your goals as a stock investor. This approach is especially important if your investment goal is growth.

Becoming a Value-Oriented Growth Investor

A stock is considered a *growth stock* when it's growing faster and at a higher rate than the overall stock market. Basically, a growth stock performs better than its peers in categories such as sales and earnings. *Value stocks* are stocks that are priced lower than the value of the company and its assets — you can identify a value stock by analyzing the company's fundamentals and looking at key financial ratios, such as the price-to-earnings (P/E) ratio. (I cover company finances in Chapter 11 and ratios in Chapter 11 and Appendix B.) Growth stocks tend to have better prospects for growth in the immediate future (from one to four years), but value stocks tend to have less risk and steadier growth over a longer term.

Over the years, a debate has quietly raged in the financial community about growth versus value investing. Some people believe that growth and value are mutually exclusive. They maintain that large numbers of people buying stock with growth as the expectation tend to drive up the stock price relative to the company's current value. Growth investors, for example, aren't put off by P/E ratios of 30, 40, or higher. Value investors, meanwhile, are too nervous to buy stocks at those P/E ratio levels.

However, you *can* have both. A value-oriented approach to growth investing serves you best. Long-term growth stock investors spend time analyzing the company's fundamentals to make sure that the company's growth prospects lie on a solid foundation. But what if you have to choose between a growth stock and a value stock? Which do you choose? Seek value when you're buying the stock and analyze the company's prospects for growth. Growth includes, but is not limited to, the health and growth of the company's specific industry, the economy at large, and the general political climate (see Chapters 13 and 15).

REMEMBER

The bottom line is that growth is much easier to achieve when you seek solid, value-oriented companies in growing industries. (To better understand industries and sectors and how they affect stock value, see Chapter 13.) It's also worth emphasizing that time, patience, and discipline are key factors in your success — especially in the tumultuous and uncertain stock investing environment of the current time (2020–2021). I cover ten major issues facing all investors during 2020–2030 in Chapter 25.

TECHNICAL STUFF

Value-oriented growth investing probably has the longest history of success compared to most stock-investing philosophies. The track record for those people who use value-oriented growth investing is enviable. Warren Buffett, Benjamin Graham, John Templeton, and Peter Lynch are a few of the more well-known practitioners. Each may have his own spin on the concepts, but all have successfully applied the basic principles of value-oriented growth investing over many years.

Choosing Growth Stocks with a Few Handy Tips

Although the information in the previous section can help you shrink your stock choices from thousands of stocks to maybe a few dozen or a few hundred (depending on how well the general stock market is doing), the purpose of this section is to help you cull the so-so growth stocks to unearth the go-go ones. It's time to dig deeper for the biggest potential winners. Keep in mind that you probably won't find a stock to satisfy all the criteria presented here. Just make sure that your selection meets as many criteria as realistically possible. But hey, if you do find a stock that meets all the criteria cited, *buy as much as you can!*

For the record, my approach to choosing a winning growth stock is probably almost the reverse method of . . . uh . . . that screaming money guy on TV (I won't mention his name!). People watch his show for "tips" on "hot stocks." The frenetic host seems to do a rapid-fire treatment of stocks in general. You get the impression that he looks over thousands of stocks and says, "I like this one," and "I don't like that one." The viewer has to decide. Sheesh.

Verifiably, 80 to 90 percent of my stock picks are profitable. People ask me how I pick a winning stock. I tell them that I don't just pick a stock and hope that it does well. In fact, my personal stock-picking research doesn't even begin with stocks; I first look at the investing environment (politics, economics, demographics, and so on) and choose which industry will benefit. After I know which industry will prosper accordingly, *then* I start to analyze and choose my stock(s).

After I choose a stock, I wait. Patience is more than just a virtue; patience is to investing what time is to a seed that's planted in fertile soil. The legendary Jesse Livermore said that he didn't make his stock market fortunes by trading stocks; his fortunes were made "in the waiting." Why?

When I tell you to have patience and a long-term perspective, it isn't because I want you to wait years or decades for your stock portfolio to bear fruit. It's because you're waiting for a specific condition to occur: for the market to discover what you have! When you have a good stock in a good industry, it takes time for the market to discover it. When a stock has more buyers than sellers, it rises — it's as simple as that. As time passes, more buyers find your stock. As the stock rises, it attracts more attention and, therefore, more buyers. The more time that passes, the better your stock looks to the investing public.

REMEMBER

When you're choosing growth stocks, you should consider investing in a company only *if* it makes a profit and *if* you understand *how* it makes that profit and from *where* it generates sales. Part of your research means looking at the industry and sector (see Chapter 13) and economic trends in general (see Chapter 15). Check out Chapter 25 for some help, too.

Looking for leaders in megatrends

A strong company in a growing industry is a common recipe for success. If you look at the history of stock investing, this point comes up constantly. Investors need to be on the alert for megatrends because they help ensure success.

A *megatrend* is a major development that has huge implications for much (if not all) of society for a long time to come. Good examples are the advent of the internet and the aging of America. Both of these trends offer significant challenges and opportunities for the economy. Take the internet, for example. Its potential for economic application is still being developed. Millions are flocking to it for many reasons. And census data tells us that senior citizens (over 65) will continue to be a fast-growing segment of the U.S. population during the next 20 years. (Millennials are another huge demographic that investors should be aware of.) How does the stock investor take advantage of a megatrend? Find out more in Chapter 13.

Because small companies can be the ones poised for the most potential growth, check out Chapter 14 to get in early on some hot stocks.

Comparing a company's growth to an industry's growth

You have to measure the growth of a company against something to figure out whether its stock is a growth stock. Usually, you compare the growth of a company with growth from other companies in the same industry or with the stock market in general. In practical terms, when you measure the growth of a stock against the stock market, you're actually comparing it against a generally accepted benchmark, such as the Dow Jones Industrial Average (DJIA) or the Standard & Poor's 500 (S&P 500). For more on stock indexes, see Chapter 5.

TIP

If a company's earnings grow 15 percent per year over three years or more, and the industry's average growth rate over the same time frame is 10 percent, then the stock qualifies as a growth stock. You can easily calculate the earnings growth rate by comparing a company's earnings in the current year to the preceding year and computing the difference as a percentage. For example, if a company's earnings (on a per-share basis) were $1 last year and $1.10 this year, then earnings grew by 10 percent. Many analysts also look at a current quarter and compare the earnings to the same quarter from the preceding year to see whether earnings are growing.

REMEMBER

A growth stock is called that not only because the company is growing but also because the company is performing well with some consistency. Having a single year where your earnings do well versus the S&P 500's average doesn't cut it. Growth must be consistently accomplished.

Considering a company with a strong niche

Companies that have established a strong niche are consistently profitable. Look for a company with one or more of the following characteristics:

>> **A strong brand:** Companies such as Coca-Cola and Microsoft come to mind. Yes, other companies out there can make soda or software, but a business needs a lot more than a similar product to topple companies that have established an almost irrevocable identity with the public.

>> **High barriers to entry:** United Parcel Service and Federal Express have set up tremendous distribution and delivery networks that competitors can't easily duplicate. High barriers to entry offer an important edge to companies that are already established. Examples of high barriers include high capital requirements (needing lots of cash to start) or special technology that's not easily produced or acquired.

>> **Research and development (R&D):** Companies such as Pfizer and Merck spend a lot of money researching and developing new pharmaceutical products. This investment becomes a new product with millions of consumers who become loyal purchasers, so the company's going to grow. You can find out what companies spend on R&D by checking their financial statements and their annual reports (more on this is in Chapters 11 and 12).

Checking out a company's fundamentals

When you hear the word *fundamentals* in the world of stock investing, it refers to the company's financial condition, operating performance, and related data. When investors (especially value investors) do *fundamental analysis,* they look at the company's fundamentals — its balance sheet, income statement, cash flow, and other operational data, along with external factors such as the company's market position, industry, and economic prospects. Essentially, the fundamentals indicate the company's financial condition. Chapter 11 goes into greater detail about analyzing a company's financial condition. However, the main numbers you want to look at include the following:

>> **Sales:** Are the company's sales this year surpassing last year's? As a decent benchmark, you want to see sales at least 10 percent higher than last year. Although it may differ depending on the industry, 10 percent is a reasonable, general yardstick.

>> **Earnings:** Are earnings at least 10 percent higher than last year? Earnings should grow at the same rate as sales (or, hopefully, better).

>> **Debt:** Is the company's total debt equal to or lower than the prior year? The death knell of many a company has been excessive debt.

TIP

A company's financial condition has more factors than I mention here, but these numbers are the most important. I also realize that using the 10-percent figure may seem like an oversimplification, but you don't need to complicate matters unnecessarily. I know someone's computerized financial model may come out to 9.675 percent or maybe 11.07 percent, but keep it simple for now.

Evaluating a company's management

The management of a company is crucial to its success. Before you buy stock in a company, you want to know that the company's management is doing a great job. But how do you do that? If you call up a company and ask, it may not even return your phone call. How do you know whether management is running the company properly? The best way is to check the numbers. The following sections tell you the numbers you need to check. If the company's management is running the business well, the ultimate result is a rising stock price.

Return on equity

REMEMBER

Although you can measure how well management is doing in several ways, you can take a quick snapshot of a management team's competence by checking the company's return on equity (ROE). You calculate the ROE simply by dividing earnings by equity. The resulting percentage gives you a good idea whether the company is using its equity (or net assets) efficiently and profitably. Basically, the higher the percentage, the better, but you can consider the ROE solid if the percentage is 10 percent or higher. Keep in mind that not all industries have identical ROEs.

To find out a company's earnings, check out the company's income statement. The *income statement* is a simple financial statement that expresses this equation: sales (or revenue) minus expenses equals net earnings (or net income or net profit). You can see an example of an income statement in Table 8-1. (I give more details on income statements in Chapter 11.)

TABLE 8-1

Grobaby, Inc., Income Statement

	2019 Income Statement	2020 Income Statement
Sales	$82,000	$90,000
Expenses	-$75,000	-$78,000
Net earnings	$7,000	$12,000

To find out a company's equity, check out that company's balance sheet. (See Chapter 11 for more details on balance sheets.) The *balance sheet* is actually a simple financial statement that illustrates this equation: total assets minus total liabilities equals net equity. For public stock companies, the net assets are called *shareholders' equity* or simply *equity*. Table 8-2 shows a balance sheet for Grobaby, Inc.

TABLE 8-2

Grobaby, Inc., Balance Sheet

	Balance Sheet as of December 31, 2019	Balance Sheet as of December 31, 2020
Total assets (TA)	$55,000	$65,000
Total liabilities (TL)	-$20,000	-$25,000
Equity (TA minus TL)	$35,000	$40,000

Table 8-1 shows that Grobaby's earnings went from $7,000 to $12,000. In Table 8-2, you can see that Grobaby increased the equity from $35,000 to $40,000 in one year. The ROE for the year 2019 is 20 percent ($7,000 in earnings divided by $35,000 in equity), which is a solid number. The following year, the ROE is 30 percent ($12,000 in earnings divided by $40,000 in equity), another solid number. A good minimum ROE is 10 percent, but 15 percent or more is preferred.

Equity and earnings growth

Two additional barometers of success are a company's growth in earnings and growth of equity:

» Look at the growth in earnings in Table 8-1. The earnings grew from $7,000 (in 2019) to $12,000 (in 2020), a percentage increase of 71 percent ($12,000 minus $7,000 equals $5,000, and $5,000 divided by $7,000 is 71 percent), which is excellent. At a minimum, earnings growth should be equal to or better than the rate of inflation, but because that's not always a reliable number, I like at least 10 percent.

» In Table 8-2, Grobaby's equity grew by $5,000 (from $35,000 to $40,000), or 14.3 percent ($5,000 divided by $35,000), which is very good — management is doing good things here. I like to see equity increasing by 10 percent or more.

Insider buying

TIP

Watching management as it manages the business is important, but another indicator of how well the company is doing is to see whether management is buying stock in the company as well. If a company is poised for growth, who knows better than management? And if management is buying up the company's stock en masse, that's a great indicator of the stock's potential. See Chapter 20 for more details on insider buying.

Noticing who's buying and/or recommending a company's stock

You can invest in a great company and still see its stock go nowhere. Why? Because what makes the stock go up is demand — when there's more buying than selling of the stock. If you pick a stock for all the right reasons and the market notices the stock as well, that attention causes the stock price to climb. The things to watch for include the following:

- » **Institutional buying:** Are mutual funds and pension plans buying up the stock you're looking at? If so, this type of buying power can exert tremendous upward pressure on the stock's price. Some resources and publications track institutional buying and how that affects any particular stock. (You can find these resources in Appendix A.) Frequently, when a mutual fund buys a stock, others soon follow. In spite of all the talk about independent research, a herd mentality still exists.

- » **Analysts' attention:** Are analysts talking about the stock on the financial shows? As much as you should be skeptical about an analyst's recommendation (given the stock market debacle of 2000–2002 and the market problems in 2008), it offers some positive reinforcement for your stock. Don't ever buy a stock solely on the basis of an analyst's recommendation. Just know that if you buy a stock based on your own research, and analysts subsequently rave about it, your stock price is likely to go up. A single recommendation by an influential analyst can be enough to send a stock skyward.

- » **Newsletter recommendations:** Independent researchers usually publish newsletters. If influential newsletters are touting your choice, that praise is also good for your stock. Although some great newsletters are out there (find them in Appendix A) and they offer information that's as good as or better than that of some brokerage firms' research departments, don't base your investment decision on a single tip. However, seeing newsletters tout a stock that you've already chosen should make you feel good.

- » **Consumer publications:** No, you won't find investment advice here. This one seems to come out of left field, but it's a source that you should notice. Publications such as *Consumer Reports* regularly look at products and services and rate them for consumer satisfaction. If a company's offerings are well received by consumers, that's a strong positive for the company. This kind of attention ultimately has a positive effect on that company's stock.

Making sure a company continues to do well

A company's financial situation does change, and you, as a diligent investor, need to continue to look at the numbers for as long as the stock is in your portfolio. You may have chosen a great stock from a great company with great numbers in 2018, but chances are pretty good that the numbers have changed since then.

WARNING

Great stocks don't always stay that way. A great selection that you're drawn to today may become tomorrow's pariah. Information, both good and bad, moves like lightning. Keep an eye on your stock company's numbers! For more information on a company's financial data, check out Chapter 11.

Heeding investing lessons from history

A growth stock isn't a creature like the Loch Ness monster — always talked about but rarely seen. Growth stocks have been part of the financial scene for nearly a century. Examples abound that offer rich information that you can apply to today's stock market environment. Look at past market winners, especially those during the bull market of the late 1990s and the bearish markets of 2000–2010, and ask yourself, "What made them profitable stocks?" I mention these two time frames because they offer a stark contrast to each other. The 1990s were booming times for stocks, whereas more recent years were very tough and bearish.

REMEMBER

Being aware and acting logically are as vital to successful stock investing as they are to any other pursuit. Over and over again, history gives you the formula for successful stock investing:

>> Pick a company that has strong fundamentals, including signs such as rising sales and earnings and low debt. (See Chapter 11.)

>> Make sure that the company is in a growing industry. (See Chapter 13.)

>> Fully participate in stocks that are benefiting from bullish market developments in the general economy. (See Chapter 15.)

>> During a bear market or in bearish trends, switch more of your money out of growth stocks (such as technology) and into defensive stocks (such as utilities).

>> Monitor your stocks. Hold onto stocks that continue to have growth potential, and sell those stocks with declining prospects.

Chapter **9**

Investing for Income and Cash Flow

Stocks are well known for their ability to appreciate (for capital gains potential), but not enough credit is given regarding stocks' ability to boost your income and cash flow. Given that income will be a primary concern for many in the coming months and years (especially baby boomers and others concerned with retirement, pension issues, and so on), I consider this to be an important chapter.

The first income feature is the obvious — dividends! I love dividends, and they have excellent features that make them very attractive, such as their ability to meet or exceed the rate of inflation and the fact that they are subject to lower taxes than, say, regular taxable interest or wages. Dividend-paying stocks (also called income stocks) deserve a spot in a variety of portfolios, especially those of investors at or near retirement. Also, I think that younger folks (such as millennials) can gain long-term financial benefits from having dividends reinvested to compound their growth (such as with dividend reinvestment plans, which are covered in Chapter 19). In this chapter, I show you how to analyze income stocks with a few handy formulas, and I describe several typical income stocks.

Dividends are the primary subject here, but I cover much more. Many stocks in your portfolio give you the firepower to generate substantial income from call and put options (sweet!). Income from options (and other income strategies) come later in this chapter, but I get to dividends first.

Understanding the Basics of Income Stocks

I certainly think that dividend-paying stocks are a great consideration for those investors seeking greater income in their portfolios. I especially like stocks with higher-than-average dividends that are known as *income stocks*. Income stocks take on a dual role in that they can not only appreciate but also provide regular income. The following sections take a closer look at dividends and income stocks.

Getting a grip on dividends and dividend rates

When people talk about gaining income from stocks, they're usually talking about dividends. Dividends are pro rata distributions that treat every stockholder the same. A *dividend* is nothing more than pro rata periodic distributions of cash (or sometimes stock) to the stock owner. You purchase dividend stocks primarily for income — not for spectacular growth potential.

Dividends are sometimes confused with interest. However, dividends are payouts to owners, whereas *interest* is a payment to a creditor. A stock investor is considered a part owner of the company he invests in and is entitled to dividends when they're issued. A bank, on the other hand, considers you a creditor when you open an account. The bank borrows your money and pays you interest on it.

A dividend is quoted as an annual dollar amount (or percentage yield) but is usually paid on a quarterly basis. For example, if a stock pays a dividend of $4 per share, you're probably paid $1 every quarter. If, in this example, you have 200 shares, you're paid $800 every year (if the dividend doesn't change during that period), or $200 per quarter. Getting that regular dividend check every three months (for as long as you hold the stock) can be a nice perk. If the company continues to do well, that dividend can grow over time. A good income stock has a higher-than-average dividend (typically 4 percent or higher).

REMEMBER

Dividend rates aren't guaranteed, and they are subject to the decisions of the stock issuer's board of directors — they can go up or down, or in some extreme cases, the dividend can be suspended or even discontinued. Fortunately, most companies that issue dividends continue them indefinitely and actually increase dividend payments from time to time. Historically, dividend increases have equaled (or exceeded) the rate of inflation.

Recognizing who's well-suited for income stocks

What type of person is best suited to income stocks? Income stocks can be appropriate for many investors, but they're especially well-suited for the following individuals:

>> **Conservative and novice investors:** Conservative investors like to see a slow-but-steady approach to growing their money while getting regular dividend checks. Novice investors who want to start slowly also benefit from income stocks.

>> **Retirees:** Growth investing (which I describe in Chapter 8) is best suited for long-term needs, whereas income investing is best suited to current needs. Retirees may want some growth in their portfolios, but they're more concerned with regular income that can keep pace with inflation.

>> **Dividend reinvestment plan (DRP) investors:** For those investors who like to compound their money with DRPs, income stocks are perfect. For more information on DRPs, see Chapter 19.

TIP

Given recent economic trends and conditions for the foreseeable future (I give you the heads-up on many of them for 2020–2030 in Chapter 25), I think that dividends should be a mandatory part of the stock investor's wealth-building approach. This is especially true for those in or approaching retirement. Investing in stocks that have a reliable track record of increasing dividends is now easier than ever. There are, in fact, exchange-traded funds (ETFs) that are focused on stocks with a long and consistent track record of raising dividends (typically on an annual basis). ETFs such as the iShares Core High Dividend ETF (symbol HDV) hold 45–50 companies that have raised their dividends every year for ten years or longer. HDV paid a dividend of 24 cents in 2011, and that dividend went to 82 cents in 2019 — a 241 percent increase in eight years. Similar ETFs are available and can be found at sites such as www.etfdb.com (use search terms such as "high dividend," "dividend growth," or "dividend yield" to find them). Discover more about ETFs in Chapter 5.

Assessing the advantages of income stocks

Income stocks tend to be among the least volatile of all stocks, and many investors view them as defensive stocks. *Defensive stocks* are stocks of companies that sell goods and services that are generally needed no matter what shape the economy is in. (Don't confuse defensive stocks with *defense stocks,* which specialize in goods and equipment for the military.) Food, beverage, and utility companies are great examples of defensive stocks. Even when the economy is experiencing tough times, people still need to eat, drink, and turn on the lights. Companies that offer relatively high dividends also tend to be large firms in established, stable industries.

TIP

Some industries in particular are known for high-dividend stocks. Utilities (such as electric, gas, and water), real estate investment trusts (REITs), and the energy sector (oil and gas royalty trusts) are places where you definitely find income stocks. Yes, you can find high-dividend stocks in other industries, but you find a higher concentration of them in these industries. For more details, see the sections highlighting these industries later in this chapter.

Heeding the disadvantages of income stocks

Before you say, "Income stocks are great! I'll get my checkbook and buy a batch right now," take a look at the following potential disadvantages (ugh!). Income stocks do come with some fine print.

What goes up . . .

Income stocks can go down as well as up, just as any stock can. The factors that affect stocks in general — politics (Chapter 15), megatrends (Chapter 13), different kinds of risk (Chapter 4), and so on — affect income stocks, too. Fortunately, income stocks don't get hit as hard as other stocks when the market is declining because high dividends tend to act as a support to the stock price. Therefore, income stocks' prices usually fall less dramatically than other stocks' prices in a declining market.

Interest-rate sensitivity

Income stocks can be sensitive to rising interest rates. When interest rates go up, other investments (such as corporate bonds, U.S. Treasury securities, and bank certificates of deposit) are more attractive. When your income stock yields

4 percent and interest rates go up to 5 percent, 6 percent, or higher, you may think, "Hmm. Why settle for a 4 percent yield when I can get better elsewhere?" As more and more investors sell their low-yield stocks, the prices for those stocks fall.

Another point to note is that rising interest rates may hurt the company's financial strength. If the company has to pay more interest, that may affect the company's earnings, which in turn may affect the company's ability to continue paying dividends.

REMEMBER

Dividend-paying companies that experience consistently falling revenues tend to cut dividends. In this case, *consistent* means two or more years.

The effect of inflation

Although many companies raise their dividends on a regular basis, some don't. Or if they do raise their dividends, the increases may be small. If income is your primary consideration, you want to be aware of this fact. If you're getting the same dividend year after year and this income is important to you, rising inflation becomes a problem.

Say that you have XYZ stock at $10 per share with an indicated annual dividend of 30 cents (the yield is 30 cents divided by $10, or 3 percent). If you have a yield of 3 percent two years in a row, how do you feel when inflation rises 6 percent one year and 7 percent the next year? Because inflation means your costs are rising, inflation shrinks the value of the dividend income you receive.

Fortunately, studies show that in general, dividends do better in inflationary environments than bonds and other fixed-rate investments. Usually, the dividends of companies that provide consumer staples (food, energy, and so on) meet or exceed the rate of inflation. This is why some investment gurus describe companies that pay growing dividends as having stocks that are "better than bonds."

Uncle Sam's cut

The government usually taxes dividends as ordinary income. Find out from your tax person whether potentially higher tax rates on dividends are in effect for the current or subsequent tax year. See Chapter 21 for more information on taxes for stock investors.

STOCK DIVIDENDS — OR COMPANY DIVIDENDS?

Hearing the phrase "stock dividend" is common in financial discussions about the stock market. However, the reality is that dividends are not paid by stocks; they are paid pro rata distributions of cash by companies. It may sound like I'm splitting hairs, but it is a fundamental difference. Stock prices are subject to the whims of market buying and selling — one day the share prices are up nicely; the next day prices go down when that day's headlines spook the market. Since the dividend is not volatile and it is paid with regularity (quarterly usually), it is more predictable, and I think that investors should be in the business of "collecting cash flows" versus fretting over the ebb and flow of the market.

What does that mean? If a hundred shares of a given dividend-paying stock provide, say, $100 per year in annual dividends, the income-minded stock investor should keep a running tally of annual dividend amounts. That way, they keep investing until they reach a desired income level (such as $2,000 annual dividend income) and feel confident that this dividend income can be relatively reliable and will keep growing as payouts grow from company operations. Lastly, keep in mind that technically a "stock dividend" is actually a pro rata distribution of stock (and not cash).

Analyzing Income Stocks

As I explain in the preceding section, even conservative income investors can be confronted with different types of risk. (Chapter 4 covers risk and volatility in greater detail.) Fortunately, this section helps you carefully choose income stocks so that you can minimize potential disadvantages.

TIP

Look at income stocks in the same way you do growth stocks when assessing the financial strength of a company. Getting nice dividends comes to a screeching halt if the company can't afford to pay them. If your budget depends on dividend income, then monitoring the company's financial strength is that much more important. You can apply the same techniques I list in Chapters 8 and 11 for assessing the financial strength of growth stocks to your assessment of income stocks.

Pinpointing your needs first

You choose income stocks primarily because you want or need income now. As a secondary point, income stocks have the potential for steady, long-term appreciation. So if you're investing for retirement needs that won't occur for another

20 years, maybe income stocks aren't suitable for you — a better choice may be to invest in growth stocks because they're more likely to grow your money faster over a lengthier investment term. (I explain who's best suited to income stocks earlier in this chapter.)

If you're certain you want income stocks, do a rough calculation to figure out how big a portion of your portfolio you want income stocks to occupy. Suppose that you need $25,000 in investment income to satisfy your current financial needs. If you have bonds that give you $20,000 in interest income, and you want the rest to come from dividends from income stocks, you need to choose stocks that pay you $5,000 in annual dividends. If you have $100,000 left to invest, you need a portfolio of income stocks that yields 5 percent ($5,000 divided by $100,000 equals a yield of 5 percent; I explain yield in more detail in the following section).

You may ask, "Why not just buy $100,000 of bonds (for instance) that may yield at least 5 percent?" Well, if you're satisfied with that $5,000, and inflation for the foreseeable future is 0 or considerably less than 5 percent, then you have a point. Unfortunately, inflation (low or otherwise) will probably be with us for a long time. Fortunately, the steady growth of the dividends that income stocks provide is a benefit to you.

TIP

If you have income stocks and don't have any immediate need for the dividends, consider reinvesting the dividends in the company's stock. For more details on this kind of reinvesting, see Chapter 19.

REMEMBER

Every investor is different. If you're not sure about your current or future needs, your best choice is to consult with a financial planner. Flip to Appendix A for helpful financial planning and investing resources.

Checking out yield

Because income stocks pay out dividends — income — you need to assess which stocks can give you the highest income. How do you do that? The main thing to look for is *yield,* which is the percentage rate of return paid on a stock in the form of dividends. Looking at a stock's dividend yield is the quickest way to find out how much money you'll earn versus other dividend-paying stocks (or even other investments, such as a bank account). Table 9-1 illustrates this point. Dividend yield is calculated in the following way:

Dividend yield = Dividend income ÷ Stock investment

TABLE 9-1	Comparing Yields			
Investment	Type	Investment Amount	Annual Investment Income (Dividend)	Yield (Annual Investment Income Divided by Investment Amount)
Smith Co.	Common stock	$20 per share	$1.00 per share	5%
Jones Co.	Common stock	$30 per share	$1.50 per share	5%
Wilson Bank	Savings account	$1,000 deposit	$10 (interest)	1%

The next two sections use the information in Table 9-1 to compare the yields from different investments and to show how evaluating yield helps you choose the stock that earns you the most money.

REMEMBER

Don't stop scrutinizing stocks after you acquire them. You may make a great choice that gives you a great dividend, but that doesn't mean the stock will continue to perform indefinitely. Monitor the company's progress for as long as the stock is in your portfolio by using resources such as www.bloomberg.com and www.marketwatch.com (see Appendix A for more resources).

Examining changes in yield

Most people have no problem understanding yield when it comes to bank accounts. If I tell you that my bank certificate of deposit (CD) has an annual yield of 3.5 percent, you can easily figure out that if I deposit $1,000 in that account, a year later I'll have $1,035 (slightly more if you include compounding). The CD's market value in this example is the same as the deposit amount — $1,000. That makes it easy to calculate.

REMEMBER

How about stocks? When you see a stock listed in the financial pages, the dividend yield is provided, along with the stock's price and annual dividend. The dividend yield in the financial pages is always calculated based on the closing price of the stock on that given day. Just keep in mind that based on supply and demand, stock prices will fluctuate throughout trading hours, so the yield changes throughout trading hours, too. So keep the following two things in mind when examining yield:

>> **The yield listed in the financial pages may not represent the yield you're receiving.** What if you bought stock in Smith Co. (see Table 9-1) a month ago at $20 per share? With an annual dividend of $1, you know your yield is 5 percent. But what if today Smith Co. is selling for $40 per share? If you look in the financial pages, the yield quoted is 2.5 percent. Gasp! Did the dividend get

cut in half?! No, not really. You're still getting 5 percent because you bought the stock at $20 rather than the current $40 price; the quoted yield is for investors who purchase Smith Co. today. They pay $40 and get the $1 dividend, and they're locked into the current yield of 2.5 percent. Although Smith Co. may have been a good income investment for you a month ago, it's not such a hot pick today because the price of the stock has doubled, cutting the yield in half. Even though the dividend hasn't changed, the yield has changed dramatically because of the stock price change.

» **Stock price affects how good of an investment the stock may be.** Another way to look at yield is by looking at the investment amount. Using Smith Co. in Table 9-1 as the example, the investor who bought, say, 100 shares of Smith Co. when they were $20 per share paid only $2,000 (100 shares multiplied by $20 — leave out commissions to make the example simple). If the same stock is purchased later at $40 per share, the total investment amount is $4,000 (100 shares multiplied by $40). In either case, the investor gets a total dividend income of $100 (100 shares multiplied by $1 dividend per share). Which investment is yielding more — the $2,000 investment or the $4,000 investment? Of course, it's better to get the income ($100 in this case) with the smaller investment (a 5 percent yield is better than a 2.5 percent yield).

Comparing yield between different stocks

All things being equal, choosing Smith Co. or Jones Co. is a coin toss. It's looking at your situation and each company's fundamentals and prospects that will sway you. What if Smith Co. is an auto stock (similar to General Motors in 2008) and Jones Co. is a utility serving the Las Vegas metro area? Now what? In 2008, the automotive industry struggled tremendously, but utilities were generally in much better shape. In that scenario, Smith Co.'s dividend is in jeopardy, whereas Jones Co.'s dividend is more secure. Another issue is the payout ratio (see the next section). Therefore, companies whose dividends have the same yield may still have different risks.

Looking at a stock's payout ratio

You can use the *payout ratio* to figure out what percentage of a company's earnings is being paid out in the form of dividends (earnings = sales − expenses). Keep in mind that companies pay dividends from their net earnings. (Technically, the money comes from the company's capital accounts, but that money ultimately comes from net earnings and capital infusions.) Given that, the company's earnings should always be higher than the dividends the company pays out. An investor wants to see total earnings growth that exceeds the total amount paid for dividends. Here's how to figure a payout ratio:

Dividend (per share) ÷ Earnings (per share) = Payout ratio

Say that the company CashFlow Now, Inc. (CFN), has annual earnings (or net income) of $1 million. Total dividends are to be paid out of $500,000, and the company has 1 million outstanding shares. Using those numbers, you know that CFN's earnings per share (EPS) are $1 ($1 million in earnings divided by 1 million shares) and that it pays an annual dividend of 50 cents per share ($500,000 divided by 1 million shares). The dividend payout ratio is 50 percent (the 50-cent dividend is 50 percent of the $1 EPS). This number is a healthy dividend payout ratio because even if CFN's earnings fall by 10 percent or 20 percent, plenty of room still exists to pay dividends.

TIP

If you're concerned about your dividend income's safety, regularly watch the payout ratio. The maximum acceptable payout ratio should be 80 percent, and a good range is 50 to 70 percent. A payout ratio of 60 percent or lower is considered very safe (the lower the percentage, the safer the dividend).

REMEMBER

When a company suffers significant financial difficulties, its ability to pay dividends is compromised. Good examples of stocks that have had their dividends cut in recent years due to financial difficulties are mortgage companies in the wake of the housing bubble bursting and the fallout from the subprime debt fiasco. Mortgage companies received less and less income due to mortgage defaults, which forced the lowering of dividends as cash inflow shrank. So if you need dividend income to help you pay your bills, you better be aware of the dividend payout ratio.

Studying a company's bond rating

Bond rating? Huh? What's that got to do with dividend-paying stocks? Actually, a company's bond rating is very important to income stock investors. The bond rating offers insight into the company's financial strength. Bonds get rated for quality for the same reasons that consumer agencies rate products like cars or toasters. Standard & Poor's (S&P) and Moody's are the major independent rating agencies that look into bond issuers. They look at the bond issuer and ask, "Does this bond issuer have the financial strength to pay back the bond and the interest as stipulated in the bond indenture?"

To understand why this rating is important, consider the following:

>> **A good bond rating means that the company is strong enough to pay its obligations.** These obligations include expenses, payments on debts, and declared dividends. If a bond rating agency gives the company a high rating

(or if it raises the rating), that's a great sign for anyone holding the company's debt or receiving dividends.

WARNING

>> **If a bond rating agency lowers the rating, that means the company's financial strength is deteriorating** — a red flag for anyone who owns the company's bonds or stock. A lower bond rating today may mean trouble for the dividend later on.

>> **A poor bond rating means that the company is having difficulty paying its obligations.** If the company can't pay all its obligations, it has to choose which ones to pay. More times than not, a financially troubled company chooses to cut dividends or (in a worst-case scenario) not pay dividends at all.

REMEMBER

The highest rating issued by S&P is AAA. The grades AAA, AA, and A are considered *investment grade,* or of high quality. Bs and Cs indicate a medium grade, and anything lower than that is considered poor or very risky (the bonds are referred to as *junk bonds*). So if you see an XXX rating, then . . . gee . . . you better stay away!

Diversifying your stocks

If most of your dividend income is from stock in a single company or single industry, consider reallocating your investment to avoid having all your eggs in one basket. Concerns about diversification apply to income stocks as well as growth stocks. If all your income stocks are in the electric utility industry, then any problems in that industry are potential problems for your portfolio as well. See Chapter 4 for more on risk.

Exploring Some Typical Income Stocks

Although virtually every industry has stocks that pay dividends, some industries have more dividend-paying stocks than others. You won't find too many dividend-paying income stocks in the computer or biotech industries, for instance. The reason is that these types of companies need a lot of money to finance expensive research and development (R&D) projects to create new products. Without R&D, the company can't create new products to fuel sales, growth, and future earnings. Computer, biotech, and other innovative industries are better for growth investors. Keep reading for the scoop on stocks that work well for income investors.

It's electric! Utilities

Public utilities are among the stock market's most reliable dividend payers. They generate a large cash flow (if you don't believe me, look at your gas and electric bills!). Many investors have at least one utility company in their portfolio. Income-minded investors (especially retirees) should seriously consider utilities — and there are great utilities ETFs as well (see Chapter 5 for more on ETFs). Investing in your own local utility isn't a bad idea — at least it makes paying the utility bill less painful.

REMEMBER

Before you invest in a public utility, consider the following:

>> **The utility company's financial condition:** Is the company making money, and are its sales and earnings growing from year to year? Make sure the utility's bonds are rated A or higher (see the earlier section "Studying a company's bond rating").

>> **The company's dividend payout ratio:** Because utilities tend to have a good cash flow, don't be too concerned if the ratio reaches 70 percent. From a safety point of view, however, the lower the rate, the better. See the earlier section "Looking at a stock's payout ratio" for more on payout ratios.

>> **The company's geographic location:** If the utility covers an area that's doing well and offers an increasing population base and business expansion, that bodes well for your stock. A good resource for researching population and business data is the U.S. Census Bureau (www.census.gov).

An interesting mix: Real estate investment trusts (REITs)

Real estate investment trusts (REITs) are a special breed of stock. A *REIT* is an investment that has elements of both a stock and a *mutual fund* (a pool of money received from investors that's managed by an investment company):

>> A REIT resembles a stock in that it's a company whose stock is publicly traded on the major stock exchanges, and it has the usual features that you expect from a stock — it can be bought and sold easily through a broker, income is given to investors as dividends, and so on.

>> A REIT resembles a mutual fund in that it doesn't make its money selling goods and services; it makes its money by buying, selling, and managing an investment portfolio of real estate investments. It generates revenue from rents and property leases, as any landlord does. In addition, some REITs own mortgages, and they gain income from the interest.

TECHNICAL
STUFF

REITs are called *trusts* only because they meet the requirements of the Real Estate Investment Trust Act of 1960. This act exempts REITs from corporate income tax and capital gains taxes as long as they meet certain criteria, such as dispensing 90 percent of their net income to shareholders. This provision is the reason why REITs generally issue generous dividends. Beyond this status, REITs are, in a practical sense, like any other publicly traded company.

The main advantages to investing in REITs include the following:

>> Unlike other types of real estate investing, REITs are easy to buy and sell (REITs are more liquid than other types of traditional real estate investing). You can buy a REIT by making a phone call to a broker or visiting a broker's website, just as you can to purchase any stock.

>> REITs have higher-than-average yields. Because they must distribute at least 90 percent of their income to shareholders, their dividends usually yield a return of 5 to 10 percent.

>> REITs involve a lower risk than the direct purchase of real estate because they use a portfolio approach diversified among many properties. Because you're investing in a company that buys the real estate, you don't have to worry about managing the properties — the company's management does that on a full-time basis. Usually, the REIT doesn't just manage one property; it's diversified in a portfolio of different properties.

>> Investing in a REIT is affordable for small investors. REIT shares usually trade in the $10 to $40 range, meaning that you can invest with very little money.

WARNING

REITs do have disadvantages. Although they tend to be diversified with various properties, they're still susceptible to risks tied to the general real estate sector. Real estate investing reached manic, record-high levels during 2000–2007, which meant that a downturn was likely. Whenever you invest in an asset (like real estate or REITs in recent years) that has already skyrocketed due to artificial stimulants (in the case of real estate, very low interest rates and too much credit and debt), the potential losses can offset any potential (unrealized) income.

TIP

When you're looking for a REIT to invest in, analyze it the way you'd analyze a property. Look at the location and type of property. If shopping malls are booming in California and your REIT buys and sells shopping malls in California, then you'll probably do well. However, if your REIT invests in office buildings across the country and the office building market is overbuilt and having tough times, you'll have a tough time, too.

Many of the dangers of the "housing bubble" have passed, and investors can start looking at real estate investments (such as REITs) with less anxiety. However, choosing REITs with a view toward quality and strong fundamentals (location, potential rents, and so forth) is still a good idea.

Business development companies (BDCs)

For those seeking a relatively high dividend with some growth potential, consider taking a look at business development companies (BDCs). They sound a little arcane but they can be bought as easily as a stock, and their setup is not that difficult to understand. A BDC is essentially a hybrid between a venture capital company and a mutual fund, and it trades like a closed-end fund. A closed-end fund functions like a regular mutual fund, but it is listed in the same way as a stock and has a finite number of total shares. Regular mutual funds are referred to as "open-ended," which means that their shares are issued (or redeemed) and there is no finite number of shares as with closed-end funds.

Like a venture capital firm, a BDC invests in companies that are small or mid-sized and that need capital to grow in their early stages of development. A BDC is like a mutual fund in that it will invest in a batch of companies so there is some sense of diversification. The companies that the BDC invests in tend to be in a particular niche such as biotech, robotics, or another "sunrise" industry. As part of the financial structure, the companies receiving the funding from the BDC pay back the financing through higher fees and interest, so BDCs tend to have a high dividend.

Given that, a BDC can provide good dividend income, but keep in mind that there is higher risk since the companies are still in the early stages of development. For more details on BDCs, check out resources such as the following:

>> CEF Connect (www.cefconnect.com)

>> Closed-End Fund Advisors (www.cefdata.com)

>> Closed-End Fund Association (www.cefa.com/)

As of this writing, there are now 49 BDCs, so there is more information on them in traditional stock investing resources (see Appendix A for more details).

Covered Call Writing for Income

The world of options can be a little tricky (and can be very risky), but there is a relatively safe options strategy that any income-minded, conservative investor should consider (even if you're a retiree). Imagine a low-risk strategy that can easily boost your stock portfolio's cash flow by 5 percent, 7 percent, 9 percent, or even more. Yes . . . it is called covered call writing.

If you do covered call writing in a disciplined way, you won't lose money, but it does come with one risk — you may be forced to sell your asset (at a profit). What a risk!

Writing a covered call means that you, as the stock investor, enter into a buy/sell transaction (the "call") whereby you (the seller or writer) will receive income (the "option premium") in exchange for the potential obligation of selling your shares to the call buyer at a set price and time frame. If, say, you own 100 shares of a stock in your brokerage account at $45 per share, you could write a call option on these 100 shares where you may have an obligation to sell those shares at, say, $50 per share. In this example, the call buyer paid you a premium of, say, $100. If your shares do not reach the higher price of $50, you continue holding onto your shares, and you also keep the $100 you received. This call option is only for a relatively brief period of time (regular options typically expire in nine months or less, but there are long-dated options that have a shelf life beyond a year), so the price move would have to occur during the short life of the call option. If the call option expires before the stock reaches $50 (referred to as the "strike price"), then the call buyer has lost money, but the call writer gets to keep the cash received from the call option.

Covered call writing is a great way to generate extra income from your stocks, and the only risk is that if the stock hits the strike price (in this case, $50 per share), the writer is obligated to sell the 100 shares at the elevated price of $50. Wow — such a risk — being obligated to sell your stock at a higher, more profitable share price!

For more comprehensive details on writing covered calls, see my book *High-Level Investing For Dummies* (published by Wiley).

Writing Puts for Income

Imagine earning income where the only risk is that you may be obligated to buy the stock of a company that you would like to own — at a lower price! I think that's cool. This sweet event can happen when you write a put option in your brokerage account.

When you write (sell) a put option, you will receive income (the premium), and in exchange you will have an obligation — you will be required to purchase the underlying security at the option's strike price. Say that there is a $50 stock you like, but you would like to purchase it at a lower price, such as $45. In that case, you write a put option with the strike price of $45. You receive the premium income (say $200 in this example). If the stock does not go down to $45 during the option time frame, the option would expire, and the good news is that you keep the $200 as income (cool!). If the stock goes down to $45 (or lower) during the time frame of the put option, you're required to buy the stock at $45. The good news is that you end up buying a stock you like at a discount (cool again!). Why? Because you really end up paying $4,300 for the underlying stock. The breakdown is that the stock costs $4,500 (100 shares multiplied by $45), but you also received $200 in put option income, meaning that your total outlay of funds was only $4,300 ($4,500 minus $200).

TIP

Given that, we come to the first golden rule of writing put options: Only write a put option on a stock (or ETF) that you would *love* to own anyway. Think of stocks that you consider an excellent addition to your brokerage portfolio. Say that the stock you are strongly considering is at $40 per share, and you would be happy to own it at $35 per share.

For more in-depth information on writing put options, you can get my book *High-Level Investing For Dummies* (published by Wiley).

Chapter **10**

Understanding Technical Analysis for Stock Investors

I n my early days as a stock investor, I rarely used technical analysis, but as time passed (and experience piled up), I came to see it as a useful part of my overall investing approach. Yes, technical analysis is . . . well . . . technical, but it can help you time your decision about when you want to buy, sell, or hold a particular stock. In short, fundamental analysis (what the rest of this book discusses) tells you *what* to buy, and technical analysis tells you *when* to buy.

I won't make this chapter an exhaustive treatment of this topic (I bet you just said "Whew!"), but I do want to alert you to techniques and resources that will give you a leg up in today's volatile and uncertain markets.

TIP

I'd like to mention some resources right out of the starting gate. Use the following resources to discover more information about technical analysis:

» Big Charts (www.bigcharts.com)

» Incredible Charts (www.incrediblecharts.com)

- » International Federation of Technical Analysts (www.ifta.org)

- » StockCharts (www.stockcharts.com)

- » *Stocks & Commodities* magazine (www.traders.com)

- » *Technical Analysis For Dummies,* 4th Edition, by Barbara Rockefeller (Wiley) (www.dummies.com)

- » TraderPlanet (www.traderplanet.com)

Comparing Technical Analysis and Fundamental Analysis

When figuring out what to do in the investment world, most professionals use one of two basic approaches: fundamental analysis or technical analysis (many use some combination of the two). Both approaches are used in a number of markets ranging from the stock market to commodities, but I limit this chapter to stock investing. The main differences between fundamental analysis and technical analysis are pretty easy to understand:

- » **Fundamental analysis** goes into the economics of the company itself, such as sales and profit data, as well as external factors affecting it, such as politics, regulations, and industry trends.

- » **Technical analysis** tries to understand where a stock's price is going based on market behavior as evidenced in its market statistics (presented in charts, price, and trading volume data). Technical analysis doesn't try to figure out the worth of an investment; it's used to figure out where the price of that stock or investment is trending.

In the following sections, I talk about the main principles of technical analysis, and I note its pros and cons as compared to fundamental analysis. I also explain how to combine technical analysis with fundamental analysis, and I list some tools of the trade.

Looking under the hood of technical analysis

To get the most benefit from using technical analysis, you need to understand how it operates and what it is that you're looking at. Technical analysis, for the purposes of this book, is based on the following assumptions.

The price is the be-all and end-all

The premise of technical analysis is that the stock's market price provides enough information to render a trading decision. Those who criticize technical analysis point out that it considers the price and its movement without paying adequate attention to the fundamental factors of the company. The argument made favoring technical analysis is that the price is a snapshot that, in fact, does reflect the basic factors affecting the company, including the company's (or investment's) fundamentals.

REMEMBER

Technical analysts (also called *technicians* or *chartists*) believe that a company's fundamentals, along with broader economic factors and market psychology, are all priced into the stock, removing the need to actually consider these factors separately. The bottom line is that technicians look at the price and its movement to extract a forecast for where the stock is going.

The trend is your friend

The price of a stock tends to move in trends. In the world of technical analysis, the phrase "the trend is your friend" is as ubiquitous as the phrase "you spoiled the broth, now you lie in it!" is in the restaurant industry. Maybe even more so. Following the trend is a bedrock principle in technical analysis, and the data either supports the trend or it doesn't. When a trend in the stock's price is established, its tendency is to continue. The three types of trends are up, down, and sideways (but you knew that). (See the later section "Staying on Top of Trends" for more information.)

If it happened before, it will happen again

Another foundational idea in technical analysis is that history tends to repeat itself, mainly in terms of price movement. The repetitive nature of price movements is attributed to market psychology; in other words, market participants tend to provide a consistent reaction to similar market stimuli over time.

Technical analysis uses chart patterns to analyze market movements and understand trends. Although many of these charts have been used for more than 100 years, they're still believed to be relevant because they illustrate patterns in price movements that often repeat themselves. (I talk about chart patterns in more detail later in this chapter.)

Examining the good and bad of technical analysis

Although technical analysis is the "star" of this chapter, it does have its shortcomings. The major drawback of technical analysis is that it's a human approach that tracks human behavior in a particular market. In other words, just because it's called technical analysis doesn't mean that it's technical à la the laws of physics. It's called technical analysis because the data you look at is technical. But the movement of the price of the underlying stock or investment is due to the cumulative decisions of many buyers and sellers who are human — and therefore, fallible.

Why mention this? Everyone is looking to make money, and many trading systems and approaches are based on technical analysis. Unfortunately, making profitable investments isn't a matter of two plus two equals four. If technical analysis made things so easy that mere computer models or trading systems could give you a voilà moneymaking decision, everyone could — and would — do it. Yet, that's not the case.

Here's my take on it. I favor fundamental analysis for long-term investing. I shun technical analysis for choosing individual stocks because I don't see the long-term value in it. Long-term investors don't have to bother with things such as triangles, pennants, cup-and-handles, or other paraphernalia. Long-term investors just ask questions like "Is the company making money?" or "Are financial and economic conditions still favorable for my investment?" When the fundamentals are in your favor, any short-term move against you is a buying opportunity (provided that you choose wisely from the start). But unfortunately, too many investors aren't patient, and they get too busy with the short-term trees to be bothered by the long-term forest. Yet that long-term forest has a lot more green, if you know what I mean (I hope I'm not meandering here).

TECHNICAL STUFF

If you were to do a nose count of successful investors in stock market history and what approaches they used, you'd find that those long-term investors who used some variation of fundamental analysis (such as those who used a value-investing approach) overwhelmingly comprise the larger category. Legendary investors like Warren Buffett and Peter Lynch rarely looked at a chart. Think about it: Warren Buffett is obviously one of history's greatest success stories in the world of stock investing. His track record and multibillion-dollar net worth attest to this. Yet he rarely (if ever) looks at any technical analysis. He isn't concerned with short-term squiggles and fluctuations. He is indeed a long-term investor, and one of his greatest assets is *patience*. He has held some stocks for decades. The point makes for an interesting observation into human nature. Everyone wants to succeed like Warren Buffett, but few are willing to go the distance.

The short term is a different animal. It requires more attention and discipline. You need to monitor all the indicators to see whether you're on track or whether the signals are warning a change in course. The technicals can be bearish one month and bullish the next. And the month after that, the signals can be mixed and give no clear warnings at all. Being a proficient technician ultimately requires more monitoring, more trading, and more hedging.

Note that all this activity also means more taxes, more transaction costs (commissions and the like), and more administrative work (tax reporting and so on). After all, who do you think will pay more in taxes: someone who buys and holds for a year or longer, or someone who makes the same profit by jumping in and out based on which way the technical winds are blowing? Short-term gains don't have the same favorable rates as long-term gains. The issue isn't what you make but what you keep (I cover taxes in Chapter 21).

REMEMBER

But before you throw out technical analysis with the bath water, read on. Those who use technical analysis in short-term trading or speculating in larger-scope investments tend to do better than those who don't use it. That means that if you apply technical analysis to something larger than a company, such as an index or a commodity, you'll tend to do better. If you're getting into trading stocks and/or stock-related exchange-traded funds (ETFs; see Chapter 5), then understanding the basics of technical analysis will make you, overall, a better (and hence more profitable) trader. Because short-term market behavior and psychology can be very mercurial and irrational (human), technical analysis has its usefulness. It's most useful for those folks who are trading and/or speculating during a relatively short time frame measured in days, weeks, or months. It isn't that useful when you're trying to forecast where a stock's price will be a year or more down the road.

Combining the best of both worlds

REMEMBER

I think a useful way to combine both fundamental analysis and technical analysis is to take advantage of the strength of each. Fundamental analysis helps you understand *what* to invest (or trade or speculate) in, whereas technical analysis guides you as to *when* to do it. Because markets ebb and flow, zig and zag, technical analysis can help you spot low-risk points to either enter or exit a trade. Technical analysis, therefore, helps you stack the deck a little more in your favor. Considering how markets have been going lately, every little bit helps.

Blending the two approaches to some extent has been done with success. Obviously, if the fundamental and the technical factors support your decision, then the chance for a profitable trade has more going for it. How does this blend occur?

For an example, look at the concepts of oversold and overbought (see the later section "Surveying the Relative Strength Index"). If you're looking at buying a stock (or other investment) because you think it's a strong investment but you're not sure about when to buy, you want to look at the technical data. If the data tells you that it has been oversold, it's a good time to buy. *Oversold* just means that the market was a little too extreme in selling that particular investment during a particular period of time.

By the way, I like to think that the technical terms *oversold* and *overbought* have a parallel to fundamental terms such as *undervalued* and *overvalued*. Because fundamental analysis is a major part of a school of thought referred to as *value investing*, the concepts make sense (yes, I'm into value investing). Just as investing in an undervalued stock is usually a good idea, so is buying a stock that has been oversold. It's logical to presume that an oversold stock is undervalued (all things being equal). Of course, the other terms (overbought and overvalued) can also run in tandem. I may as well finish here before you're overwhelmed and underinterested.

On the other hand, the fundamentals can help a technical analyst make a better trading decision. Say that a technical analyst has a profitable position in a particular stock called Getting Near a Cliff Corp. (GNAC). If the technical indicators are turning bearish and the new quarterly earnings report for GNAC indicates a significantly lower profit, then selling GNAC's stock is probably a good idea. (Of course, because you're reading this book, you're doing something better like immediately putting on a trailing stop, right? See Chapter 17 for details on trailing stops.)

Using the technician's tools

When you roll up your sleeves and get into technical analysis, what will you be dealing with? It depends on what type of technical analyst you are. In technical analysis, there are two subcategories: those who predominantly use charts (these technicians are called . . . chartists!) and those who predominantly use data (such as price and volume data). Of course, many technicians use a combination of both (and I discuss both later in this chapter):

>> **Charts:** Charts are the neat pictures that graph price movements (such as chart patterns).

>> **Data:** Data includes price and volume information (along with technical and behavioral indicators derived from it).

Technical analysts don't look at the fundamentals because they believe that the marketplace (as depicted in the charts, price, and volume data) already take into account the fundamentals.

Staying on Top of Trends

Identifying trends is a crucial part of technical analysis. A *trend* is just the overall direction of a stock (or another security or a commodity); you can see trends in technical charts (I provide details about charts later in this chapter). Which way is the price headed? In the following sections, I describe different types of trends, talk about trend length, and discuss trendlines and channel lines.

Distinguishing different trends

Three basic trends exist:

>> **An uptrend or bullish trend** is when each successive high is higher than the previous high and each successive low is higher than the previous low.

>> **A downtrend or bearish trend** is when each successive high is lower than the previous high and each successive low is lower than the previous low.

>> **A sideways trend or horizontal trend** shows that the highs and the lows are both in a generally sideways pattern with no clear indication of trending up or down (at least not yet).

It's easy to see which way the stock is headed in Figure 10-1. Unless you're a skier, that's not a pretty picture. The bearish trend is obvious.

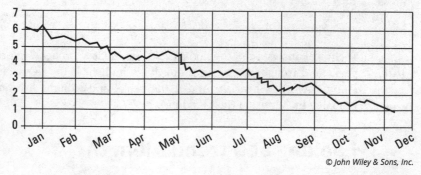

FIGURE 10-1: Generic chart sloping in a definite downward direction.

© John Wiley & Sons, Inc.

What do you do with a chart like Figure 10-2? Yup . . . looks like somebody's heart monitor while he's watching a horror movie. A sideways or horizontal trend just shows a consolidation pattern that means that the stock will break out into an uptrend or downtrend.

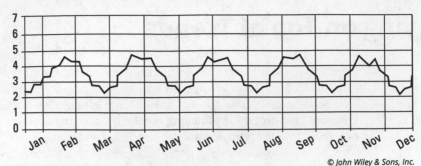

FIGURE 10-2: Generic chart showing a sideways pattern.

© John Wiley & Sons, Inc.

Regardless of whether a trend is up, down, or sideways, you'll notice that it's rarely (closer to never) in a straight line. The line is usually jagged and bumpy because it's really a summary of all the buyers and sellers making their trades. Some days the buyers have more impact, and some days it's the sellers' turn. Figure 10-3 shows all three trends.

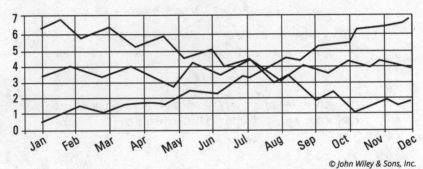

FIGURE 10-3: Chart that simultaneously shows an up, down, and sideways trend.

© John Wiley & Sons, Inc.

REMEMBER

Technical analysts call the highs *peaks* and the lows *troughs*. In other words, if the peaks and troughs keep going up, that's bullish. If the peaks and troughs keep going down, it's bearish. And if the peaks and troughs are horizontal, you're probably in California (just kidding).

Looking at a trend's length

With trends, you're not just looking at the direction; you're also looking at the trend's *duration*, or the length of time that it goes along. Trend durations can be (you guessed it) short-term, intermediate-term, or long-term:

>> **A short-term (or near-term) trend** is generally less than a month.

>> **An intermediate-term trend** is up to a quarter (three months) long.

» **A long-term trend** can last up to a year. And to muddy the water a bit, the long-term trend may have several trends inside it (don't worry; the quiz has been canceled).

Using trendlines

A *trendline* is a simple feature added to a chart: a straight line designating a clear path for a particular trend. Trendlines simply follow the peaks and troughs to show a distinctive direction. They can also be used to identify a trend reversal, or a change in the opposite direction. Figure 10-4 shows two trendlines: the two straight lines that follow the tops and bottoms of the jagged line (which shows the actual price movement of the asset in question).

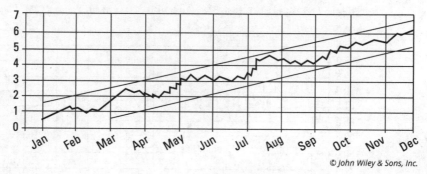

FIGURE 10-4: Chart that shows the jagged edge going upward along with the trendlines.

© John Wiley & Sons, Inc.

Watching the channel for resistance and support

REMEMBER

The concepts of resistance and support are critical to technical analysis the way tires are to cars. When the rubber meets the road, you want to know where the price is going:

» **Resistance** is like the proverbial glass ceiling in the market's world of price movement. As a price keeps moving up, how high can or will it go? That's the $64,000 question, and technical analysts watch this closely. Breaking through resistance is considered a positive sign for the price, and the expectation is definitely bullish.

» **Support** is the lowest point or level that a price is trading at. When the price goes down and hits this level, it's expected to bounce back, but what happens when it goes below the support level? It's then considered a bearish sign, and technical analysts watch closely for a potential reversal even though they expect the price to head down.

Channel lines are lines that are added to show both the peaks and troughs of the primary trend. The top line indicates resistance (of the price movement), and the lower line indicates support. Resistance and support form the trading range for the stock's price. The channel can slope or point upward or downward, or go sideways. Technical traders view the channel with interest because the assumption is that the price will continue in the direction of the channel (between resistance and support) until technical indicators signal a change. (To me, this tells me to change to a cable channel, but that's just me. Please continue reading. . . .)

Check out the channel in Figure 10-5; it shows you how the price is range-bound. The emphasis on trends is to help you make more profitable decisions because you're better off trading with the trend than not.

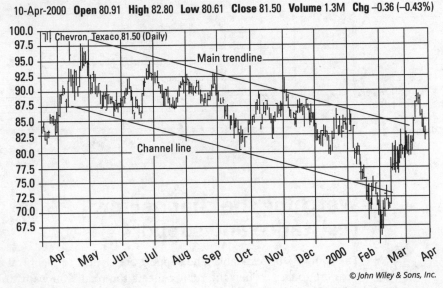

FIGURE 10-5: Chart showing a channel.

© *John Wiley & Sons, Inc.*

In Figure 10-5, you see a good example of a channel for a particular stock. In this case, the stock is zigzagging downward, and toward the end of the channel, it indicates that the stock is getting more volatile as the stock's price movement is outside the original channel lines. This tells the trader/investor to be cautious and on the lookout for opportunities or pitfalls (depending on your outlook for the stock).

Getting the Scoop on Technical Charts

Charts are to technical analysis what pictures are to photography. You can't avoid them 'cause you're not supposed to. If you're serious about trading stocks (or ETFs, commodities, or whatever), charts and the related technical data come in handy. In the following sections, I describe different types of charts and chart patterns.

Checking out types of charts

Technical analysts use charts to "diagnose" an investment's situation the same way any analyst uses different tools and approaches. Different charts provide fresh angles for viewing the data. In terms of visualization and utility, the following are the four most common charts used in technical analysis.

Line charts

A line chart simply shows a series of prices plotted in a graph that displays how the price has moved over a period of time. The period of time can be a day, week, month, year, or longer. The prices that are usually chosen for a line chart are the closing prices for those market days.

With a yearlong line chart (like those that appear earlier in this chapter), you can see how the stock has progressed during the 12-month period, and you can do some simple analysis. When were the peaks? How about the troughs? What were the strongest seasons for this stock's price movement?

TIP

I prefer to use five-year charts; I like to encourage my clients, students, and readers to focus on the longer term because positive results can be easier to achieve.

Bar charts

Bar charts are a little fancier. Whereas the line chart only gives you the closing prices for each market day, the bar chart gives you the range of trading prices for each day during the chosen time period. Each trading day is a vertical line that represents the price movements, and you see the stock's high, low, and closing prices.

In a bar chart, the vertical line has two notches. The notch on the left indicates the opening price, and the notch on the right indicates the closing price. If the opening price notch is higher than the closing price notch, the line is in red to indicate that the closing price of the stock declined versus the opening price. An up day is in black, and the closing price notch is higher than the opening price notch.

Candlestick charts

Candlestick charts have been all the rage in recent years. They're basically bar charts, but they're a little more complex. A candlestick chart provides a more complete picture by adding a visualization of other data that simple charts don't contain, such as the high, low, and closing price of the security the chart is tracking. It stands to reason that because candlestick charts provide more information in a visual form than bar charts, they can provide more guidance in trading. Candlestick charting is too complex to adequately describe in this space, so please continue your research with the resources provided at the start of this chapter.

TECHNICAL STUFF

The full name for these charts is Japanese candlestick charts because they originated as a form of technical analysis in the 17th century, when the Japanese were trading in rice markets. You know, they do look like candlesticks (but I'm waxing eloquent here).

Point-and-figure charts

A more obscure chart that chartists use is the point-and-figure chart. When you look at it, you'll notice a series of Xs and Os. The Xs represent upward price trends, and the Os represent downward price trends. This type of chart enables the stock trader to easily determine which prices are "support levels" and which are "resistance levels" to better judge buy and sell prices.

Picking out chart patterns

Chart patterns are the graphical language of technical analysis, and a very interesting language at that. For technical analysts, the pattern is important because it provides a potential harbinger for what is to come. It's not 100 percent accurate, but it's usually accurate better than 50 percent of the time as odds go. In the world of trading, being right more than 50 percent of the time can be enough. Usually a proficient technician is better than that. The following sections cover common chart patterns.

REMEMBER

Technical analysts don't say that the next step after a particular pattern is a certainty; it's a probability. Probable outcomes, more times than not, tend to materialize. Increasing the probability of success for more profitable decision-making (entering or exiting a trade) is the bottom-line mission of technical analysis.

Above the rest: The head and shoulders

The head and shoulders pattern is essentially bearish. It's usually a signal that an uptrend has ended and the pattern is set to reverse and head downward. Technical analysts consider this to be one of the most reliable patterns.

The pattern shows three peaks and two troughs. The three peaks break down into the tall center peak (the head) and the shorter peaks (the shoulders) that are on either side of the center peak. The two troughs form the neckline.

The head and shoulders pattern tells technical analysts that the preceding trend basically ran out of gas. The selling pressures build up and overpower the buyers. Hence, the price starts to come down. The shoulder on the right is like a last effort for the bullish trend to regain its traction, but to no avail. Keep in mind that the neckline in this pattern is the support (which I discuss in the earlier section "Watching the channel for resistance and support"). As support is broken, the tendency is a bearish expectation.

In reverse: The reverse head and shoulders

As you can infer, this pattern is the opposite of the prior chart pattern, and it's essentially bullish. This pattern signals that a downtrend has ended and is set to reverse and head upward. In this pattern, you have three troughs and two peaks. The middle trough is usually the deepest one. The small trough on the right is an interim low, which is higher than the middle trough low and typically indicates the trend is moving upward.

In this pattern, buying pressures build up and form a base from which to spring upward. Note that a bullish pattern is a series of higher highs and higher lows. In the reverse head and shoulders pattern, the neckline is resistance (which I discuss earlier in this chapter). After resistance is broken, the expectation is for an upward move.

Wake up and smell the coffee: The cup and handle

This pattern is generally bullish. In the pattern, the price first peaks and then craters into a bowl-shaped trough (the cup). It peaks again at the end with a small downward move (the handle) before it moves up.

This pattern basically tells the technician that the stock's price took a breather to build support and then continued its bullish pattern.

Twice as nice: The double top and the double bottom

Both the double top and the double bottom chart patterns indicate a trend reversal:

>> **The double top** is essentially a bearish pattern wherein the price makes two attempts (the double top) to break through resistance but fails to do so. The

bottom of the trough between the two peaks indicates support. However, the two failed attempts at the resistance level are more significant than the support at the trough, so this pattern signals a potential downturn for that stock's price.

>> **The double bottom** is the opposite reversal pattern. It's a bullish pattern because the support level indicators are stronger than the resistance. This pattern signals a potential upturn in the stock's price. Because this indicates a support level, bullish traders tend to look at it as a generally safe entry point to get positioned for the next potential up-move in the stock.

TECHNICAL STUFF

Triple tops and triple bottoms are variations of double tops and double bottoms. These are sideways or horizontal patterns that do portend a trend reversal. Don't even ask about quadruple tops and bottoms!

Triangles (And I don't mean Bermuda!)

A triangle is formed when the resistance line and the support line converge to form the triangle point that shows a general direction in the stock's price movement. There are three types of triangles: symmetrical, ascending, and descending.

>> **Symmetrical:** The symmetrical triangle points sideways, which tells you it's a horizontal pattern that becomes a setup for a move upward or downward when more price movement provides a bullish or bearish indicator.

>> **Ascending:** The ascending triangle is a bullish pattern.

>> **Descending:** The descending triangle is bearish.

Of course, if you see a divergent trapezoidal and octagonal candlestick formation supported in a bowl-shaped isosceles triangle, do nothing! Just take two aspirin and try again tomorrow.

Time to cheer: Flags and pennants

Flags and pennants are familiar chart patterns that are short-term in nature (usually not longer than a few weeks). They're continuation patterns that are formed immediately after a sharp price movement, which is usually followed by a sideways price movement. Both the flag and the pennant are similar except that the flag is triangular, whereas the pennant is in a channel formation (I talk about channels earlier in this chapter).

Cut it up: Wedges

The wedge pattern can be either a continuation or reversal pattern. It seems to be much like a symmetrical triangle, but it slants (up or down), whereas the symmetrical triangle generally shows a sideways movement. In addition, the wedge forms over a longer period of time (typically three to six months).

Watch your step: Gaps

A gap in a chart is an empty space between two trading periods. This pattern occurs when the difference in the price between those two periods is substantial. Say that in the first period, the trading range is $10 to $15. The next trading session opens at $20. That $5 discrepancy will appear as a large gap between those two periods on the chart. These gaps are typically found on bar and candlestick charts. Gaps may happen when positive (or negative) news comes out about the company, and initial buying pressure causes the price to jump in the subsequent period as soon as trading commences.

There are three types of gaps: breakaway, runaway, and exhaustion. The breakaway gap forms at the start of a trend, and the runaway gap forms during the middle of the trend. So what obviously happens when the trend gets tired at the end? Why, the exhaustion gap of course! See, this stuff isn't that hard to grasp.

Surveying the Relative Strength Index

An *indicator* is a mathematical calculation that can be used with the stock's price and/or volume. The end result is a value that's used to anticipate future changes in price. The two types of indicators are leading and lagging:

>> *Leading* indicators help you profit by attempting to forecast what prices will do next. Leading indicators provide greater rewards at the expense of increased risk. They perform best in sideways or trading markets. They work by measuring how overbought or oversold a stock is.

>> *Lagging* (or *trend-following*) indicators are best suited to price movements in relatively long trends. They don't warn you of any potential changes in price. Lagging indicators have you buy and sell in a mature trend, when the risk is reduced.

As noted in the earlier section "Combining the best of both worlds," the technical conditions of overbought and oversold are important to be aware of. They're good warning flags to help you time a trade, whether that means getting in or getting out of a position. The Relative Strength Index (RSI) is a convenient metric for measuring the overbought/oversold condition. Generally, the RSI quantifies the condition and gives you a number that acts like a barometer. On a reading of 0 to 100, the RSI becomes oversold at about the 30 level and overbought at about the 70 level.

The RSI is a metric usually calculated and quoted by most charting sources and technical analysis websites. It's generally considered a leading indicator because it forewarns potential price movements.

TIP

For stock investors, I think the RSI is particularly useful for timing the purchase or sale of a particular stock. I know when I'm looking at a favorite stock that I like and notice that its RSI is below 30, I check to see whether anything is wrong with the stock (did the fundamentals change?). If nothing is wrong and it's merely a temporary, market-driven event, I consider buying more of the stock. After all, if I loved a great stock at $40 and it's now cheaper at $35, all things being equal, I have a great buying opportunity. Conversely, if I'm not crazy about a stock and I see that it's overbought, I consider either selling it outright or at least putting a stop-loss order on the stock (see Chapter 17).

3 Picking Winners

Use basic accounting and find financial information that helps you uncover value stocks that can power your prosperity.

Invest in the hottest sectors that will be growing in the coming years.

Locate small cap stocks that offer huge potential, and discover initial public offerings (IPOs), motif investing, and business development companies (BDCs).

Know which stocks and sectors will benefit from economic and political trends.

Chapter **11**

Using Basic Accounting to Choose Winning Stocks

Too often, the only number investors look at when they look at a stock is the stock's price. Yet what determines the stock price is the company behind that single number. To make a truly good choice in the world of stocks, you have to consider the company's financial information. What does it take to see these important numbers?

This book, and a little work on your part are all you need to succeed. This chapter takes the mystery out of the numbers behind the stock. The most tried-and-true method for picking a good stock starts with picking a good company. Picking a company means looking at its products, services, industry, and financial strength. Considering the problems that the market has witnessed in recent years — such as subprime debt problems and derivative meltdowns wreaking havoc on public companies and financial firms — this chapter is more important than ever. Understanding the basics behind the numbers can save your portfolio.

Recognizing Value When You See It

If you pick a stock based on the value of the underlying company that issues it, you're a *value investor* — an investor who looks at a company's value to judge whether you can purchase the stock at a good price. Companies have value the same way many things have value, such as eggs or elephant-foot umbrella stands. And there's a fair price to buy them at, too. Take eggs, for example. You can eat them and have a tasty treat while getting nutrition as well. But would you buy an egg for $1,000 (and no, you're not a starving millionaire on a deserted island)? Of course not. But what if you could buy an egg for 5 cents? At that point, it has value *and* a good price. This kind of deal is a value investor's dream.

Value investors analyze a company's *fundamentals* (sales, earnings, assets, net worth, and so on) to see whether the information justifies purchasing the stock. They see whether the stock price is low relative to these verifiable, quantifiable factors. Therefore, value investors use *fundamental analysis,* whereas other investors may use technical analysis. *Technical analysis* looks at stock charts and statistical data, such as trading volume and historical stock prices (I take a closer look at technical analysis for investors in Chapter 10). Some investors use a combination of both strategies.

History has shown that the most successful long-term investors have typically been value investors using fundamental analysis as their primary investing approach. The most consistently successful long-term investors were — and are — predominately value investors (yes, I count myself in this crowd as well).

In the following sections, I describe different kinds of value and explain how to spot a company's value in several places.

Understanding different types of value

Value may seem like a murky or subjective term, but it's the essence of good stock-picking. You can measure value in different ways (as you discover in the following sections), so you need to know the differences and understand the impact that value has on your investment decisions.

Market value

REMEMBER

When you hear someone quoting a stock at $47 per share, that price reflects the stock's market value. The total market valuation of a company's stock is also referred to as its *market cap* or *market capitalization.* How do you determine a company's market cap? With the following simple formula:

Market capitalization = Share price × Number of shares outstanding

If Bolshevik Corp.'s stock is $35 per share, and it has 10 million shares outstanding (or the number of shares issued less treasury shares), its market cap is $350 million. Granted, $350 million may sound like a lot of money, but Bolshevik Corp. is considered a small cap stock. (For more information about small cap stocks, dip into Chapter 14.)

Who sets the market value of stock? The market, of course! Millions of investors buying and selling directly and through intermediaries such as mutual funds determine the market value of any particular stock. If the market perceives that the company is desirable, investor demand for the company's stock pushes up the share price.

WARNING

The problem with market valuation is that it's not always a good indicator of a good investment. In recent years, plenty of companies have had astronomical market values, yet they've proven to be very risky investments. For example, think about a company that was set to go public (in an initial public offering, or IPO, which is covered in Chapter 14) in 2019. WeWork was expected to have a market value (before going public) as high as $47 billion. Investors such as you and I couldn't obtain complete financial information on this highly anticipated company, but we assumed it was a big deal due to its multibillion-dollar market value and the involvement of notable financial institutions such as JP Morgan and Soft-Bank. Hey, what could go wrong? After the discovery of financial difficulties and large losses, WeWork's IPO was cancelled, and the market value totally evaporated and hit zero. Yikes! Because market value is a direct result of buying and selling by stock investors, it can be a fleeting thing. This precariousness is why investors must understand the company behind the stock price and its market valuation.

Book value and intrinsic value

Book value (also referred to as *accounting value*) looks at a company from a balance sheet perspective (assets minus liabilities equals net worth, or *stockholders' equity*). It's a way of judging a firm by its net worth to see whether the stock's market value is reasonable compared to the company's intrinsic value. *Intrinsic value* is tied to what the market price of a company's assets — both *tangible* (such as equipment) and *intangible* (such as patents) — would be if they were sold.

Generally, market value tends to be higher than book value. If market value is substantially higher than book value, the value investor becomes more reluctant to buy that particular stock because it's overvalued. The closer the stock's market capitalization is to the book value, the safer the investment.

WARNING

I like to be cautious with a stock whose market value is more than five times its book value. If, for example, the market value is north of $2 billion and the book value is less than $500 million, that's a good indicator that the business may be *overvalued*, or valued at a higher price than its book value and ability to generate a profit. Just understand that the farther the market value is from the company's book value, the more you'll pay for the company's real potential value. And the more you pay for the company's real value, the greater the risk that the company's market value (the stock price, that is) can decrease.

Sales value and earnings value

A company's intrinsic value is directly tied to its ability to make money. For this reason, many analysts like to value stocks from the perspective of the company's income statement. Two common barometers of value are expressed in ratios: the price to sales ratio (PSR) and the price-to-earnings (P/E) ratio. In both instances, the price is a reference to the company's market value (as reflected in its share price). Sales and earnings are references to the firm's ability to make money. I cover these two ratios more fully in the later section "Tooling around with ratios."

REMEMBER

For investors, the general approach is clear. The closer the market value is to the company's intrinsic value, the better. And, of course, if the market value is lower than the company's intrinsic value, you have a potential bargain worthy of a closer look. Part of looking closer means examining the company's income statement (which I discuss later in this chapter), also called the *profit and loss statement,* or simply the *P&L.* A low price-to-sales ratio is 1, a medium PSR is between 1 and 2, and a high PSR is 3 or higher.

Putting the pieces together

REMEMBER

When you look at a company from a value-oriented perspective, here are some of the most important items to consider (see the later section "Accounting for Value" for more information):

>> **The balance sheet, to figure out the company's net worth:** A value investor doesn't buy a company's stock because it's cheap; she buys it because it's *undervalued* (the company is worth more than the price its stock reflects — its market value is as close as possible to its book value).

>> **The income statement, to figure out the company's profitability:** A company may be undervalued from a simple comparison of the book value and the market value, but that doesn't mean it's a screaming buy. For example, what if you find out that a company is in trouble and losing money this year? Do you buy its stock then? No, you don't. Why invest in the stock of a losing company? (If you do, you aren't investing — you're gambling or speculating.) The heart of a firm's value, besides its net worth, is its ability to generate profit.

>> **Ratios that let you analyze just how well (or not so well) the company is doing:** Value investors basically look for a bargain. That being the case, they generally don't look at companies that everyone is talking about, because by that point, the stock of those companies ceases to be a bargain. The value investor searches for a stock that will eventually be discovered by the market and then watches as the stock price goes up. But before you bother digging into the fundamentals to find that bargain stock, first make sure that the company is making money.

The more ways that you can look at a company and see value, the better:

>> **Examine the P/E ratio.** The first thing I look at is the P/E ratio. Does the company have one? (This question may sound dumb, but if the company is losing money, it may not have one.) Does the P/E ratio look reasonable or is it in triple-digit, nosebleed territory?

>> **Check out the debt load.** Next, look at the company's *debt load* (the total amount of liabilities). Is it less than the company's equity? Are sales healthy and increasing from the prior year? Does the firm compare favorably in these categories versus other companies in the same industry?

TIP

>> **Think in terms of 10s.** Simplicity to me is best. You'll notice that the number 10 comes up frequently as I measure a company's performance, juxtaposing all the numbers that you need to be aware of. If net income is rising by 10 percent or more, that's fine. If the company is in the top 10 percent of its industry, that's great. If the industry is growing by 10 percent or better (sales and so on), that's terrific. If sales are up 10 percent or more from the prior year, that's wonderful. A great company doesn't have to have all these things going for it, but it should have as many of these things happening as possible to ensure greater potential success.

Does every company/industry have to neatly fit these criteria? No, of course not. But it doesn't hurt you to be as picky as possible. You need to find only a handful of stocks from thousands of choices. (Hey, this approach has worked for me, my clients, and my students for more than three decades — 'nuff said.)

TIP

Value investors can find thousands of companies that have value, but they can probably buy only a handful at a truly good price. The number of stocks that can be bought at a good price is relative to the market. In mature *bull markets* (markets in a prolonged period of rising prices), a good price is hard to find because most stocks have probably seen significant price increases, but in *bear markets* (markets in a prolonged period of falling prices), good companies at bargain prices are easier to come by.

Accounting for Value

Profit is to a company what oxygen is to you and me. Without profit, a company can't survive, much less thrive. Without profit, it can't provide jobs, pay taxes, and invest in new products, equipment, or innovation. Without profit, the company eventually goes bankrupt, and the price of its stock plummets toward zero.

In the heady days leading up to the bear market of 2008–2009, many investors lost a lot of money simply because they invested in stocks of companies that weren't making a profit. Lots of public companies ended up like bugs that just didn't see the windshield coming their way. Companies such as Bear Stearns entered the graveyard of rather-be-forgotten stocks. Stock investors as a group lost trillions of dollars investing in glitzy companies that sounded good but weren't making money. When their brokers were saying, "buy, buy, buy," their hard-earned money was saying, "bye, bye, bye!" What were they thinking?

Stock investors need to pick up some rudimentary knowledge of accounting to round out their stock-picking prowess and to be sure that they're getting a good value for their investment dollars. Accounting is the language of business. If you don't understand basic accounting, you'll have difficulty being a successful investor. Investing without accounting knowledge is like traveling without a map. However, if you can run a household budget, using accounting analysis to evaluate stocks is easier than you think, as you find out in the following sections.

TIP

Finding the relevant financial data on a company isn't difficult in the age of information and 24-hour internet access. Websites such as www.nasdaq.com can give you the most recent balance sheets and income statements of most public companies. You can find out more about public information and company research in Chapter 6.

Breaking down the balance sheet

REMEMBER

A company's balance sheet gives you a financial snapshot of what the company looks like in terms of the following equation:

Assets – Liabilities = Net worth (or net equity)

In the following sections, I list the questions that a balance sheet can answer and explain how to judge a company's strength over time from a balance sheet.

Answering a few balance sheet questions

Analyze the following items that you find on the balance sheet:

- >> **Total assets:** Have they increased from the prior year? If not, was it because of the sale of an asset or a write-off (uncollectable accounts receivable, for example)?

- >> **Financial assets:** In recent years, many companies (especially banks and brokerage firms) had questionable financial assets (such as subprime mortgages and specialized bonds) that went bad, and they had to write them off as unrecoverable losses. Does the company you're analyzing have a large exposure to financial assets that are low-quality (and hence, risky) debt?

- >> **Inventory:** Is inventory higher or lower than last year? If sales are flat but inventory is growing, that may be a problem.

- >> **Debt:** Debt is the biggest weakness on the corporate balance sheet. Make sure that debt isn't a growing item and that it's under control. In recent years, debt has become a huge problem.

- >> **Derivatives:** A *derivative* is a speculative and complex financial instrument that doesn't constitute ownership of an asset (such as a stock, bond, or commodity) but is a promise to convey ownership. Some derivatives are quite acceptable because they're used as protective or hedging vehicles (this use isn't my primary concern). However, they're frequently used to generate income and can then carry risks that can increase liabilities. Standard options and futures are examples of derivatives on a regulated exchange, but the derivatives I'm talking about here are a different animal and in an unregulated part of the financial world. They have a book value exceeding $600 trillion and can easily devastate a company, sector, or market (as the credit crisis of 2008 showed).

WARNING

  Find out whether the company dabbles in these complicated, dicey, leveraged financial instruments. Find out (from the company's 10K report; see Chapter 12) whether it has derivatives and, if so, the total amount. Having derivatives that are valued higher than the company's net equity may cause tremendous problems. Derivatives problems sank many organizations ranging from stodgy banks (Barings Bank of England) to affluent counties (Orange County, California) to once-respected hedge funds (LTCM) to infamous corporations (Enron in 2001 and Glencore in 2015).

- >> **Equity:** *Equity* is the company's net worth (what's left in the event that all the assets are used to pay off all the company debts). The stockholders' equity should be increasing steadily by at least 10 percent per year. If not, find out why.

Table 11-1 shows you a brief example of a balance sheet.

TABLE 11-1

XYZ Balance Sheet — December 31, 2019

Assets (What the Company Owns)	Amount
1. Cash and inventory	$5,000
2. Equipment and other assets	$7,000
3. TOTAL ASSETS (Item 1 plus Item 2)	$12,000
Liabilities (What the Company Owes)	Amount
4. Short-term debt	$1,500
5. Other debt	$2,500
6. TOTAL LIABILITIES (Item 4 plus Item 5)	$4,000
7. NET EQUITY (Item 3 minus Item 6)	$8,000

By looking at a company's balance sheet, you can address the following questions:

>> **What does the company own (assets)?** The company can own assets, which can be financial, tangible, and/or intangible. An *asset* is anything that has value or that can be converted to or sold for cash. Financial assets can be cash, investments (such as stocks or bonds of other companies), or accounts receivable. Assets can be tangible items such as inventory, equipment, and/or buildings. They can also be intangible things such as licenses, trademarks, or copyrights.

>> **What does the company owe (liabilities)?** A *liability* is anything of value that the company must ultimately pay someone else for. Liabilities can be invoices (accounts payable) or short-term or long-term debt.

REMEMBER

>> **What is the company's net equity (net worth)?** After you subtract the liabilities from the assets, the remainder is called *net worth, net equity,* or *net stockholders' equity.* This number is critical when calculating a company's book value.

Assessing a company's financial strength over time

The logic behind the assets/liabilities relationship of a company is the same as that of your own household. When you look at a snapshot of your own finances (your personal balance sheet), how can you tell whether you're doing well? Odds are that you start by comparing some numbers. If your net worth is $5,000, you may say, "That's great!" But a more appropriate remark is something like, "That's great compared to, say, a year ago."

TIP

Compare a company's balance sheet at a recent point in time to a past time. You should do this comparative analysis with all the key items on the balance sheet, which I list in the preceding section, to see the company's progress (or lack thereof). Is it growing its assets and/or shrinking its debt? Most important, is the company's net worth growing? Has it grown by at least 10 percent since a year ago? All too often, investors stop doing their homework after they make an initial investment. You should continue to look at the firm's numbers regularly so that you can be ahead of the curve. If the business starts having problems, you can get out before the rest of the market starts getting out (which causes the stock price to fall).

To judge the financial strength of a company, ask yourself the following questions:

>> **Are the company's assets greater in value than they were three months ago, a year ago, or two years ago?** Compare current asset size to the most recent two years to make sure that the company is growing in size and financial strength.

>> **How do the individual items compare with prior periods?** Some particular assets that you want to take note of are cash, inventory, and accounts receivable.

>> **Are liabilities such as accounts payable and debt about the same, lower, or higher compared to prior periods? Are they growing at a similar, faster, or slower rate than the company's assets?** Debt that rises faster and higher than items on the other side of the balance sheet is a warning sign of pending financial problems.

>> **Is the company's net worth or equity greater than the preceding year? And is that year's equity greater than the year before?** In a healthy company, the net worth is constantly rising. As a general rule, in good economic times, net worth should be at least 10 percent higher than the preceding year. In tough economic times (such as a recession), 5 percent is acceptable. Seeing the net worth grow at a rate of 15 percent or higher is great.

Looking at the income statement

REMEMBER

Where do you look if you want to find out what a company's profit is? Check out the firm's income statement. It reports, in detail, a simple accounting equation that you probably already know:

Sales – Expenses = Net profit (or net earnings, or net income)

Look at the following figures found on the income statement:

>> **Sales:** Are they increasing? If not, why not? By what percentage are sales increasing? Preferably, they should be 10 percent higher than the year before. Sales are, after all, where the money comes from to pay for all the company's activities (such as expenses) and create subsequent profits.

>> **Expenses:** Do you see any unusual items? Are total expenses reported higher than the prior year, and if so, by how much? If the total is significantly higher, why? A company with large, rising expenses will see profits suffer, which isn't good for the stock price.

>> **Research and development (R&D):** How much is the company spending on R&D? Companies that rely on new product development (such as pharmaceuticals or biotech firms) should spend at least as much as they did the year before (preferably more) because new products mean future earnings and growth.

>> **Earnings:** This figure reflects the bottom line. Are total earnings higher than the year before? How about earnings from operations (leaving out expenses such as taxes and interest)? The earnings section is the heart and soul of the income statement and of the company itself. Out of all the numbers in the financial statements, earnings have the greatest single impact on the company's stock price.

Table 11-2 shows you a brief example of an income statement.

TABLE 11-2

XYZ Income Statement — December 31, 2019

Total Sales (Or Revenue)	Amount
1. Sales of products	$11,000
2. Sales of services	$3,000
3. TOTAL SALES (Item 1 plus Item 2)	$14,000
Expenses	Amount
4. Marketing and promotion	$2,000
5. Payroll costs	$9,000
6. Other costs	$1,500
7. TOTAL EXPENSES (Item 4 plus Item 5 plus Item 6)	$12,500
8. NET INCOME (Item 3 minus Item 7) (In this case, it's a net profit)	$1,500

Looking at the income statement, an investor can try to answer the following questions:

>> **What sales did the company make?** Businesses sell products and services that generate revenue (known as *sales* or *gross sales*). Sales also are referred to as the *top line.*

>> **What expenses did the company incur?** In generating sales, companies pay expenses such as payroll, utilities, advertising, administration, and so on.

>> **What is the net profit?** Also called *net earnings* or *net income,* net profit is the *bottom line.* After paying for all expenses, what profit did the company make?

The information you glean should give you a strong idea about a firm's current financial strength and whether it's successfully increasing sales, holding down expenses, and ultimately maintaining profitability. You can find out more about sales, expenses, and profits in the sections that follow.

Sales

Sales refers to the money that a company receives as customers buy its goods and/ or services. It's a simple item on the income statement and a useful number to look at. Analyzing a business by looking at its sales is called *top line analysis.*

As an investor, you should take into consideration the following points about sales:

>> **Sales should be increasing.** A healthy, growing company has growing sales. They should grow at least 10 percent from the prior year, and you should look at the most recent three years.

>> **Core sales (sales of those products or services that the company specializes in) should be increasing.** Frequently, the sales figure has a lot of stuff lumped into it. Maybe the company sells widgets (what the heck is a widget, anyway?), but the core sales shouldn't include other things, such as the sale of a building or other unusual items. Take a close look. Isolate the firm's primary offerings and ask whether these sales are growing at a reasonable rate (such as 10 percent).

>> **Does the company have odd items or odd ways of calculating sales?** In the late 1990s, many companies boosted their sales by aggressively offering affordable financing with easy repayment terms. Say you find out that Suspicious Sales Inc. (SSI) had annual sales of $50 million, reflecting a 25 percent increase from the year before. Looks great! But what if you find out that $20 million of that sales number comes from sales made on credit that the company extended to buyers? Some companies that use this approach later have to write off losses as uncollectable debt because the customers ultimately can't pay for the goods.

TIP

If you want to get a good clue as to whether a company is artificially boosting sales, check its accounts receivable (listed in the asset section of its balance sheet). *Accounts receivable* refers to money that is owed to the company for goods that customers have purchased on credit. If you find out that sales went up by $10 million (great!) but accounts receivable went up by $20 million (uh-oh), something just isn't right. That may be a sign that the financing terms were too easy, and the company may have a problem collecting payment (especially in a recession).

Expenses

How much a company spends has a direct relationship to its profitability. If spending isn't controlled or held at a sustainable level, it may spell trouble for the business.

When you look at a company's expense items, consider the following:

>> **Compare expense items to the prior period.** Are expenses higher than, lower than, or about the same as those from the prior period? If the difference is significant, you should see commensurate benefits elsewhere. In other words, if overall expenses are 10 percent higher compared to the prior period, are sales at least 10 percent more during the same period?

>> **Are some expenses too high?** Look at the individual expense items. Are they significantly higher than the year before? If so, why?

>> **Have any unusual items been expensed?** An unusual expense isn't necessarily a negative. Expenses may be higher than usual if a company writes off uncollectable accounts receivable as a bad debt expense. Doing so inflates the total expenses and subsequently results in lower earnings. Pay attention to nonrecurring charges that show up on the income statement and determine whether they make sense.

Profit

Earnings or profit is the single most important item on the income statement. It's also the one that receives the most attention in the financial media. When a company makes a profit, it's usually reported in both absolute dollars and as earnings per share (EPS). So if you hear that XYZ Corporation (yes, the infamous XYZ Corp.!) beat last quarter's earnings by a penny, here's how to translate that news. Suppose that the company made $1 per share this quarter and 99 cents per share last quarter. If that company had 100 million shares of stock outstanding, its profit this quarter is $100 million (the EPS times the number of shares outstanding), which is $1 million more than it made in the prior quarter ($1 million is 1 cent per share times 100 million shares).

TIP

Don't simply look at current earnings as an isolated figure. Always compare current earnings to earnings in past periods (usually a year). For example, if you're looking at a retailer's fourth-quarter results, don't compare them with the retailer's third-quarter outcome. Doing so is like comparing apples to oranges. What if the company usually does well during the December holidays but poorly in the fall? In that case, you don't get a fair comparison.

A strong company should show consistent earnings growth from the period before (such as the prior year or the same quarter from the prior year), and you should check the period before that, too, so that you can determine whether earnings are consistently rising over time. Earnings growth is an important barometer of the company's potential growth and bodes well for the stock price.

When you look at earnings, here are some things to consider:

>> **Total earnings:** This item is the most watched. Total earnings should grow year to year by at least 10 percent.

>> **Operational earnings:** Break down the total earnings, and look at a key subset — that portion of earnings derived from the company's core activity. Is the company continuing to make money from its primary goods and services?

>> **Nonrecurring items:** Are earnings higher (or lower) than usual or than expected, and if so, why? Frequently, the difference results from items such as the sale of an asset or a large depreciation write-off.

TIP

I like to keep percentages as simple as possible. Ten percent is a good number because it's easy to calculate, and it's a good benchmark. However, 5 percent isn't unacceptable if you're talking about tough times, such as a recession. Obviously, if sales, earnings, and/or net worth are hitting or surpassing 15 percent, that's great.

Tooling around with ratios

A *ratio* is a helpful numerical tool that you can use to find out the relationship between two or more figures found in a company's financial data. A ratio can add meaning to a number or put it in perspective. Ratios sound complicated, but they're easier to understand than you may think.

Say that you're considering a stock investment and the company you're looking at has earnings of $1 million this year. You may think that's a nice profit, but in order for this amount to be meaningful, you have to compare it to something. What if you find out that the other companies in the industry (of similar size and scope) had earnings of $500 million? Does that change your thinking? Or what if the same company had earnings of $75 million in the prior period? Does that change your mind?

Two key ratios to be aware of are

>> Price-to-earnings (P/E) ratio

>> Price to sales ratio (PSR)

TIP

Every investor wants to find stocks that have a 20 percent average growth rate over the past five years and have a low P/E ratio (sounds like a dream). Use stock screening tools available for free on the internet to do your research. A *stock screening tool* lets you plug in numbers, such as sales or earnings, and ratios, such as the P/E ratio or the debt to equity ratio, and then click! — up come stocks that fit your criteria. These tools are a good starting point for serious investors. Many brokers have them at their websites (such as Charles Schwab at www.schwab.com and E*TRADE at www.etrade.com). You can also find some excellent stock screening tools at Yahoo! Finance (finance.yahoo.com), Bloomberg (www.bloomberg.com), Nasdaq (www.nasdaq.com), and MarketWatch (www.marketwatch.com). Check out Appendix B for even more on ratios.

The P/E ratio

The *price-to-earnings (P/E) ratio* is very important in analyzing a potential stock investment because it's one of the most widely regarded barometers of a company's value, and it's usually reported along with the company's stock price in the financial page listing. The major significance of the P/E ratio is that it establishes a direct relationship between the bottom line of a company's operations — the earnings (or net profit) — and the stock price.

The *P* in P/E stands for the stock's current price. The *E* is for earnings per share (typically the most recent 12 months of earnings). The P/E ratio is also referred to as the *earnings multiple* or just *multiple*.

REMEMBER

You calculate the P/E ratio by dividing the price of the stock by the earnings per share. If the price of a single share of stock is $10 and the earnings (on a per-share basis) are $1, then the P/E is 10. If the stock price goes to $35 per share and the earnings are unchanged, then the P/E is 35. Basically, the higher the P/E, the more you pay for the company's earnings.

Why would you buy stock in one company with a relatively high P/E ratio instead of investing in another company with a lower P/E ratio? Keep in mind that investors buy stocks based on expectations. They may bid up the price of the stock (subsequently raising the stock's P/E ratio) because they feel that the company will have increased earnings in the near future. Perhaps they feel that the company has great potential (a pending new invention or lucrative business deal) that will eventually make it more profitable. More profitability in turn has a beneficial impact on the firm's stock price. The danger with a high P/E is that if the company doesn't achieve the hoped-for results, the stock price can fall.

TIP

You should look at two types of P/E ratios to get a balanced picture of the company's value:

>> **Trailing P/E:** This P/E is the most frequently quoted because it deals with existing data. The trailing P/E uses the most recent 12 months of earnings in its calculation.

>> **Forward P/E:** This P/E is based on projections or expectations of earnings in the coming 12-month period. Although this P/E may seem preferable because it looks into the near future, it's still considered an estimate that may or may not prove to be accurate.

The following example illustrates the importance of the P/E ratio. Say that you want to buy a business, and I'm selling a business. You come to me and say, "What do you have to offer?" I say, "Have I got a deal for you! I operate a retail business downtown that sells spatulas. The business nets a cool $2,000 profit per year." You reluctantly say, "Uh, okay, what's the asking price for the business?" I reply, "You can have it for only $1 million! What do you say?"

If you're sane, odds are that you politely turn down that offer. Even though the business is profitable (a cool $2,000 a year), you'd be crazy to pay a million bucks for it. In other words, the business is way overvalued (too expensive for what you're getting in return for your investment dollars). The million dollars would generate a better rate of return elsewhere and probably with less risk. As for the business, the P/E ratio of 500 ($1 million divided by $2,000) is outrageous. This is definitely a case of an overvalued company — and a lousy investment.

What if I offered the business for $12,000? Does that price make more sense? Yes. The P/E ratio is a more reasonable 6 ($12,000 divided by $2,000). In other words, the business pays for itself in about 6 years (versus 500 years in the prior example).

REMEMBER

Looking at the P/E ratio offers a shortcut for investors asking the question, "Is this stock overvalued?" As a general rule, the lower the P/E, the safer (or more conservative) the stock is. The reverse is more noteworthy: The higher the P/E, the greater the risk.

When someone refers to a P/E as high or low, you have to ask the question, "Compared to what?" A P/E of 30 is considered very high for a large cap electric utility but quite reasonable for a small cap, high-technology firm. Keep in mind that phrases such as *large cap* and *small cap* are just a reference to the company's market value or size (see Chapter 1 for details on these terms). *Cap* is short for *capitalization* (the total number of shares of stock outstanding multiplied by the share price).

The following basic points can help you evaluate P/E ratios:

>> **Compare a company's P/E ratio with its industry.** Electric utility industry stocks, for example, generally have a P/E that hovers in the 9–14 range. Therefore, an electric utility with a P/E of 45 indicates that something is wrong with that utility. (I touch on sectors and industries in Chapter 13.)

>> **Compare a company's P/E with the general market.** If you're looking at a small cap stock on the Nasdaq that has a P/E of 100 and the average P/E for established companies on the Nasdaq is 40, find out why. You should also compare the stock's P/E ratio with the P/E ratio for major indexes such as the Dow Jones Industrial Average (DJIA), the Standard & Poor's 500 (S&P 500), and the Nasdaq Composite. Stock indexes are useful for getting the big picture, and I include them in Chapter 5 and Appendix A.

>> **Compare a company's current P/E with recent periods** (such as this year versus last year). If it currently has a P/E ratio of 20 and it previously had a P/E ratio of 30, you know that either the stock price has declined or that earnings have risen. In this case, the stock is less likely to fall. That bodes well for the stock.

>> **Low P/E ratios aren't necessarily a sign of a bargain,** but if you're looking at a stock for many other reasons that seem positive (solid sales, strong industry, and so on) and it also has a low P/E, that's a good sign.

>> **High P/E ratios aren't necessarily bad,** but they do mean that you should investigate further. If a company is weak and the industry is shaky, heed the high P/E as a warning sign. Frequently, a high P/E ratio means that investors have bid up a stock price, anticipating future income. The problem is that if the anticipated income doesn't materialize, the stock price can fall.

WARNING

>> **Watch out for a stock that doesn't have a P/E ratio.** In other words, it may have a price (the *P*), but it doesn't have earnings (the *E*). No earnings means no P/E, meaning that you're better off avoiding the stock. Can you still make money buying a stock with no earnings? You can, but you aren't investing; you're speculating.

The PSR

The *price to sales ratio (PSR)* is a company's stock price divided by its sales. Because the sales number is rarely expressed as a per-share figure, it's easier to divide a company's total market value (I explain market value earlier in this chapter) by its total sales for the last 12 months.

TIP

As a general rule, stock trading at a PSR of 1 or less is a reasonably priced stock worthy of your attention. For example, say that a company has sales of $1 billion, and the stock has a total market value of $950 million. In that case, the PSR is 0.95. In other words, you can buy $1 of the company's sales for only 95 cents. All things being equal, that stock may be a bargain.

Analysts frequently use the PSR as an evaluation tool in the following circumstances:

>> In tandem with other ratios to get a more well-rounded picture of the company and the stock.

>> When they want an alternative way to value a business that doesn't have earnings.

>> When they want a true picture of the company's financial health, because sales are tougher for companies to manipulate than earnings.

>> When they're considering a company offering products (versus services). PSR is more suitable for companies that sell items that are easily counted (such as products). Firms that make their money through loans, such as banks, aren't usually valued with a PSR because deriving a usable PSR for them is more difficult.

REMEMBER

Compare the company's PSR with other companies in the same industry, along with the industry average, so that you get a better idea of the company's relative value.

Chapter **12**

Decoding Company Documents

Financial documents — good grief! Some people would rather suck a hospital mop than read some dry corporate or government report. Yet if you're serious about choosing stocks, you should be serious about your research. Fortunately, it's not as bad as you think (put away that disgusting mop). When you see that some basic research helps you build wealth, it gets easier.

In this chapter, I discuss the basic documents that you come across (or should come across) most often in your investing life. These documents include essential information that all investors need to know, not only at the time of the initial investment decision, but also for as long as that stock remains in their portfolio.

REMEMBER

If you plan to hold a stock for the long haul, reading the annual report and other reports covered in this chapter will be very helpful. If you intend to get rid of the stock soon or plan to hold it only for the short term, reading these reports diligently isn't that important.

A Message from the Bigwigs: Reading the Annual Report

When you're a regular stockholder, the company sends you its annual report. If you're not already a stockholder, contact the company's shareholder services (or investor relations) department for a hard copy or to get a copy emailed to you. Virtually all the websites for public companies have publicly filed documents (or links to where they can be found at the Securities and Exchange Commission, or SEC).

You can also often view a company's annual report at its website. Any major search engine can help you find it. Downloading or printing the annual report is easy.

TIP

The following resources also provide access to annual reports:

>> **Check out The Public Register's Annual Report Service.** Go to www.prars.com to order a hard copy or to www.annualreportservice.com to view reports online. This organization maintains an extensive collection of annual reports.

>> **Use the free annual report service of *The Wall Street Journal*.** If you read this newspaper's financial pages and see a company with the club symbol (like the one you see on a playing card), then you can order that company's annual report by visiting the website (www.wsj.com).

You need to carefully analyze an annual report to find out the following:

>> **How well the company is doing:** Are earnings higher, lower, or the same as the year before? How are sales doing? You can find these numbers clearly presented in the annual report's financial section.

>> **Whether the company is making more money than it's spending:** How does the balance sheet look? Are assets higher or lower than the year before? Is debt growing, shrinking, or about the same as the year before? For more details on balance sheets, see Chapter 11.

>> **What management's strategic plan is for the coming year:** How will management build on the company's success? This plan is usually covered in the beginning of the annual report — frequently in the letter from the chairman of the board.

Your task boils down to figuring out where the company has been, where it is now, and where it's going. As an investor, you don't need to read the annual report like a novel — from cover to cover. Instead, approach it like a newspaper and jump around to the relevant sections to get the answers you need to decide whether you should buy or hold onto the stock. I describe the makeup of the annual report and proxy materials in the following sections.

Analyzing the annual report's anatomy

Not every company puts its annual report together in exactly the same way — the style of presentation varies. Some annual reports have gorgeous graphics or coupons for the company's products, whereas others are in a standard black-and-white typeface with no cosmetic frills at all. But every annual report does include common basic content, such as the income statement and the balance sheet. The following sections present typical components of an average annual report. (Keep in mind that not every annual report presents the sections in the same order.)

The letter from the chairman of the board

The first thing you see is usually the letter from the chairman of the board. It's the "Dear Stockholder" letter that communicates views from the head muckety-muck. The chairman's letter is designed to put the best possible perspective on the company's operations during the past year. Be aware of this bias; no one in upper management wants to panic stockholders. If the company is doing well, the letter will certainly point it out. If the company is having hard times, the letter will probably put a positive spin on the company's difficulties. If the *Titanic* had had an annual report, odds are that the last letter would have reported, "Great news! A record number of our customers participated in our spontaneous moonlight swimming program. In addition, we confidently project no operating expenses whatsoever for the subsequent fiscal quarter." You get the point.

REMEMBER

To get a good idea of what issues the company's management team feels are important and what goals it wants to accomplish, keep the following questions in mind:

>> What does the letter say about changing conditions in the company's business? How about in the industry?

>> If any difficulties exist, does the letter communicate a clear and logical action plan (cutting costs, closing money-losing plants, and so on) to get the company back on a positive track?

>> What's being highlighted and why? For example, is the firm focusing on research and development for new products or on a new deal with China?

>> Does the letter offer apologies for anything the company did? If, for example, it fell short of sales expectations, does the letter offer a reason for the shortcoming?

>> Did the company make (or will it make) new acquisitions or major developments (say, selling products to China or a new marketing agreement with a Fortune 500 company)?

TIP

Read an annual report (or any messages from upper management) in the same way you read or hear anything from a politician — be more concerned with means than ends. In other words, don't tell me what the goal is (greater profitability or peace on earth); tell me how you're going to get there. Executives may say "we will increase sales and profits," but saying "we will increase sales and profits by doing X, Y, and Z" is a better message because you can then decide for yourself whether the road map makes sense.

The company's offerings

This section of an annual report can have various titles (such as "Sales and Marketing"), but it generally covers what the company sells. You should understand the products or services (or both) that the business sells and why customers purchase them. If you don't understand what the company offers, then understanding how it earns money, which is the driving force behind its stock, is more difficult.

Are the company's core or primary offerings selling well? If, for example, the earnings of McDonald's are holding steady but earnings strictly from burgers and fries are fizzling, that's a cause for concern. If a business ceases making money from its specialty, you should become cautious. Here are some other questions to ask:

>> **How does the company distribute its offerings?** Through a website, malls, representatives, or some other means? Does it sell only to the U.S. market, or is its distribution international? Generally, the greater the distribution, the greater the potential sales and, ultimately, the higher the stock price.

>> **Are most of the company's sales to a definable marketplace?** For example, if most of the sales are to a war-torn or politically unstable country, you should worry. If the company's customers aren't doing well, that has a direct impact on the company and, eventually, its stock.

>> **How are sales doing versus market standards?** In other words, is the company doing better than the industry average? Is it a market leader in what it offers? The firm should be doing better than (or as well as) its peers in the industry. If the company is falling behind its competitors, that doesn't bode well for the stock in the long run.

>> **Does the report include information on the company's competitors and related matters?** You should know who the company's competitors are because they have a direct effect on the company's success. If customers are choosing the competitor over your firm, the slumping sales and earnings will ultimately hurt the stock's price.

Financial statements

Look over the various financial statements and find the relevant numbers. Every annual report should have (at the very least) a balance sheet (for the beginning of the year and the end of year), three years (typically) of income statements, and cash flow statements for the years in question. Catching the important numbers on a financial statement isn't that difficult to do. However, it certainly helps when you pick up some basic accounting knowledge. Chapter 11 can give you more details on evaluating financial statements.

First, review the *income statement* (also known as the *profit and loss statement*, or simply *P&L*). It gives you the company's sales, expenses, and the results (net income or net loss).

Next, look at the *balance sheet.* It provides a snapshot of a point in time (annual reports are required to provide two years of year-end balance sheets) that tells you what the company owns *(assets),* what it owes *(liabilities),* and the end result *(net worth).* For a healthy company, assets should always be greater than liabilities.

WARNING

Carefully read the footnotes to the financial statements. Sometimes big changes are communicated in small print. In current times, especially be wary of small print pointing out other debt or derivatives. *Derivatives* are complicated and (lately) very risky vehicles. Problems with derivatives were one of the major causes of the market turmoil that destroyed financial firms on Wall Street during late 2008. AIG, for example, is a major insurer that had to be bailed out by the Federal Reserve before it went bankrupt (shareholders suffered huge losses).

WARNING

Derivatives are a huge land mine, and large money center banks still carry them. According to the Bank for International Settlements (www.bis.org), major money center banks are carrying more than 1 quadrillion dollars' worth of derivatives. (Whew! Now I see why they give away so many toasters.) Derivatives are especially worth being aware of if you're considering bank or other financial stocks for your portfolio.

Summary of past financial figures

The summary of past financial figures gives you a snapshot of the company's overall long-term progress. How many years does the annual report summarize? Some reports summarize three years, but most go back two years.

Management issues

The annual report's management issues section includes a reporting of current trends and issues, such as new developments happening in the industry that affect the company. See whether you agree with management's assessment of economic and market conditions that affect the firm's prospects. What significant developments in society does management perceive as affecting the company's operations? Does the report include information on current or pending lawsuits?

CPA opinion letter

Annual reports typically include comments from the company's independent accounting firm. It may be an opinion letter or a simple paragraph with the accounting firm's views regarding the financial statements.

TIP

The CPA opinion letter offers an opinion about the accuracy of the financial data presented and information on how the statements were prepared. Check to see whether the letter includes any footnotes regarding changes in certain numbers or how they were reported. For example, a company that wants to report higher earnings may use a conservative method of measuring depreciation rather than a more aggressive approach. In any case, you should verify the numbers by looking at the company's 10K document filed with the Securities and Exchange Commission (SEC; I describe this document in more detail later in this chapter).

Company identity data

The company identity data section informs you about the company's subsidiaries (or lesser businesses that it owns), brands, and addresses. It also contains standard data such as the headquarters' location and names of directors and officers. Many reports also include data on the directors' and officers' positions in stock ownership at year's end.

Stock data

The stock data section may include a history of the stock price, along with information such as what exchange the stock is listed on, the stock symbol, the company's dividend reinvestment plan (if any), and so on. It also includes information on stockholder services and who to contact for further information.

Going through the proxy materials

As a shareholder (or stockholder — same thing), you're entitled to vote at the annual shareholders meeting. If you ever get the opportunity to attend one, do so. You get to meet other shareholders and ask questions of management and other company representatives. Usually, the shareholder services department (or investor relations department) provides you with complete details. At the meetings, shareholders vote on company matters, such as approving a new accounting firm or deciding whether a proposed merger with another company will go forward.

If you can't attend (which is usually true for the majority of shareholders), you can vote by proxy. *Voting by proxy* essentially means that you vote by mail or electronically. You indicate your votes on the proxy statement (or card) and authorize a representative to vote at the meeting on your behalf. The proxy statement is usually sent to all shareholders, along with the annual report, just before the meeting.

Dig Deeper: Getting a Second Opinion

A wealth of valuable information is available for your investing pursuits. The resources in this section are just a representative few — a good representation, though. To get a more balanced view of the company and its prospects (instead of relying only on the annual report that I describe in the preceding section), take a look at several different sources of information for the stocks you're researching.

TIP

The information and research they provide can be expensive if you buy or subscribe on your own, but fortunately, most of the resources mentioned are usually available in the business reference section of a well-stocked public library.

Company documents filed with the SEC

The serious investor doesn't overlook the wealth of information that he can cull from documents filed with the SEC. Take the time and effort to review the documents in the following sections because they offer great insight regarding a company's activities.

Here's how to obtain the main documents that investors should be aware of:

>> **Drop by the company itself.** Stockholder services departments keep these publicly available documents on hand and usually give them out at no cost to interested parties.

TIP

>> **Visit the SEC, either in person or online.** These documents are available for public viewing at the SEC offices. You can find out more by contacting the Securities and Exchange Commission, Publications Unit, 450 Fifth St. NW, Washington, DC 20549.

At the SEC's website (www.sec.gov), you can check out EDGAR (the Electronic Data Gathering, Analysis, and Retrieval system) to search public documents filed. It's a tremendous source of documents that date back to 1994. You can search, print, or download documents very easily. Documents can be located either by document number or keyword search.

Form 10K

Gee, how intimidating. Just the report name alone makes you scratch your head. To some people, 10K refers to running a race of 10 kilometers. But if you're reading a 10K, you may wish you were running one instead.

Form 10K is a report that companies must file with the SEC annually. It works like the annual report that you get from the company, except that it provides more detailed financial information. It can be a little intimidating because the text can be dry and cumbersome. It's not exactly Shakespeare (although 10K reports would've also driven Lady Macbeth insane); then again, the data isn't laden with as much spin as the annual report the company sends to shareholders. Without going crazy, go through each section of the 10K. Take some extra time to scrutinize the section on financial data. Ask the same questions that you do when you're looking at the annual report.

TIP

The following websites can help you make sense of 10K reports:

>> Investopedia (www.investopedia.com)

>> Investor.gov (www.investor.gov)

>> Last10K.com (www.last10k.com)

>> SEC Info (www.secinfo.com)

Form 10Q

Form 10Q is a quarterly report that gives you the same basic information as the 10K, but it details only three months' worth of activity. Because a long time can pass between 10Ks (after all, it is a year), don't wait 12 months to see how your company is progressing. Make a habit of seeing how the company is doing by comparing its recent 10Q with one that covers the same quarter last year. Is the profit higher or lower? How about sales? Debt?

REMEMBER

Keep in mind that not every company has the same fiscal year. A company with a calendar year fiscal year (ending December 31), for example, files a 10Q for each of the first three quarters and files a 10K for the final quarter (the last three months of the year). The company reports its fourth quarter data in the 10K, along with the statistics for the full year.

Insider reports

Two types of insiders exist: those who work within a company and those outside the company who have a significant (5 percent or more) ownership of company stock. Tracking insider activity is very profitable for investors who want to follow in the footsteps of the people in the know. See Chapter 20 for information about monitoring and benefiting from insider activity.

REMEMBER

Every time an insider (such as the CEO or controller) buys or sells stock, the transaction has to be reported to the SEC. The insider actually reports the trade prior to transacting it. These reports are publicly available documents that allow you to see what the insiders are actually doing. Hearing what they say in public is one thing, but seeing what they're actually doing with their stock transactions is more important.

Value Line

The Value Line Investment Survey, one of many information products provided by Value Line Publishing, Inc., is considered a longtime favorite by many stock investing professionals. You can look it over at any library that has a good business reference department. In the survey, Value Line covers the largest public companies and ranks them according to financial strength and several other key business factors. To get more information about Value Line, either head to the library or visit www.valueline.com.

Standard & Poor's

Another ubiquitous and venerable publisher is Standard & Poor's (S&P). Although it has a number of quality information products and services for both individual and institutional investors, the three you should take a look at are the following:

>> ***S&P Stock Reports:*** Available at many libraries, this guide comes out periodically and reports on stocks on the New York Stock Exchange and the largest firms listed on Nasdaq. It gives a succinct, two-page summary of each stock, offering a snapshot of the company's current finances, along with a brief history and commentary on the company's activities. This guide also rates companies based on their financial strength.

>> **The S&P Industry Survey:** S&P gives detailed reports on the top industries, cramming a lot of information about a given industry in four to seven pages. This annual publication provides a nice summary of what's happened in each industry in the past 12 months, what the industry looks like today, and what the prospects are for the coming year. It also provides the important numbers (earnings, sales, and industry ranking) for the top 50 to 100 firms in each industry.

>> **S&P Bond Reports:** Yes, I know this book is about stocks. But a company's bond rating is invaluable for stock investors. S&P analyzes the strength of the bond issuer and ranks the bond for creditworthiness. If S&P gives a company a high rating, you have added assurance that the company is financially strong. You want the company to have a bond rating of AAA, AA, or A, because these ratings tell you that the company is "investment-grade."

Check out S&P's website at www.standardandpoors.com for more information about its publications.

Moody's Investment Service

Another stalwart publisher, Moody's offers vital research on stocks and bonds. *Moody's Handbook of Common Stocks* is usually available in the reference section of a well-stocked library. It offers stock and bond guides similar to S&P and also provides an independent bond-rating service. Check out www.moodys.com for more information.

TIP

A stock rated highly by both Moody's and S&P is a great choice for investors hunting for value investments.

Brokerage reports: The good, the bad, and the ugly

Clint Eastwood, where are you? Traditionally, brokerage reports have been a good source of information for investors seeking informed opinions about stocks. And they still are, but in recent years some brokers have been penalized for biased reports. Brokers should never be your sole source of information. (Otherwise, Clint may ask them whether they're feeling lucky, punks.) The following sections describe the good, the bad, and the ugly of brokerage reports.

The good

Research departments at brokerage firms provide stock reports and make them available for their clients and investment publications. The firms' analysts and market strategists generally prepare these reports. Good research is critical, and brokerage reports can be very valuable. What better source of guidance than full-time experts backed up by million-dollar research departments? Brokerage reports have some strong points:

>> The analysts are professionals who should understand the value of a company and its stock. They analyze and compare company data every day.

>> Analysts have at their disposal tremendous information and historical data that they can sift through to make informed decisions.

>> If you have an account with the firm, you can usually access the information at no cost.

The bad

WARNING

Well, brokerage reports may not be bad in every case, but at their worst, they're quite bad. Brokers make their money from commissions and investment banking fees (nothing bad here). However, they can find themselves in the awkward position of issuing brokerage reports on companies that are (or could be) customers of the brokerage firm that employs them (hmmm — could be bad). Frequently, this relationship results in a brokerage report that paints an overly positive picture of a company that can be a bad investment (yup, that's bad). The bottom line is that you should always be wary of a conflict of interest when brokers are too pushy or optimistic about a particular security.

The ugly

During 1998–2000, an overwhelming number of brokerage reports issued glowing praise of companies that were either mediocre or dubious. Investors bought up stocks such as tech stocks and internet stocks. The sheer demand pushed up stock prices, which gave the appearance of genius to analysts' forecasts, yet the stock prices rose essentially as a self-fulfilling prophecy. The stocks were way overvalued and were cruisin' for a bruisin'. Analysts and investors were feeling lucky.

Investors, however, lost a ton of money (ooh, ugly). Money that people painstakingly accumulated over many years of work vanished in a matter of months as the bear market of 2000 hit (ooh, ugly). Of course, the bear market that hit in 2008–2009 was even more brutal. Retirees who had trusted the analysts saw nest eggs lose 40 to 70 percent in value (yikes, very ugly). Investors lost trillions during these major downturns, much of it needlessly. I'm sure that lots of those folks thought that they should have put that money in things that had enduring value instead — such as cookies and cases of merlot.

REMEMBER

During that bear market of 2000–2002, a record number of lawsuits and complaints were filed against brokerage firms. Wall Street and Main Street learned some tough lessons. Regarding research reports from brokerage firms, the following points can help you avoid getting a bad case of the uglies:

>> Always ask yourself, "Is the provider of the report a biased source?" In other words, is the broker getting business in any way from the company she's recommending?

>> Never, never, *never* rely on just one source of information, especially if it's the same source that's selling you the stock or other investment.

>> Do your research first before you rely on a brokerage report. Check out annual reports and the other documents I recommend earlier in this chapter.

>> Do your due diligence before you buy stocks anyway. Look at Parts 1 and 2 to understand your need for diversification, risk tolerance, and so on.

>> Verify the information provided to you with a trip to the library or websites (see Appendix A).

TIP

Although I generally don't rely on Wall Street brokerage analysts, I do track some independent investment analysts. I mention some of my favorites in Appendix A.

Do It Yourself: Compiling Your Own Research Department

You don't need to spend an excessive amount of time or money, but you should maintain your own library of resources. You may need only one shelf (or a small amount of memory on your computer's hard drive), but why not have a few investment facts and resources at your fingertips? I maintain my own library loaded with books, magazines, newsletters, and tons of great stuff downloaded on my computer for easy search and reference. When you start your own collection, follow these tips:

>> **Keep some select newspapers.** *Barron's, The Wall Street Journal,* and *Investor's Business Daily* regularly have some editions that are worth keeping. For example, *The Wall Street Journal* and *Investor's Business Daily* usually publish a year-in-review issue the first business week in January. *Barron's* has special issues reviewing brokers and financial websites.

>> **Subscribe to financial magazines.** Publications such as *Forbes* and *Money* magazines offer great research and regularly review stocks, brokers, and resources for investors.

>> **Keep annual reports.** Regarding the stocks that are the core holdings in your portfolio, keep all the annual reports (at the very least, the most recent three).

>> **Go to the library's business reference section periodically to stay updated.** Hey, you pay the taxes that maintain the public library — you may as well use it to stay informed.

>> **Use the internet for research.** The web offers plenty of great sites to peruse; I list some of the best in Appendix A.

TIP

Financial reports are very important and easier to read than most people think. An investor can easily avoid a bad investment by simply noticing the data in what seems like a jumble of numbers. Figure out how to read them. For a great book to help you with reading financial reports (without needless technicality), check out the latest edition of *How to Read a Financial Report: Wringing Vital Signs Out of the Numbers,* by John A. Tracy and Tage C. Tracy, or the latest edition of *Fundamental Analysis For Dummies* by Matt Krantz (both published by Wiley).

Chapter **13**

Emerging Sector and Industry Opportunities

S uppose that you have to bet your entire nest egg on a one-mile race. All you need to do is select a winning group. Your choices are the following:

Group A: Thoroughbred racehorses

Group B: Overweight Elvis impersonators

Group C: Lethargic snails

This isn't a trick question, and you have one minute to answer. Notice that I didn't ask you to pick a single winner out of a giant mush of horses, Elvii, and snails; I only asked you to pick the winning group in the race. The obvious answer is the thoroughbred racehorses (and no, they weren't ridden by the overweight Elvis impersonators because that would take away from the eloquent point I'm making). In this example, even the slowest member of Group A easily outdistances the fastest member of either Group B or C.

Industries, like Groups A, B, and C in my example, aren't equal, and life isn't fair. After all, if life were fair, Elvis would be alive, and the impersonators wouldn't exist. Fortunately, picking stocks doesn't have to be as difficult as picking a winning racehorse. The basic point is that it's easier to pick a successful stock from a group of winners (a growing, vibrant industry). Understanding industries only enhances your stock-picking strategy.

A successful, long-term investor looks at the industry (or the basic sector) just as carefully as he looks at the individual stock. Luckily, choosing a winning industry to invest in is easier than choosing individual stocks, as you find out in this chapter. I know some investors who can pick a winning stock in a losing industry, and I also know investors who've chosen a losing stock in a winning industry (the former is far outnumbered by the latter). Just think how well you do when you choose a great stock in a great industry! Of course, if you repeatedly choose bad stocks in bad industries, you may as well get out of the stock market altogether (maybe your calling is to be a celebrity impersonator instead!).

Telling the Difference between a Sector and an Industry

Very often, investors confuse an industry with a sector. Even though it may not be a consequential confusion, some clarity is needed here.

A *sector* is simply a group of interrelated industries. An *industry* is typically a category of business that performs a more precise activity; you can call an industry a *subsector*. Investing in a sector and investing in an industry can mean different things for the investor. The result of your investment performance can also be very different.

Healthcare is a good example of a sector that has different industries. The sector of healthcare includes such industries as pharmaceuticals, drug retailers, health insurance, hospitals, medical equipment manufacturers, and so on.

REMEMBER

Healthcare is actually a good (great!) example of why you should know the distinction between a sector and an industry. Within a given sector (like healthcare), you have industries that behave differently during the same economic conditions. Some of the industries are cyclical (like medical equipment manufacturers), whereas some are defensive (like drug retailers). In a bad economy, cyclicals tend to go down while defensive stocks tend to hold their value. In a good or booming economy, cyclicals do very well while defensive stocks tend to lag behind. (I talk more about cyclical and defensive industries later in this chapter.)

Given that fact, an exchange-traded fund (ETF) that reflected the general healthcare sector would be generally flat because some of the industries that went up would be offset by those that went down. Flip to Chapter 5 for more about ETFs.

Interrogating the Sectors and Industries

Your common sense is an important tool in choosing sectors and industries with winning stocks. This section explores some of the most important questions to ask yourself when you're choosing a sector or industry.

Which category does the industry fall into?

Most industries can neatly be placed in one of two categories: cyclical or defensive. In a rough way, these categories generally translate into what society wants and what it needs. Society buys what it *wants* when times are good and holds off when times are bad. It buys what it *needs* in both good and bad times. A want is a "like to have," whereas a need is a "must have." Got it?

Cyclical industries

Cyclical industries are industries whose fortunes rise and fall with the economy's rise and fall. In other words, if the economy and the stock market are doing well, consumers and investors are confident and tend to spend and invest more money than usual, so cyclical industries tend to do well. Real estate and automobiles are great examples of cyclical industries.

Your own situation offers you some common-sense insight into the concept of cyclical industries. Think about your behavior as a consumer, and you get a revealing clue into the thinking of millions of consumers. When you (and millions of others) feel good about your career, your finances, and your future, you have a greater tendency to buy more (and/or more expensive) stuff. When people feel financially strong, they're more apt to buy a new house or car or make some other large financial commitment. Also, people take on more debt because they feel confident that they can pay it back. In light of this behavior, what industries do you think would do well?

The same point holds for business spending. When businesses think that economic times are good and foresee continuing good times, they tend to spend more money on large purchases such as new equipment or technology. They think that when they're doing well and are flush with financial success, it's a good idea to reinvest that money in the business to increase future success.

Defensive industries

Defensive industries are industries that produce goods and services that are needed no matter what's happening in the economy. Your common sense kicks in here, too. What do you buy even when times are tough? Think about what millions of people buy no matter how bad the economy gets. A good example is food — people still need to eat regardless of good or bad times. Other examples of defensive industries are utilities and healthcare.

REMEMBER

In bad economic times, defensive stocks tend to do better than cyclical stocks. However, when times are good, cyclical stocks tend to do better than defensive stocks. Defensive stocks don't do as well in good times because people don't necessarily eat twice as much or use up more electricity.

So how do defensive stocks grow? Their growth generally relies on two factors:

>> **Population growth:** As more and more consumers are born, more people become available to buy.

>> **New markets:** A company can grow by seeking out new groups of consumers to buy its products and services. Coca-Cola, for example, found new markets in Asia during the 1990s. As communist regimes fell from power and more societies embraced a free market and consumer goods, the company sold more beverages, and its stock soared.

TIP

One way to invest in a particular industry is to take advantage of exchange-traded funds (ETFs), which have become very popular in recent years. ETFs are structured much like mutual funds but are fixed portfolios that trade like a stock. If you find a winning industry, but you can't find a winning stock (or don't want to bother with the necessary research), then ETFs are a great consideration. You can find out more about ETFs at websites such as www.etfdb.com or by turning to Chapter 5.

Is the sector growing?

The question may seem obvious, but you still need to ask it before you purchase stock. The saying "the trend is your friend" applies when choosing a sector in which to invest, as long as the trend is an upward one. If you look at three different stocks that are equal in every significant way, but you find that one stock is in a sector growing 15 percent per year while the other two stocks are in sectors that either have little growth or are shrinking, which stock would you choose?

WARNING

Sometimes the stock of a financially unsound or poorly run company goes up dramatically because the sector it's in is very exciting to the public. A recent example is marijuana stocks during 2018–2019. Their stock prices generally soared during 2018, but generally crashed during 2019. Investors and speculators went nuts buying up stocks as widespread legalization by key states opened the floodgates of interest. However, stock prices came down significantly from their highs (you were expecting a pun, right?), and investors soon smelled the coffee and remembered that fundamentals matter (as they eventually do!). Whatever new area interests you, be sure to look at the company's fundamentals (see Chapter 11 to find out how to do this) and the prospects for the industry's growth before settling on a particular stock.

To judge how well a sector or industry is doing, various information sources monitor all the sectors and industries and measure their progress. Some reliable sources include the following:

>> MarketWatch (www.marketwatch.com)

>> Standard & Poor's (www.standardandpoors.com)

>> D&B Hoovers (www.hoovers.com)

>> Yahoo! Finance (finance.yahoo.com)

>> *The Wall Street Journal* (www.wsj.com)

The preceding sources generally give you in-depth information about the major sectors and industries. Visit their websites to read their current research and articles along with links to relevant sites for more details. For example, *The Wall Street Journal* (published by Dow Jones & Co.), whose website is updated daily (or more frequently), publishes indexes for all the major sectors and industries so that you can get a useful snapshot of how well each one is doing.

Standard and Poor's (S&P) Industry Survey is an excellent source of information on U.S. industries. Besides ranking and comparing industries and informing you about their current prospects, the survey also lists the top companies by size, sales, earnings, and other key information. What I like is that each industry is covered in a few pages, so you get the critical information you need without reading a novel. The survey and other S&P publications are available on the S&P website or in the business reference section of most libraries (your best bet is to head for the library because the survey is rather expensive).

Will demand for the sector's products and/or services see long-term growth?

Look at the products and services that the sector or industry provides. Do they look like things that society will continue to want? Are there products and services on the horizon that could replace them? What does the foreseeable future look like for the sector?

REMEMBER

When evaluating future demand, look for a *sunrise industry* — one that's new or emerging or has promising appeal for the future. Good examples of sunrise industries in recent years are biotech and internet companies. In contrast, a *sunset industry* is one that's either declining or has little potential for growth. For example, you probably shouldn't invest in the DVD manufacturing industry because demand has shifted toward digital delivery instead. Owning stock in a strong, profitable company in a sunrise industry is obviously the most desirable choice.

Current research unveils the following megatrends:

>> **The aging of the United States:** More senior citizens than ever before are living in the United States. Because of this fact, healthcare and financial services that touch on eldercare or financial concerns of the elderly will prosper.

>> **Advances in high technology:** Internet, telecom, medical, and biotechnology innovations will continue.

>> **Security concerns:** Terrorism, international tensions, and security issues on a personal level mean more attention for national defense, homeland security, and related matters.

>> **Energy challenges:** Traditional and nontraditional sources of energy (such as solar, fuel cells, and so on) will demand society's attention as it transitions from fossil fuels to new forms of energy.

TIP

One of my favorite resources for anticipating megatrends is Gerald Celente and his Trends Journal (www.trendsresearch.com). They have been spot-on with forecasting megatrends as they unfold.

What does the industry's growth rely on?

An industry doesn't exist in a vacuum. External factors weigh heavily on its ability to survive and thrive. Does the industry rely on an established megatrend? Then it will probably be strong for a while. Does it rely on factors that are losing relevance? Then it may begin to decline soon. Technological and demographic changes are other factors that may contribute to an industry's growth or fall.

REMEMBER

Keep in mind that a sector will either continue to grow, shrink, or be level, but individual industries can grow, shrink, or even be on a track to disappear. If a sector is expanding, you may see new industries emerge. For example, the graying of the United States is an established megatrend. As millions of Americans climb into their later years, profitable opportunities await companies that are prepared to cater to them. Perhaps an industry (subsector) offers great new medical products for senior citizens. What are the prospects for growth?

Does the industry depend on another industry?

This twist on the prior question is a reminder that industries frequently are intertwined and can become codependent. When one industry suffers, you may find it helpful to understand which industries will subsequently suffer. The reverse can also be true — when one industry is doing well, other industries may reap the benefits.

In either case, if the stock you choose is in an industry that's highly dependent on other industries, you should know about it. If you're considering stocks of resort companies and you see the headlines blaring, "Airlines losing money as public stops flying," what do you do? This type of question forces you to think logically and consider cause and effect. Logic and common sense are powerful tools that frequently trump all the number-crunching activity performed by analysts.

Who are the leading companies in the industry?

After you've chosen the industry, what types of companies do you want to invest in? You can choose from two basic types:

>> **Established leaders:** These companies are considered industry leaders or have a large share of the market. Investing in these companies is the safer way to go; what better choice for novice investors than companies that have already proven themselves?

>> **Innovators:** If the industry is hot and you want to be more aggressive in your approach, investigate companies that offer new products, patents, or technologies. These companies are probably smaller but have a greater potential for growth in a proven industry.

Is the industry a target of government action?

You need to know whether the government is targeting an industry because intervention by politicians and bureaucrats (rightly or wrongly) can have an impact on an industry's economic situation. Find out about any political issues that face a company, industry, or sector (see Chapter 15 for political considerations).

WARNING

Investors need to take heed when political "noise" starts coming out about a particular industry. An industry can be hurt either by direct government intervention or by the threat of it. Intervention can take the form of lawsuits, investigations, taxes, regulations, or sometimes an outright ban. In any case, being on the wrong end of government intervention is the greatest external threat to a company's survival.

REMEMBER

Sometimes, government action helps an industry. Generally, beneficial action takes two forms:

>> **Deregulation and/or tax decreases:** Government sometimes reduces burdens on an industry. During the late 1990s, for example, government deregulation led the way to more innovation in the telecommunications industry. This trend, in turn, laid the groundwork for more innovation and growth in the internet and expansion of cellphone service.

>> **Direct funding:** Government has the power to steer taxpayer money toward business as well. In recent years, federal and state governments have provided tax credits and other incentives for alternative energy such as solar power.

Outlining Key Sectors and Industries

In this section, I highlight some up-and-coming sectors and industries that investors should take note of, as well as established sectors and industries that have strong potential for the coming years. Consider investing some of your stock portfolio in those that look promising (and, of course, avoid those that look problematic).

REMEMBER

Keep in mind everything you read in earlier chapters (like Chapters 11 and 12) regarding the fundamentals (sales, profits, and so on) of the best companies within these sectors and industries. No matter how new, glamourous, and popular some companies seem to be, always go back to the fundamentals. Don't get excited when you hear pundits say that these companies or trends are "groundbreaking" with "game-changing" technologies or "glitzy" inventions.

The internet in the late 1990s, for example, was indeed extremely significant for the economy and society at large, but the initial wave of companies ultimately had more losers than winners. Hundreds of dot-com companies ended up in the graveyard of barely remembered failures. The real growth opportunities emerged with the second wave, which meant those companies that survived, made a profit, and went on to become leaders of the pack.

Robotics and artificial intelligence

Robotics and artificial intelligence are a promising new area of growth in the economy. Companies big and small are getting in on the action. This technology ranges from drones to actual, lifelike robots. The growth in this technology has been tremendous, and because there are so many applications for it, ranging from robots that perform basic services to military uses such as defusing bombs and other traditionally hazardous tasks, growth in this venue looks strong going forward.

TIP

My favorite way to invest in this venue is through ETFs so that I can invest in a wide swath of companies; the industry has strong growth prospects, but it's not always easy to discern winning individual companies. For individual companies to choose from, why not take a look at the top holdings of a robotics ETF? A good example of a leading robotics ETF is ROBO (the Global Robotics and Automation Index ETF). When you see some suitable companies in an ETF, review their fundamentals before you add them to your growth portfolio. Flip to Chapter 5 for more about ETFs; Chapters 11 and 12 are a good start for reviewing company fundamentals.

Ecommerce

Amazon (AMZN) is considered the quintessential ecommerce site as more and more of the public are turning to the internet for their consumer purchases. I think that AMZN is very expensive — not only on a per-share basis but also based on fundamentals. (It has a very high P/E ratio; compare it to others by reading up on P/E ratios in Chapter 6 and Appendix B.) I think there are better ways to profit from ecommerce.

TIP

Consider companies that make money every time someone buys something online such as Visa Inc. (V) or PayPal (PYPL). And yes, there are ETFs in this venue too.

Marijuana investing

For 2020, marijuana investing will probably enter a period of normal growth after two years of bubble-ish gains and the subsequent declines. As marijuana usage continues to expand both for recreational and medicinal purposes, investors can start looking at these companies through the lens of fundamentals in the same way a stock investor would view other, conventional stock investments.

TIP

Many companies in this space experienced losses, so investors would be best off waiting for winners to emerge. Fortunately, new ETFs have emerged (at least nine are currently found on www.etfdb.com), and so has a spate of new investor websites such as www.MarijuanaStocks.com. Conventional sites such as www.investopedia.com and www.marketwatch.com now carry regular news and views on this growing industry.

Commodities

In the year 2000, the general commodities complex went on a multiyear bull market and resulted in some spectacular gains for early investors. Then the mega crisis of 2008 hit, and commodities collapsed. As economies struggled and contracted, demand for general commodities was generally down, and stocks and ETFs tied to this sector sputtered and declined in the ensuing years.

Keep in mind that commodities do not move in lockstep — some commodities can do well when others do not. Supply and demand factors are primary considerations. Commodities tied to food (such as grains), for example, tend to keep moderately growing as investment vehicles as the world population continues to grow. Commodities tied to building and infrastructure (such as base metals like copper and zinc), on the other hand, tend to do well when good economic times translate into more things being built such as highways, skyscrapers, and so forth. Energy-related commodities such as oil and natural gas do well when the economy is booming and demand for energy increases.

How to play commodities? Of course, many assume that commodities are all about trading and speculating, but there are plenty of ways for stock investors to participate. Virtually every major commodity has a variety of ways for you to play it.

If you believe that soybeans will be doing very well in the coming years, you can invest in a company such as Bunge Ltd. (BG), or you can do the ETF in soybeans (the Teucrium Soybean fund — symbol SOYB). If you think that corn will do well and you want to stalk some profits there (see what I did?), you can consider companies such as Archer Daniels Midland (ADM) or the corn ETF (the Teucrium Corn Fund — symbol CORN). If you think grains in general will do well but are not sure which ones will have more fertile profits, than consider ETFs exposed to grains such as DBA (the PowerShares DB Agriculture Fund). It has soybeans and corn but also includes wheat and even cattle and hogs, too.

Precious metals

Precious metals are an important hedge in the case of financial crises tied to paper assets. I can safely forecast that paper assets such as bonds (government, corporate, and so on) are reaching unsustainable levels, which could have dangerous effects on many portfolios and retirement accounts. Additionally, central banks such as the federal reserve typically resort to opening up the spigots for cash and more debt in attempts to placate any looming financial crisis.

Given that, hard asset alternatives tend to be treated by the investing public as safe harbors. Precious metals did very well in the late 1970s when inflation and an energy crisis erupted, and they repeated their bullish runs during 2000–2010, so conditions are ripe for bullish moves during 2020–2030. Speculators should consider precious metals mining stocks, while investors may consider large cap mining stocks and also precious metals industry ETFs.

Good examples of precious metals ETFs are SPDR Gold Shares (symbol GLD) and iShares Silver Trust (SLV). To find out more about precious metals (along with stocks and ETFs related to them), take a look at my book *Precious Metals Investing For Dummies* (published by Wiley).

Cryptocurrency opportunities

Cryptocurrencies are another market that was initially overheated when opportunities rose in 2017–2018. Cryptocurrencies became a new alternative to traditional paper currencies and precious metals a few years ago. It was an incredible bubble that pushed cryptocurrencies such as Bitcoin (BTC) soaring to a unit value of $13,800 during late 2017 and early 2018 and then crashing to $3,500 by the start of 2019. Then it soared again to $ 10,000 before falling to $7,300 at the end of 2019. I'm getting dizzy just writing about this incredible volatility. Rival cryptocurrencies such as Ethereum (ETH) and Litecoin (LTC) had similar roller-coaster rides.

TIP

Investing (actually speculating) in cryptocurrencies is not for the faint-hearted and should be done only with a relatively small portion of your investable funds. Given that, here are two considerations for you:

>> If you want to be involved with cryptocurrencies, find out about using them as a transactional medium and not an investment vehicle. This means that if you have a business — even a part-time one from home or through freelancing — consider making it a payment option so that you can receive, say, Bitcoin as a payment for your services.

>> If you want to invest, consider companies that make money from the products and services tied to cryptocurrencies such as blockchain technology. That way you can participate in the growth of cryptocurrencies with less exposure to their risks and volatility.

TIP

My favorite resource for folks who are beginners and are serious about getting directly involved with cryptocurrencies is the book *Cryptocurrency Investing For Dummies* by Kiana Danial (published by Wiley).

Driving it home

Tesla (TSLA) and Uber (UBER) are the newest darlings of the auto world, so you may be curious about their stocks. As of early 2020, both companies have been running losses, though, so please consider them only for speculation since profitability should be considered the primary consideration (in my book, at least) before you can call it an investment.

WARNING

Yes, both stocks may be suitable vehicles for short-term speculating and trading (especially for options traders), but they haven't yet achieved reliable profitability in their income statements and they still have large debt loads, so investors are best served to wait until their fundamentals improve.

Chapter **14**

Small Cap Stocks, IPOs, and Motif Investing

I f you're an investor (or a speculator) who wants to use a relatively small amount of money to buy stock in a single company or a set of companies (much like a mutual fund but requiring less money), this chapter is for you! Many investors dream of buying a cheap stock (referred to as *micro caps* and *small caps*) and watching it become a real investment powerhouse. It can be done, but you need to do it right; the first part of this chapter addresses this topic.

Another consideration is investing in a company's *IPO* (initial public offering). The right IPO can make you a fortune, but too many people lose money because they miss some crucial points (which, of course, I cover here).

One way to potentially turn a small grubstake like a few hundred dollars into big money is through a relatively new innovation called motif investing. *Motif investing* gives you the ability to invest as little as $250 into a batch of stocks and/or exchange-traded funds (ETFs) that have a particular theme or a specific outlook that you expect to occur. You can get the scoop later in this chapter.

Exploring Small Caps

Everyone wants to get in early on a hot new stock. Why not? You buy Shlobotky, Inc., at $1 per share and hope it zooms to $98 before lunchtime. Who doesn't want to buy a cheapy-deepy stock today that could become the next Apple or Walmart? This possibility is why investors are attracted to small cap stocks.

Small cap (or small capitalization) is a reference to the company's market value, as I explain in Chapter 1. *Small cap stocks* are stocks that have a market value under $1 billion (some consider the cutoff to be $2 billion). And small cap stocks that are valued under $250 million are referred to as *micro caps*. (**Note:** Some consider micro caps to be under $100 million, and the stocks of these relatively small companies are often referred to as *penny stocks.* For the most part, I simply refer to them as small caps.) Investors may face more risk with small caps, but they also have the chance for greater gains.

Out of all the types of stocks, small cap stocks continue to exhibit the greatest amount of growth. In the same way that a tree planted last year has more opportunity for growth than a mature 100-year-old redwood, small caps have greater growth potential than established large cap stocks. Of course, a small cap doesn't exhibit spectacular growth just because it's small. It grows when it does the right things, such as increasing sales and earnings by producing goods and services that customers want to buy.

WARNING

For every small company that becomes a Fortune 500 firm, hundreds of companies don't grow at all or go out of business. When you try to guess the next great stock before any evidence of growth, you're not investing — you're speculating. Even worse than speculating is buying the stock of a company that's losing money (net loss instead of net profit), and then hoping or expecting that it will go up (and stay up if it does go up).

Don't get me wrong — there's nothing wrong with speculating in small cap stocks (of companies that aren't proven in sales and profits). But it's important to *know* that you're speculating when you're doing it. If you're going to speculate in small stocks hoping for the next Microsoft or Apple, use the guidelines I present in the following sections to increase your chances of success.

Checking that a small cap stock is making money

REMEMBER

I emphasize two points when investing in stocks:

>> **Make sure that a company is established.** Being in business for at least three years is a good minimum.

>> **Make sure that a company is profitable.** It should show net profits of 10 percent or more over two years or longer.

These points are especially important for investors in small stocks. Plenty of start-up ventures lose money but hope to make a fortune down the road. A good example is a company in the biotechnology industry. Biotech is an exciting area, but it's esoteric, and at this early stage, companies are finding it difficult to use the technology in profitable ways. You may say, "But shouldn't I jump in now in anticipation of future profits?" You may get lucky, but understand that when you invest in unproven, small cap stocks, you're speculating.

Analyzing small cap stocks before you invest

REMEMBER

The only difference between a small cap stock and a large cap stock is a few zeros in their numbers and the fact that you need to do more research with small caps. By sheer dint of size, small caps are riskier than large caps, so you offset the risk by accruing more information on yourself and the stock in question. Plenty of information is available on large cap stocks because they're widely followed. Small cap stocks don't get as much press, and fewer analysts issue reports on them. Here are a few points to keep in mind:

>> **Understand your investment style.** Small cap stocks may have more potential rewards, but they also carry more risk. No investor should devote a large portion of his capital to small cap stocks. If you're considering retirement money, you're better off investing in large cap stocks, ETFs (see Chapter 5), investment-grade bonds, bank accounts, and/or mutual funds. Retirement money should be in investments that are either very safe or have proven track records of steady growth over an extended period of time (five years or longer).

>> **Check with the Securities and Exchange Commission (SEC).** Get the financial reports that the company must file with the SEC (such as its 10Ks and 10Qs — see Chapter 12 for more details). These reports offer more complete information on the company's activities and finances. Go to the SEC website at www.sec.gov, and check its massive database of company filings at EDGAR (the Electronic Data Gathering, Analysis, and Retrieval system). You can also check to see whether any complaints have been filed against the company.

>> **Check other sources.** See whether brokers and independent research services, such as Value Line (`www.valueline.com/`), or venues such as Seeking Alpha (`https://seekingalpha.com/`) and Yahoo! Finance (`https://finance.yahoo.com/`) follow the stock. If two or more different sources like the stock, it's worth further investigation. Check the resources in Appendix A for additional sources of information before you invest.

Picking out principles for small cap success

Micro caps and small cap stocks are perfect for speculators. Whether you're doing short-term speculating (such as trading) or long-term speculating (hoping your choice eventually becomes a major investment later), you're gambling. You may not be putting a fortune on the line, but it is your hard-earned money. Here are some small cap guidelines to keep you sane — and hopefully profitable:

>> **Know your goals.** You should know as much about yourself as you know about the company and its small cap stock potential. What is your approach? What do you aim to do with small cap stocks?

- **Short-term speculation:** There's nothing wrong with seeking quick gains if you don't mind the risks. With speculating, a company's fundamentals aren't that great of a concern because you don't plan on holding the stock for very long. As a speculator, you use technical analysis to evaluate the stock (see Chapter 10).

- **Long-term investing:** Here you approach the stock as a value investor, much as you would with larger cap stocks. Think growing sales and increasing earnings (net profits). Use fundamental analysis, which I cover in Chapter 8.

>> **Designate risk capital.** You allocate your funds for a variety of purposes — emergency funds in the bank, investment funds in your IRA and/or 401(k) plan, and so on. For small cap stocks, allocate a sum of money that you're comfortable losing in a worst-case scenario; this sum is called *risk capital*.

TIP

This sum has to be high enough for you to diversify your small cap holdings but small enough that losing the money won't alter your life or general prosperity. Unless you're more experienced with small cap stocks, consider limiting your exposure to less than 10 percent (or less than 5 percent for novice investors).

>> **Become proficient in an industry.** When an industry does well, many of the stocks in that industry tend to do well, and the small cap stocks tend to do very well. The more you know about an industry and the major factors that influence it, the better you'll be as a stock picker. Check out Chapter 13 for an introduction to sectors and industries.

>> **Diversify.** Yes, if you have 100,000 shares of one small cap stock, you'll have a fortune if you're right. But the odds are definitely against you. Losing all or most of your money is too strong of a possibility to ignore. You're better off having, say, 20,000 shares in each of five different companies.

In the world of small cap stocks, you could have a situation where you end up with four losers and one winner and still come out ahead in total market value.

TIP

>> **Buy some, sell some.** If you bought 1,000 shares of a stock and it's up a few hundred percent, take some money off the table and cash out enough to get (at the very least) your original investment back. Then hold the remaining stock for the long term if you're an investor. If the worst case occurs and the company goes bankrupt, then at least you got back your original grubstake.

>> **Get to know the company through a phone call (or a visit if possible).** Usually company executives like to discuss the business with investors and other interested parties, and a call or visit gives you the opportunity to pick up some valuable information. Ask about the company's short-term and long-term objectives. If possible, get on the company's distribution list for email updates and press releases.

>> **Check for news and insider disclosure.** Many financial websites give you the ability to receive alerts when major events happen with your stock. Many financial websites also let you see what the insiders are doing. Take advantage of that (see Chapter 20 for more details).

>> **Use limit orders.** Use what brokerage orders are available to minimize risk and potential losses and to maximize gains. Use limit orders rather than market orders with small cap stocks so you can control what prices you pay or receive when you enter or exit positions. Find out more about these types of orders in Chapter 17.

TIP

>> **Choose a batch of potential winners.** When you're investing in micro caps and/or small caps, get five to ten in your chosen industry or sector. This strategy enhances your chance of a total winning portfolio. When you choose a hot industry or sector, then your chance of getting one or more winning stocks is greatly enhanced. Keep in mind that in lieu of choosing a batch of winning stocks, an ETF (see Chapter 5) or motif investing (covered later in this chapter) may suffice for those who can't or won't do the necessary research.

Reading up on what history's great investors have done is always a good idea, and one of my favorites is John Templeton. He started his legendary multimillion-dollar fortunes (which later turned into billions) investing in micro cap stocks during the Great Depression. Templeton made sure that the companies he invested in had true value (profitability, valuable assets, and so on), where the stock price was significantly below the company's value. To find out more about John Templeton and his successful stocking investing career, head over to www.sirjohntempleton.org.

TIP

Consider reading up on small caps and micro caps. A good book on the topic is *Penny Stocks For Dummies*, 2nd Edition, by Peter Leeds (published by Wiley). The term "penny stocks" is frequently synonymous with micro cap stocks.

Finding small cap gems

Consider starting your search for good small cap stocks by checking out top organizations that already have those stocks in their portfolios. If experts chose small cap stocks for an ETF portfolio or for a mutual fund that specializes in small cap stocks, those stocks probably offer a good starting point for your research. These experts did the heavy lifting of choosing small caps for their portfolios, so you can learn from them and use this approach as a shortcut in finding quality small cap stocks.

TIP

To look for micro caps and small caps, go to sites such as the following (along with other sources in Appendix A):

>> **Nasdaq** (www.nasdaq.com): This is a premier site for stocks, but it's also the hub of activity for small cap stocks. You can find stock reports and SEC filings for virtually any small cap (or larger) company.

>> **OTC Markets** (www.otcmarkets.com): Find small cap stock listings and prices as well as the most active small cap stocks.

>> **Stockwatch** (www.stockwatch.com): This very active site is packed with news and views of stocks in general but emphasizes small cap stocks.

>> **SmallCap Network** (www.smallcapnetwork.com): This extensive site has research and reports on small cap stocks.

>> **Small Cap Directory** (www.smallcapdirectory.com): This site is a search engine for doing research on small cap stocks.

Also, consider alternatives to directly owning small cap stocks. Buying ETFs that have a diversified portfolio of small cap stocks can be a safer and more convenient way of adding small cap stocks to your portfolio. To find great ETFs on small cap stocks, do a search at www.etfdb.com.

Investigating IPOs

Initial public offerings (IPOs) are the birthplaces of publicly held stocks, or the proverbial ground floor. The IPO is the first offering to the public of a company's stock. The IPO is also referred to as "going public." Because a company going public is frequently an unproven enterprise, investing in an IPO can be risky. Here are the two types of IPOs:

>> **Start-up IPO:** This is a company that didn't exist before the IPO. In other words, the entrepreneurs get together and create a business plan. To get the financing they need for the company, they decide to go public immediately by approaching an investment banker. If the investment banker thinks that it's a good concept, the banker will seek funding (selling the stock to investors) via the IPO.

>> **A private company that decides to go public:** In many cases, the IPO is done for a company that already exists and is seeking expansion capital. The company may have been around for a long time as a smaller private concern but now decides to seek funding through an IPO to grow even larger (or to fund a new product, promotional expenses, and so on).

Which of the two IPOs do you think is less risky? That's right — the private company going public. Why? Because it's already a proven business, which is a safer bet than a brand-new start-up. Some great examples of successful IPOs in recent years are United Parcel Service and Google (they were established companies *before* they went public). A great example of a failed IPO that lost mega-billions was 2019's WeWork (which . . . uh . . . didn't work.)

Great stocks started as small companies going public. You may be able to recount the stories of Federal Express, Dell, United Parcel Service, Home Depot, and hundreds of other great successes. But do you remember an IPO by the company Lipschitz & Farquar? No? I didn't think so. It's among the majority of IPOs that don't succeed.

WARNING

IPOs have a dubious track record of success in their first year. Studies periodically done by the brokerage industry have revealed that IPOs actually decline in price 60 percent of the time (more often than not) during the first 12 months. In other words, an IPO has a better-than-even chance of dropping in price.

REMEMBER

For investors, the lesson is clear: Wait until a track record appears before you invest in a company. If you don't, you're simply rolling the dice (in other words, you're speculating, not investing!). Don't worry about missing that great opportunity; if it's a bona fide opportunity, you'll still do well after the IPO.

Getting the Scoop on Motif Investing

For many investors, choosing a small cap stock or considering an IPO may be a daunting task. Fortunately, there are innovative ways to invest in stocks today that weren't around when I first started investing.

There are ETFs as well as mutual funds in small cap stocks. There are also investment vehicles called "motifs" that specialize in small cap stocks and in IPOs. A motif is a relatively new way to invest and offers an interesting twist on mutual funds and ETFs.

REMEMBER

A *motif* is a basket of stocks and/or ETFs that mirror a specific idea, trend, or theme. Some motifs are designed to be very targeted and can fit any person's outlook or expectation. The motif may be as few as 1 or 2 stocks and/or ETFs or as many as 30. It may be a predefined motif designed by the brokerage firm (also called *professional motifs*; as of October 2019, about 140 different motifs were available). You can create your own motif or modify an existing one (these are called *community motifs* because they are user-defined by customers). Find out the basics of motif investing in the following sections.

Discovering what you get with motifs

When you look at the interesting variety of motifs, it will make you go "ooh!" Here's a sample of available motifs (as of this writing):

>> **Caffeine Fix:** This basket of stocks is for those who want to profit from the public's enjoyment of coffee and related caffeine products.

>> **Rising Food Prices:** If you expect (or see) rising food prices, this motif is designed to profit from that scenario.

>> **High Spirits:** Profit from owning stocks of companies that sell adult beverages.

>> **Drug Patent Cliffs:** Own stocks that benefit when drug patents expire.

>> **Online Gaming:** Profit from the growth of gambling on the internet.

>> **Political Donors:** Invest in a portfolio of stocks that could benefit from the ebb and flow of politics.

>> **Cleantech:** As the world seeks to "go green and clean," this basket of stocks is for investors seeking clean technology profits.

LOOKING AT MOTIFS' PERFORMANCE

When you look at the range of available motifs, the performance (how well did the basket of stocks and ETFs do for the year?) is as varied as the selection. Here are the top three performing motifs for the 12-month period that ended October 2019 (as of this writing):

- Software as a Service: As specialized software apps grow, this motif was up 34.72%.

- Precious Metals: Up 32.42% as investors sought alternatives to paper investments.

- Renter Nation: Up 30.69% as providers of products/services to renters do well.

Of course, there were losing motifs in that same time frame too:

- Shale Gas: Down 47% as the energy markets took a drubbing.

- Frack Attack: This motif of fracking-related companies was down 42%.

- Shale Oil: Another energy-related motif took a hit — down 34%.

Two other motifs with a bear market theme were also down sharply since 2019 was a bullish (up) year.

Keep in mind that the preceding lists (both good and bad performances) were for a single, 12-month period. Don't assume that they will experience the same in 2020 and beyond as the economy and financial markets keep ebbing and flowing.

It seems like you're limited only by your imagination and the types of securities available. These are the securities that can be in a motif:

>> Stocks (both large and small cap)

>> Exchange-traded funds (ETFs)

>> American depository receipts (ADRs), which are essentially foreign securities that trade on U.S. exchanges (see Chapter 18 for details)

Focusing on motif features

A motif is more than a theme–based approach to investing; it's also a broker. You open an account with the company (at www.motif.com/) just as you would with any traditional broker. Here are the main features:

>> You can open an account with as little as $250 (cash account). For a margin account, the minimum is $2,000. (See Chapter 17 for details on using margin.)

>> The cash account can be a regular account or an Individual Retirement Account (IRA) — either a traditional or a Roth. Margin trading is available only as a regular account.

>> You can choose a preexisting motif (and modify it if you like), or you can build your own on the company's website. You can even suggest a theme for a motif, and the company can create one for its catalog.

>> The transaction cost (as of this writing) is an annual fee of 0.50 percent for Motif thematic portfolios and 0.25 percent for Motif impact portfolios.

>> You have to view a detailed profile (and the securities) of the motif at the site (the catalog) before you buy it.

Considering motif categories

All these varied motifs do fall into definable categories, so start your search there:

>> **General:** This is the catch-all for new and trendy motifs and those that may not be neatly categorized.

>> **Values-based:** If you want your investing approach to embrace a particular social cause or political theme, check out this category.

>> **Sectors:** Whether you like healthcare, technology, or financial services, you'll find a suitable motif here. (Find out more about sectors in Chapter 13.)

>> **Global opportunities:** Want to invest in developed markets or emerging markets? Check them out here.

>> **Asset allocation:** Here you find motifs that try to emulate portfolios for a particular target date (such as for those retiring in a specific year, like 2030 or 2035).

>> **Income strategies:** If you want income from dividends or from bond interest (through an ETF), this category is for you.

>> **Trading strategies:** Want to trade with technical analysis or based on short-term events? Check out the motifs in this category.

>> **Special situations:** As new and/or innovative securities or assets emerge (such as cryptocurrencies), new or unique motifs come on the scene.

Understanding the risks

Motifs sound pretty good, but what are the risks? A motif, much like an ETF or a traditional mutual fund, is only as good as the securities in the portfolio. All the risks of buying and holding stocks, ETFs, and ADRs are present in the motif, just as they would be in any other investment.

WARNING

The risk with a motif is really tied to your viewpoint. If you believe that a certain scenario will play out, such as a bear market, inflation, or some other economic or social scenario, and it doesn't materialize, then your motif's performance will suffer.

For more details on motif investing, check out www.motif.com/.

Chapter 15

The Big Economic and Political Picture

E ven if politics doesn't amuse or interest you, you can't ignore it. The point is not whether you vote for or against a particular candidate; the point is that you vote for or against their policies and legislative agendas. You don't vote because the candidate is Mother Teresa or Attila the Hun; you vote not only for the policies that will ultimately govern your life (career, business, and so on) but primarily for which set of policies will generate the greatest economic good, which in turn can set an environment for your stocks (those underlying companies) to succeed or not.

REMEMBER

What people must understand (especially government policymakers) is that a new tax, law, regulation, or government action has a *macro* effect on a stock, an industry, a sector, or even an entire economic system, whereas a typical company has a *micro* effect on an economy. The following gives you a simple snapshot of these effects:

Politics → policy → economy → sector → industry → company → stock → stock investor

This chapter doesn't moralize about politics or advocate a political point of view; after all, this book is about stock investing. In general, policies can be good or bad regardless of their effect on the economy — some policies are enacted to achieve greater purposes even if they kick you in the wallet. However, in the context of this chapter, politics is covered from a cause-and-effect perspective: How does politics affect prosperity in general and stock investing in particular?

REMEMBER

A proficient stock investor can't — must not — look at stocks as though they exist in a vacuum. My favorite example of this rule is the idea of fish in a lake. You can have a great fish (your stock) among a whole school of fish (the stock market) in a wonderful lake (the economy). But what if the lake gets polluted (bad policy)? What happens to the fish? Politics controls the lake and can make it hospitable — or dangerous — for the participants. You get the point. The example may sound too simple, yet it isn't. So many people — political committees, corporate managers, bureaucrats, and politicians — still get this picture so wrong time and time again, to the detriment of the economy and stock investors. Heck, I don't mind if they get it wrong with *their* money, but their actions make it tough for *your* money.

Although the two inexorably get intertwined, I do what I can to treat politics and economics as separate issues.

Tying Together Politics and Stocks

The campaigns heat up. Democrats, Republicans, and smaller parties vie for your attention and subsequent votes. Conservatives, liberals, socialists, moderates, and libertarians joust in the battlefield of ideas. But after all is said and done, voters make their decisions. Election Day brings a new slate of politicians into office, and they in turn joust and debate on new rules and programs in the legislative halls of power. Before and after election time, investors must keep a watchful eye on the proceedings. In the following sections, I explain some basic political concepts that relate to stock investing.

Seeing the general effects of politics on stock investing

For stock investors, politics manifests itself as a major factor in investment-making decisions in the ways shown in Table 15-1.

REMEMBER

When many of the factors in Table 15-1 work concurrently, they can have a magnified effect that can have tremendous consequences for your stock portfolio. Alert investors keep a constant vigil when the legislature is open for business, and they adjust their portfolios accordingly.

TABLE 15-1   **Politics and Investing**

Possible Legislation	Effect on Investing
Taxes	Will a new tax affect a particular stock (industry, sector, or economy)? Generally, more or higher taxes ultimately have a negative impact on stock investing. Income taxes and capital gains taxes are good examples.
Laws	Will Congress (or, in some instances, state legislatures) pass a law that will have a negative impact on a stock, the industry, the sector, or the economy? Price controls — laws that set the price of a product, service, or commodity — are examples of negative laws. I discuss price controls in more detail later in this chapter.
Regulations	Will a new (or existing) regulation have a negative (or positive) effect on the stock of your choice? Generally, more or tougher regulations have a negative impact on stocks.
Government spending and debt	If government agencies spend too much or misallocate resources, they may create greater burdens on society, which in turn will be bearish for the economy and the stock market.
Money supply	The U.S. money supply — the dollars you use — is controlled by the Federal Reserve. It's basically a governmental agency that serves as America's central bank. How can it affect stocks? Increasing or decreasing the money supply results in either an inflationary or a deflationary environment, which can help or hurt the economy, specific sectors and industries, and your stock picks. When the money supply flows into goods and services, you get higher consumer prices. When it flows into assets (such as stocks), you get asset inflation, which typically precedes an asset bubble.
Interest rates	The Federal Reserve has crucial influence here. It can raise or lower key interest rates that in turn can have an effect on the entire economy and the stock market. When interest rates go up, it makes credit more expensive for companies. When interest rates go down, companies can get cheaper credit, which can be better for profits.
Government bailouts	A *bailout* is when the government intervenes directly in the marketplace and uses either tax money or borrowed money to bail out a troubled enterprise. This is generally a negative because funds are diverted by force from the healthier private economy to an ailing enterprise.

Ascertaining the political climate

The bottom line is that you ignore political realities at your own (economic) risk. To be and stay aware, ask yourself the following questions about the stock of each company in which you invest:

>> What laws will directly affect my stock investment adversely?

>> Will any laws affect the company's industry and/or sector?

>> Will any current or prospective laws affect the company's sources of revenue?

>> Will any current or prospective laws affect the company's expenses or supplies?

>> Am I staying informed about political and economic issues that may possibly have a negative impact on my investment?

>> Will such things as excessive regulations, price controls, or new taxes have a negative impact on my stock's industry?

Regardless of the merits (or demerits) of the situation, investors must view it through the lens of economic causes and effects, which in turn leads to their decisions on which companies (and their stocks) are impacted positively or negatively.

Distinguishing between nonsystemic and systemic effects

Politics can affect your investments in two basic ways: nonsystemic and systemic.

>> *Nonsystemic* means that the system isn't affected but a particular participant is affected.

>> *Systemic* means that all the players in the system are affected. Laws typically affect more than just one company or group of companies; rather, they affect an entire industry, sector, or the entire economy — more "players" in the economic system.

In this case, the largest system is the economy at large; to a lesser extent, an entire industry or sector can be the system that's affected. Politics imposes itself (through taxes, laws, regulations, and so on) and can have an undue influence on all (or most) of the members of that system.

Nonsystemic effects

Say that you decide to buy stock in a company called Golf Carts Unlimited, Inc. (GCU). You believe that the market for golf carts has great potential and that GCU stands to grow substantially. How can politics affect GCU?

What if politicians believe that GCU is too big and that it controls too much of the golf cart industry? Maybe they view GCU as a monopolistic entity and want the federal government to step in to shrink GCU's reach and influence for the sake of competition and for the ultimate benefit of consumers. Maybe the government believes that GCU engages in unfair or predatory business practices and that it's in violation of antitrust (or antimonopoly) laws. If the government acts against GCU, the action is a nonsystemic issue: The action is directed toward the participant (in this case, GCU) and not the golf cart industry in general.

What happens if you're an investor in GCU? Does your stock investment suffer as a result of government action directed against the company? Let's just say that the stock price will "hook left" and could end up "in the sand trap."

Systemic effects

Say that politicians want to target the golf industry for intervention because they maintain that golf should be free or close to free for all to participate in and that a law must be passed to make it accessible to all, especially those people who can't afford to play. So to remedy the situation, the following law is enacted: "Law #67590305598002 declares that from this day forward, all golf courses must charge only one dollar for any golfer who chooses to participate."

POLITICS RUN AMOK — SO COMPANIES RUN

In recent years we have seen how government jurisdictions, both domestic and international, have made the political and governmental environment too toxic for companies, their customers, and the investors. Right now states such as California and Illinois have gone too far with taxes and regulations and have poisoned the economic environment to the point that companies and taxpayers (and investors) have fled to friendlier venues. Overseas, socialist Venezuela went to official totalitarian status, which caused a massive flight by people and businesses.

What lessons do these disparate places have for stock investors? When a jurisdiction — a state or country — becomes too onerous to do business in, then investors will be left with losses when the dust settles. Excessive regulations, burdensome mandates, and high taxes harm business formation and lead to investor losses.

The point is to be sensitive to changing laws and how they affect economic behavior. Many companies have seen their factories and facilities become worthless when socialist governments nationalized (in other words, expropriated) property causing huge losses for the company and subsequently falling stock prices (if those companies were public). Always be mindful and watchful of politics going the extreme statist route so you can change course before it's too late. Some of my favorite sources that watch for politics and government to give you an "early warning" can be found in Appendix A.

That law sounds great to any golfer. But what are the unintended effects when such a law becomes reality? Many people may agree with the sentiment of the law, but what about the actual cause-and-effect aspects of it? Obviously, all things being equal, golf courses will be forced to close. Staying in business is uneconomical if their costs are higher than their income. If they can't charge any more than a dollar, how can they possibly stay open? Ultimately (and ironically), no one can play golf. The law would be a "triple bogey" for sure!

What happens to investors of Golf Carts Unlimited, Inc.? If the world of golf shrinks, demand for golf carts shrinks as well. The value of GCU's stock will certainly be stuck in a sand trap.

REMEMBER

Examples of politics creating systemic problems are endless, but you get the point. Companies are ultimately part of a system, and those that control or maintain the rules overseeing that system can have far-reaching effects. All investors are advised to be vigilant about systemic effects on their stocks.

Understanding price controls

Stock investors should be very wary of price controls, which are a great example of regulation. A *price control* is a fixed price on a particular product, commodity, or service mandated by the government.

WARNING

Price controls have been tried continuously throughout history, and they've continuously been removed because they ultimately do more harm than good. It's easy to see why (unless, of course, you're an overzealous politician or bureaucrat eager to apply them). Imagine that you run a business that sells chairs, and a law is passed that states, "From this point onward, chairs can only be sold for $10." If all your costs stay constant at $9 or less, the regulation wouldn't be harmful at that point. However, price controls put two dynamics in motion:

>> First, the artificially lower price encourages consumption — more people buy chairs.

>> Second, production is discouraged. What company wants to make chairs if it can't sell them for a decent profit (or at the very least cover its costs)?

What happens to the company with a fixed sales price (in this example, $10) coupled with rising costs? Profits shrink, and depending on how long the price controls are in effect, the company eventually experiences losses. The chair producer is eventually driven out of business. The chair-building industry shrinks, and the result is a chair shortage. Profits (and jobs) soon vanish. So what happens if you own stock in a company that builds chairs? I'll just say that if I tell you how badly the stock price is pummeled, you'd better be sitting down (if, of course, you have a chair).

Looking at the role of central banks

Central banks are the governmental entities that are charged with the responsibility of managing the supply of currency that's used in the economy. The problem with this is the tendency of central banks to overproduce the supply of currency. This overproduction leads to the condition of having too much currency, which leads to the problematic condition of inflation. If too many units of currency (such as dollars or yen, for example) are chasing a limited supply of goods and services, consumers end up paying more money for goods and services (ugh!), but this is the reality that occurs when central banks (in the case of the United States, the Federal Reserve) create too much of the currency.

Poking into Political Resources

Ignoring what's going on in the world of politics is like sleepwalking near the Grand Canyon — a bad idea! You have to be aware of what's going on. Governmental data, reports, and political rumblings are important clues to the kind of environment that's unfolding for the economy and financial markets. Do your research with the following resources so you can stay a step ahead in your stock-picking strategies.

TIP

I know this section is laden with economic terms and the like, but fear not! Take your time with the terms and concepts, and don't forget that plenty of good sites provide easy-to-understand definitions and explanations. Look up any term in this chapter (or book) and do a search at venues such as Investopedia (www. investopedia.com) and Investor Words (www.investorwords.com). More sources are in Appendix A.

Government and other reports to watch out for

The best analysts look at economic reports from both private and government sources. The following sections list some reports/statistics to watch out for. For additional private reports and commentaries on the economy, investors can turn to sources such as Mish's Global Economic Trend Analysis (mishtalk.com), the Mises Institute (www.mises.org), and Moody's (www.economy.com). General sources, such as MarketWatch (www.marketwatch.com), Bloomberg (www.bloomberg.com), Shadow Statistics (www.shadowstats.com) and Yahoo! Finance (http://yahoo.com/finance), are good as well.

CORONAVIRUS INFECTS THE STOCK MARKET

Combine governmental mismanagement with a deadly virus and you get the coronavirus pandemic sweeping across the global landscape, which caused massive panic selling in February 2020. The coronavirus (officially referred to as COVID-19) started its contagion in the Wuhan area of mainland China. Unfortunately for the world, the epidemic was grossly mismanaged by China's communist party. It quickly spread across China and traveled across the border to 60-plus countries within a few weeks to became a global health pandemic. This, in turn, shut down assembly lines and thousands of businesses in China and related areas and industries.

The health panic soon became an international financial panic, resulting in sharp and massive losses hitting major stock markets everywhere. The Dow Jones Industrial Average plunged over 3,500 points during the week of February 24–28, 2020. This was a painful correction (meaning a drop of at least 10 percent). Quality stocks with good fundamentals can rebound from such a loss, but weak companies and companies that are overly exposed to such a danger can become vulnerable to even deeper losses. The lessons for stock investors are to make sure that 80 percent or more of your stock portfolio is in financially sound companies and to always be diversified with money outside the stock market, such as bank accounts, quality bonds, and other nonstock assets.

For more health information on this particular issue, check out the Centers for Disease Control and Prevention (www.cdc.gov). For financial news and information on issues such as this one, check out the resources in Appendix A.

Gross domestic product

Gross domestic product (GDP), which measures a nation's total output of goods and services for the quarter, is considered the broadest measure of economic activity. Although the U.S. GDP is measured in dollars (as of 2018, annual GDP is in the ballpark of $20.5 trillion), it's usually quoted as a percentage. You typically hear a news report that says something like, "The economy grew by 2.5 percent last quarter." Because the GDP is an important overall barometer of the economy, the number should be a positive one. The report on the GDP is released quarterly by the U.S. Department of Commerce (www.doc.gov).

REMEMBER

You should regularly monitor the GDP along with economic data that relates directly to your stock portfolio. The following list gives some general guidelines for evaluating the GDP:

>> **More than 3 percent:** This number indicates strong growth and bodes well for stocks. At 5 percent or higher, the economy is sizzling!

>> **1 to 3 percent:** This figure indicates moderate growth and can occur either as the economy is rebounding from a recession or as it's slowing down from a previously strong period.

>> **0 percent or negative (as low as –3 percent):** This number isn't good and indicates that the economy either isn't growing or is actually shrinking a bit. A negative GDP is considered *recessionary* (meaning that the economy's growth is receding).

>> **Worse than –3 percent:** A GDP this low indicates a very difficult period for the economy. A GDP worse than –3 percent, especially for two or more quarters, indicates a serious recession or possibly a depression.

TIP

Looking at a single quarter isn't that useful. Track the GDP over many consecutive quarters to see which way the general economy is trending. When you look at the GDP for a particular quarter of a year, ask yourself whether it's better (or worse) than the quarter before. If it's better (or worse), then ask yourself to what extent it has changed. Is it dramatically better (or worse) than the quarter before? Is the economy showing steady growth or is it slowing? If several quarters show solid growth, the overall economy is generally bullish.

Higher economic growth typically translates into better sales and profits for companies, which in turn bodes well for their stocks (and, of course, the investors who hold those stocks).

Traditionally, if two or more consecutive quarters show negative growth (an indication that economic output is shrinking), the economy is considered to be in a recession. A recession can be a painful necessity; it usually occurs when the economy can't absorb the total amount of goods being produced because of too much excess production. A bear market in stocks usually accompanies a recession.

REMEMBER

The GDP is just a rough estimate at best. It can't possibly calculate all the factors that go into economic growth. For example, crime has a negative effect on economic growth, but it's not reflected in the GDP. Still, most economists agree that the GDP provides an adequate ballpark snapshot of the overall economy's progress.

Unemployment

The National Unemployment Report is provided by the Bureau of Labor Statistics (www.bls.gov). It gives investors a snapshot of the health and productivity of the economy. If the level of jobs (especially full-time jobs) meets or exceeds the number of jobs needed to keep able-bodied adults employed, the economy is growing, and that is a positive for both the economy and the stock market.

In recent years (2017–2020), the unemployment rate has been very strong across the board, which in turn has resulted in greater investment capital (through pension plans such as 401Ks). That became a contributing factor to the bullish performance of the stock market during the same period. For more information on employment data, check out the sites mentioned at the end of this chapter.

The Consumer Price Index

The Consumer Price Index (CPI) is a statistic that tracks the prices of a representative basket of goods and services monthly. This statistic, which is also computed by the Bureau of Labor Statistics, is meant to track price inflation. *Inflation* is the expansion of the money supply. This is referred to as *monetary inflation,* and it usually leads to *price inflation,* which means that the prices of goods and services rise. Inflation, therefore, is not the price of goods and services going up; it's actually the price or value of money going down. Investors should pay attention to the CPI because a low-inflation environment is generally good for stocks (and bonds, too), whereas high inflation is generally more favorable for sectors such as commodities and precious metals.

Leading Economic Indicators

The full title is the "Composite Index of Leading Indicators." Leading Economic Indicators (LEI) is one of the most widely tracked economic statistics because it's made up of ten economic components whose changes typically precede changes in the economy at large. Investors and analysts watch this carefully so they can spot a major trend unfolding in the economy and determine whether that trend is positive or negative. The index is published by the Conference Board (www. conference-board.org).

There are also "lagging indicators" and "coincident indicators" that the Conference Board publishes, but investors are more concerned about the future, so the LEI is more closely watched.

The Producer Price Index

The Producer Price Index (PPI) tracks the prices that are paid at the wholesale level by manufacturers and other producers. Investors watch this because if producers are paying more for commodities and other materials, then higher prices will subsequently occur for consumers. The PPI is calculated monthly by the Bureau of Labor Statistics.

The Consumer Confidence Index

The Consumer Confidence Index (CCI) is published by the Conference Board and is a survey of 5,000 consumers and businesspeople about the economy. Consumer confidence being up is generally seen as a positive for investors because it indicates that people are more upbeat, and that leads to a tendency to either spend more or be more apt to make big-ticket purchases. This expected consumer activity bodes well for the economy and stocks in general.

Websites to surf

To find out about new laws being passed or proposed, check out Congress and what's going on at its primary websites: the U.S. House of Representatives (www. house.gov) and the U.S. Senate (www.senate.gov). For presidential information and proposals, check the White House's website at www.whitehouse.gov.

TIP

You also may want to check out the advanced legislative search engine at www. congress.gov/. The search engine helps you find any piece of legislation, either by bill number or keyword. This search engine is an excellent way to find out whether an industry is being targeted for increased regulation or deregulation. In the late 1980s, real estate was hit hard when the government passed new regulations and tax rules (related stocks went down). When the telecom industry was deregulated in the mid-1990s, the industry grew dramatically (related stocks went up).

Turn to the following sources for economic data:

>> Bureau of Labor Statistics (investors' information page): http://www.bls.gov/audience/investors.htm

>> Census Bureau's Economic Indicators page: http://www.census.gov/economic-indicators/

>> Conference Board: www.conference-board.org/us

>> Grandfather Economic Report: www.grandfather-economic-report.com

>> Investing.com: www.investing.com

>> The Federal Reserve: www.federalreserve.gov

>> U.S. Department of Commerce: www.doc.gov

TIP

You can find more resources in Appendix A. The more knowledge you pick up about how politics and government actions can help (or harm) an investment, the better you'll be at growing (and protecting) your wealth.

4

Investment Strategies and Tactics

Use powerful stock screening tools to unearth great stock picks.

Discover how brokerage orders can help you maximize profits and minimize losses (even in bear markets).

Get the scoop on international stock investing opportunities.

Understand how to buy top stocks for as little as $50 (and no brokerage commissions).

See how insiders trade so you can have a profitable edge in the markets.

Find out how you can keep the tax bite on your profits to a minimum — especially with the new tax laws.

Chapter **16**

Discovering Screening Tools

When you're spanning the stock-investing world, it can be daunting to see literally thousands of stocks to choose from — and that's just the U.S. stock markets. Many thousands more are across the global stock market realm. Where would a stock investor (especially a novice investor) begin to look?

Well, you're doing the right thing by first reading a book like this (thank you and, uh, you're welcome!). Why? Because a book like this gives you some parameters and guidelines to help you make a sound choice among the companies that are available as publicly traded stocks. As I often emphasize, you may be purchasing a stock, but you're really investing in a company. That company has financial data and other information that you can review and use to narrow your search by keeping to some definable (and searchable) standards.

This is why I love stock screening tools! A *stock screening tool* is an online program found on many financial websites and brokerage sites that sifts through tons of stocks and their relevant data (profits, sales, and so on) with parameters that you set. It works like a search engine but within a huge closed database that is regularly updated with public company data. You'll find one or more stocks that fit the parameters you set.

In this chapter, I provide the most common parameters for tools that screen stocks and exchange-traded funds (ETFs). But first, I give you some basics about these tools. Keep in mind that with these tools, you're looking for companies based on your search criteria. You can find stocks and ETFs based on a variety of critical standards and metrics that you define and set.

TIP

For some great sites that have stock screening tools (especially for fundamental analysis), check out the following:

>> Investing.com (www.investing.com)

>> MarketWatch (www.marketwatch.com)

>> Nasdaq (www.nasdaq.com)

>> TradingView (www.tradingview.com)

>> Yahoo! Finance (http://finance.yahoo.com)

Understanding the Basics of Screening Tools

After you familiarize yourself with the components and practicality of stock screening tools, you'll be hooked, and you'll wish that you had used them sooner. In the following sections, I break down the essentials.

Choosing the category

The first thing you typically see with a stock screening tool is the category. Actually, this means the sector or industry (see Chapter 13 for an introduction to industries). Many screeners (such as the one at Yahoo! Finance, https://finance.yahoo.com/screener) go into subcategories. Yahoo! Finance can help you screen stocks in the equity screener found at the top of the page; also useful are a mutual fund screener and an ETF screener.

If, for example, you're looking to invest in a technology company, you click the equity screener link, go to the sector choice Technology, and then go to the industries within it. The industry choices (I found 12 at the time of writing) range from Information Technology Services and Electronic Components to the last one, Solar.

Distinguishing "min" versus "max"

Min and max are the yin and yang of the stock screening world. When you set your parameters for stocks, you need to set a minimum and a maximum. Some sites use terms such as "greater than," "less than," and "equals," or they let you set a definable range between two specific numbers. If a stock screening tool uses the term "profitable stock," that means you need to set a parameter of minimum profit. The stock investor takes the long view and stays patient and focused for successful value investing (find out more about this topic in Chapter 8).

REMEMBER

Keep in mind that some stock screeners use a different approach than "min" and "max," such as "less than" and "greater than," but it essentially serves the same purpose for your searches.

Setting value ranges

In some cases, you may need to choose a range. Perhaps you're looking for stocks in a particular price range. A stock screening tool may provide choices such as 0–10, 10–20, 20–30, 30–40, 40–50, and over 50. Other typical ranges you may see are market capitalization (the total market value of the company's stock) and dividend yields (the dividend amount divided by the stock price).

Searching regardless of your entry

Most screening tools allow you to do a search whether you enter one value or parameter or many. If you choose to search for a stock in all categories and enter only, say, a dividend yield with a minimum value of 2 and a maximum value of 999 and no other entries, you'll get hundreds of stocks.

However, if you input plenty of parameters, then you'll get very few stocks (or none at all). If you ask for stocks with features A, B, C, D, and E, then you won't get as many results. Be selective — that's the whole point of using stock screeners — but don't go overboard trying to find the perfect stock because it may not exist.

REMEMBER

Getting close to perfection is probably good enough, but the more important point is to avoid the bad choices such as companies that have too little income, have net losses, or carry too much debt.

Touring a Stock Screening Tool

Most stock screening tools have some basic elements that are very useful in helping you narrow your search for the right stocks in your portfolio. Figure 16-1 shows a typical stock screener from Yahoo! Finance (https://finance.yahoo.com/screener); the following sections walk you through the major fields of this tool.

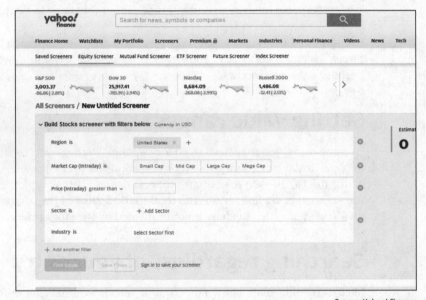

FIGURE 16-1: A typical stock screening tool.

Source: Yahoo! Finance

REMEMBER Keep in mind that with the minimums and maximums in the following sections, there will be variations. Also, some market analysts and financial advisors are more or less lenient than I am with these numbers. Don't sweat it. Do your research and come up with similar numbers that you're comfortable with.

Before you begin: Selecting your screener

At the Yahoo! Finance stock screener page (https://finance.yahoo.com/screener), you see the following links at the top:

>> **Saved screeners:** When you design your own screeners, you can save them for future use. This option will come in handy as you become experienced and proficient with screeners.

>> **Equity screener:** This option is for finding and analyzing stocks. I work with this particular screener in the upcoming sections.

>> **Mutual fund and ETF screeners:** When you're looking for the right mutual fund or ETF, these screeners will help. (Check out Chapter 5 for an introduction to ETFs.)

>> **Future and index screeners:** These categories are more for the speculators and traders in the world of futures and indexes, so I don't cover them in this chapter (or book).

First up: The major categories

After you choose the equity (stock) screener in Yahoo! Finance, you have to address a few major categories first before you get to the "guts" of screening stock data (refer to Figure 16-1):

>> **Region:** Here you enter data about your chosen country to refine your search. If you're looking for U.S. stocks, the choice of course is "United States." In the menu, you see countries with public stock exchanges ranging from Argentina to Vietnam.

>> **Market cap:** In the Market Cap (Intraday) category, you can designate the criteria for your search based on market capitalization and choose Small Cap, Mid Cap, Large Cap, or Mega Cap.

TIP

Looking for growth potential? Go for small cap or mid cap. Looking for more safety? Go to large cap or mega cap. Find out more about market capitalization in Chapter 1.

>> **Price:** In the Price (Intraday) field, enter criteria based on share price, such as "greater than" or "less than" your chosen price. There are also options for "equals" and "between."

>> **Sector and industry:** A *sector* is a group of interrelated industries. For example, the healthcare sector has varied industries such as hospitals, medical device manufacturers, pharmaceuticals, drug retailers, and so on. Choosing an industry rather than a sector narrows your choices, as you find out in the earlier section "Choosing the category." Flip to Chapter 13 for more information on sectors and industries.

The main event: Specific filters

After you make choices in the major categories covered in the preceding section, you drill down to find stocks that meet your standards with various filters. I don't cover all the metrics here since there are literally too many to cover, but in the following sections, I briefly touch on the most relevant subcategories and then you can dive in. (To get to these filters in the Yahoo! Finance screener, just click Add Another Filter, as shown in Figure 16-1.)

Share statistics

In the Share Statistics menu in the Yahoo! Finance screener, you find over 40 stock-related criteria ranging from share price action (the 52-week high or low) to fundamentals such as total assets or total liabilities. One area I like to focus on is the price-to-earnings (P/E) ratio. This ratio is one of the most widely followed ratios, and I consider it the most important valuation ratio (it can be considered a profitability ratio as well). It ties a company's current stock price to the company's net earnings. The net earnings are the heart and soul of the company, so always check this ratio.

All things being considered, I generally prefer low ratios (under 15 is good, and under 25 is acceptable). If I'm considering a growth stock, I definitely want a ratio under 40 (unless there are extenuating circumstances that I like and that aren't reflected in the P/E ratio).

WARNING

Generally, beginning investors should stay away from stocks that have P/Es higher than 40, and definitely stay away if the P/E is in triple digits (or higher), because that's too pricey. Pricey P/Es can be hazardous, as those stocks have high expectations and are very vulnerable to a sharp correction. In addition, definitely stay away from stocks that either have no P/E ratio or show a negative P/E. In these instances, it's a stock where the company is losing money (net losses). Buying stock in a company that's losing money is *not* investing — it's speculating.

REMEMBER

Make sure your search parameters have a minimum P/E of, say, 1 and a maximum of between 15 (for large cap, stable, dividend-paying stocks) and 40 (for growth stocks) so that you have some measure of safety (or sanity!).

If you want to speculate and find stocks to go short on (or buy put options on), two approaches apply:

>> You can put in a minimum P/E of, say, 100 and an unlimited maximum (or 9,999 if a number is needed) to get very pricey stocks that are vulnerable to a correction.

>> A second approach is putting in a maximum P/E of 0, which would indicate that you're searching for companies with losses (earnings under zero).

Income

In the Income menu in the Yahoo! Finance screener, there are some important metrics tied to sales and profits. Keep in mind that income in terms of sales and profits are among your most important screening criteria.

For sales revenue (called Total Revenue in the Yahoo! Finance tool), there may be absolute numbers or percentages. In some stock screeners, there may be ranges such as "under $1 million in sales" up to "over $1 billion in sales." On a percentage basis, some stock screeners may have a minimum and a maximum. An example of this is if you wanted companies that increased their sales by at least 10 percent. You'd enter 10 in the minimum percentage and either leave the maximum blank or plug in a high number such as 999. Another twist is that you may find a stock screener that shows sales revenue with an average percentage over three or five years so you can see more consistency over an extended period.

Profit margin (called Net Income Margin % in the Yahoo! Finance tool) is basically what percent of sales is the company's net profit. If a company has $1 million in sales and $200,000 in net profit, the profit margin is 20 percent ($200,000 divided by $1,000,000). For this metric, you'd enter a minimum of 20 percent and a maximum of 100 percent because that's the highest possible (but improbable) profit margin you can reach.

REMEMBER

Keep in mind that the data you can sift through isn't just for the most recent year; some stock screeners give you a summary of three years or longer, such as what a company's profit margin has been over a three-year period, so you can get a better view of the company's consistent profitability. The only thing better than a solid profit in the current year is a solid profit year after year (three consecutive years or more).

Valuation measures

For value investors (who embrace fundamental analysis), the following parameters are important to help home in on the right values (check out Appendix B for more details on ratios):

>> **Price-to-sales ratio:** A price-to-sales (PSR) ratio close to 1 is positive. When market capitalization greatly exceeds the sales number, then the stock leans to the pricey side. In the stock screener's PSR field, consider entering a minimum of 0, or leave it blank. A good maximum value is 3.

>> **PEG ratio:** You obtain the PEG ratio (price/earnings to growth) when you divide the stock's P/E ratio by its year-over-year earnings growth rate. Typically, the lower the PEG, the better the value of the stock. A PEG ratio over 1 suggests that the stock is overvalued, and a ratio under 1 is considered undervalued. Therefore, when you use the PEG ratio in a stock screening tool, leave the minimum blank (or 0), and use a maximum of 1.

>> **Other valuation ratios:** Some stock screeners may include other ratios. A good one is the average five-year ROI (return on investment), which gives

you a good idea of the stock's long-term financial strength. Others may have an average three-year ROI.

Because this is an average (in percentage terms) over five years, do a search for a minimum of 10 percent and an unlimited maximum (or just plug in 999 percent). If you do get one that's anywhere near 999 percent, by the way, call me and let me know!

SCREENING STOCKS WITH TECHNICAL ANALYSIS

In this chapter, I use criteria and financial data (the "fundamentals"), but many stock screeners have the ability to use technical analysis (see Chapter 10) by using technical indicators. Technical analysis is more important for those with a short-term focus, such as stock traders and short-term speculators. Here are some common technical indicators:

- **Moving averages:** Looking for stocks that are trading above their 50-day moving average or have fallen below it? How about the 200-day moving average, which can be a more reliable indicator of the stock's near-term strength (or weakness)?

- **Relative Strength Index:** The RSI is one of my favorite technical indicators. It basically tracks a stock in terms of being overbought or oversold in the near term. If a stock has an RSI of over 70, it's overbought, and the stock is vulnerable to declining in the near future. A stock with an RSI under 30 is considered oversold, and that's potentially an opportunity for the stock to rally in the near term.

Don't use the RSI to determine what to buy, but certainly consider it as a way to time a purchase (or sale). In other words, if you're attracted to a stock and want to buy, consider getting it in the event that it's oversold. That gives you the chance to get a stock you want at a favorable price.

When you do your search and you're using the RSI as one of your criteria, consider using a maximum RSI of 50, which is essentially in the middle of the range, with a minimum RSI of 0. If you're looking to speculate by going short, make sure your minimum RSI is 70, and the maximum is unlimited.

Here are some popular screening tools online for technical analysis:

- StockCharts (www.stockcharts.com)

- StockFetcher (www.stockfetcher.com)

- MarketInOut (www.marketinout.com)

Dividends and splits

For income-minded folks, go to the Dividends and Splits menu in the Yahoo! Finance screener to enter criteria such as Dividend Per Share (DPS) and Dividend Yield %. For more information on dividends, head to Chapter 9.

ESG scores

For many investors in recent years, nonfinancial and nonmarket aspects of corporate governance have gained greater importance. In the category of ESG Scores (environmental, social, and governance criteria) in the Yahoo! Finance screener, you can enter aspects of corporate behavior that you seek (or want to avoid) in the public company that you're considering for investment.

Checking Out an ETF Screening Tool

In addition to stock screeners, there are also screeners for bonds, mutual funds, and now exchange-traded funds (ETFs; see Chapter 5). Figure 16-2 is a typical ETF screener like many online.

You won't find minimum and maximum with ETF screeners as much as with stock screeners. There are more varied categories to filter through and different performance criteria. The following sections cover the main categories.

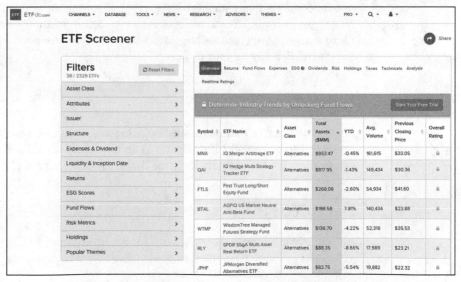

FIGURE 16-2:
A typical ETF screening tool.

Courtesy of ETFdb.com

TIP

Keep in mind that most of the popular financial sites (such as Yahoo! Finance and MarketWatch) have good ETF screeners (as well as stock screeners); most of the stock brokerage sites have search and screening tools as well. Some other popular sites that have ETF screening tools include the following:

>> ETF.com (www.etf.com)

>> ETF Database (www.etfdb.com/screener); you see this screener in Figure 16-2

>> ETF Screen (www.etfscreen.com)

Asset class

Choosing your asset class is the first search criteria, and of course in a book like this, the focus is stocks (equity). However, this category shows the range of choices that ETFs have to offer. There are ETFs that concentrate on bonds, currencies, precious metals, real estate, basic commodities, or "multi-asset" portfolios. There are also inverse ETFs, which have within their portfolio speculative derivatives such as put and call options (found in the asset category called "alternatives").

Attributes

TIP

In the Attributes category in the ETF Database tool (refer to Figure 16-2), you can choose Active, Passive, or Any. ETFs, by and large, are passive, meaning that the portfolio isn't actively managed like a typical mutual fund portfolio. However, in recent years some ETFs have become more active in their portfolios (meaning more active buying and selling of positions within the portfolio). If you aren't sure, just click Any as your choice.

Issuer

Looking for an ETF that was issued by a financial institution such as iShares, State Street SPDR, or VanEck? If the issuer is an important consideration, check out the comprehensive list of financial firms that issue and sponsor ETFs.

Structure

Although you're most likely looking for a conventional ETF, you can find other structures, such as a commodity pool or exchange-traded notes (ETNs). For most beginners, the standard ETFs are fine.

Expenses and dividends

In the Expenses & Dividend category in the ETF Database screener, you can perform your search using an expense ratio and/or a dividend yield. Maybe you want an ETF with a relatively low expense ratio — say, under 2 percent. You can then adjust your search with this criteria, and the search will exclude all ETFs with expense ratios higher than 2 percent.

As for the dividend yield (and you know I am a big fan of dividends if you read earlier chapters), you can adjust it based on your preference. Indicate that, for example, you want ETFs with a minimum yield of 2.5 percent, and the screener will exclude all ETFs with a reported dividend yield lower than that percentage.

Liquidity and inception

TIP

The typical criteria in the Liquidity & Inception Date category shown in Figure 16-2 are the following:

>> **Assets ($MM):** This field measures the market capitalization of the ETF in case you want to make sure that you're buying a large ETF versus a smaller ETF that has a lower market capitalization. For novice ETF investors, go for the higher market capitalization (larger asset size).

>> **Average Daily Volume:** This field refers to how many shares of a particular ETF are traded in the market on a typical trading day. Novice ETF investors want a higher trading volume, which indicates greater liquidity and hence is easier to buy and/or sell.

>> **Share Price:** Here you indicate whether you have a limit as to share price. For example, if you can afford ETFs only at $50 per share or lower, use that criteria. Easy!

>> **Inception Date:** Here you put in the criteria, if you wish, regarding how long an ETF has been around. All things being equal, an ETF around for 15 years or longer is a safer investing vehicle to choose than one that started just last year.

Returns

Looking for ETFs based on how well they have performed over a year or longer? Then the Returns search criteria shown in Figure 16-2 is for you. You can designate a time frame such as year to date or a longer one such as one year, three years, or five years.

TIP

I take seriously the admonition that "past performance is not necessarily indicative of future results," but check out the returns since they help confirm that an ETF's portfolio is a good consideration. After all, all things being equal and you're choosing between one ETF that went up 87 percent in the past three years and another ETF that dropped 12 percent in the same time frame, your choice should be a no-brainer (Put away that coin! No heads or tails here).

ESG scores

Are social or other nonfinancial considerations important to you? Perhaps you're worried about the environmental effects of corporate activity. Maybe moral considerations are important because you want to invest in companies that are "good citizens" or that do not exhibit practices you disagree with. Given that, the ESG Scores category in Figure 16-2 will be a prime consideration in your search criteria.

In the ETF Database screener, there is a single composite ESG score ranging from 0 to 10, with 10 being the most favorable — the higher, the better.

Fund flows

The Fund Flows metric in the ETF Database screener tracks how much money is flowing into an ETF over a given period such as one week, one year, or five years. *Fund flow* essentially means that when you tally money coming into and out of various financial assets, you can gauge the popularity (or unpopularity) of a given asset. If there is a net inflow of money for a given asset, then ETFs with that asset are in a bullish position (and that's a good thing for your ETF's share price).

Risk

The Risk Metrics category in Figure 16-2 touches on volatility and beta characteristics of a particular ETF. It also includes the price-to-earnings (P/E) ratio if available. You can find out whether an ETF has lower or higher volatility (compared to the total market).

REMEMBER

Higher volatility means ultimately greater risk. A tech stock ETF, for example, has higher volatility than a utilities stock ETF. ETFs with portfolios that have a higher P/E ratio can be riskier than those with a lower P/E ratio. The bottom line is that if you're concerned about risk, select search criteria with low P/E ratio and low volatility. Flip to Chapter 4 for more about risk.

Holdings

Holdings criteria cover what asset(s) are in an ETF. Does the ETF have one asset or 50? In addition, this category covers how balanced and deep an ETF is relative to its peer group. In other words, is this ETF's holdings in the top 10 percent, 15 percent, or 50 percent of their peers in the category?

Themes

You can see the top ETFs in terms of popular themes in the final category in Figure 16-2. At the time of writing, the most popular themes are artificial intelligence, blockchain, marijuana, and FAANG (referring to Facebook, Apple, Amazon, Netflix, and Google).

REMEMBER

The problem here is that what is popular today may not do well next year, so novice investors should focus on long-term profitability and the fundamentals for more assured success over time.

A Few Final Points to Keep in Mind

Listen: Don't go nuts with all the parameters and search criteria because you want to find the "perfect stock" (although if you do find it, let me know). For investors, your best approach is to use criteria that focuses on the key fundamentals:

>> **A winning sector/industry:** Make sure that the sector/industry is enduring and growing. This is why I focus on "human need" such as food and beverage, utilities, and so on.

>> **Market leadership:** Does the company rank among the best in its industry?

>> **Profit:** Make sure the company is consistently profitable.

>> **Sales:** Make sure the company has growing sales.

>> **A good balance sheet:** Ensure that assets are greater than liabilities (in other words, the company has low debt).

>> **Dividends:** Where possible, make sure the company has dividends.

That should hold you for now, grasshopper. Now go forth and search!

Chapter 17

Understanding Brokerage Orders and Trading Techniques

I nvestment success isn't just about *which* stocks to choose; it's also about *how* you choose those stocks. Frequently, investors think that good stock-picking means doing your homework and then making that buy (or sell). However, you can take it a step further to maximize profits (or minimize losses).

In 2008, millions of investors were slammed mercilessly by a tumultuous market; many could have used some simple techniques and orders that could have saved them some grief. Investors who used stop-loss orders avoided some of the trillion-dollar carnage that hit the stock market during that scary time. As a stock investor, you can take advantage of this technique and others available through your standard brokerage account (see Chapter 7 for details). This chapter presents some of the best ways you can use these powerful techniques, which are useful whether you're buying or selling stock.

Checking Out Brokerage Orders

Orders you place with your stockbroker fit neatly into three categories:

>> Time-related orders

>> Condition-related orders

>> Advanced orders (which are combinations of the preceding two)

At the very least, get familiar with the first two types of orders because they're easy to implement, and they're invaluable tools for wealth-building and (more importantly) wealth-saving!

TIP

Using a combination of orders helps you fine-tune your strategy so that you can maintain greater control over your investments. Speak with your broker about the different types of orders you can use to maximize the gains (or minimize the losses) from your stock-investing activities. You also can read the broker's policies on stock orders at the brokerage website.

On the clock: Time-related orders

A *time-related order* is just that — the order has a time limit. Typically, investors use these orders in conjunction with condition-related orders, which I describe later in this chapter. The two most common time-related orders are day orders and good-til-canceled (GTC) orders.

Day orders

A *day order* is an order to buy or sell a stock that expires at the end of that particular trading day. If you tell your broker, "Buy BYOB, Inc., at $37.50 and make it a day order," you mean that you want to purchase the stock at $37.50. But if the stock doesn't hit that price, your order expires, unfilled, at the end of the trading day.

Why would you place such an order? Maybe BYOB is trading at $39, but you don't want to buy it at that price because you don't believe the stock is worth it. Consequently, you have no problem not getting the stock that day.

When would you use day orders? It depends on your preferences and personal circumstances. I rarely use day orders because few events cause me to say, "Gee, I'll just try to buy or sell between now and the end of today's trading action." However, you may feel that you don't want a specified order to linger beyond today's market action. Perhaps you want to test a price. ("I want to get rid of stock

A at $39 to make a quick profit, but it's currently trading at $37.50. However, I may change my mind tomorrow.") A day order is the perfect strategy to use in this case.

If you make a trade and don't specify a time limit with the order, most (if not all) brokers will automatically treat it as a day order.

Good-til-canceled orders

A *good-til-canceled (GTC) order* is the most commonly requested order by investors, and it's one that I use and recommend often. The GTC order means just what it says: The order stays in effect until it's transacted or until the investor cancels it. Although GTC orders are time-related, they're always tied to a condition, such as the stock achieving a certain price.

Although the order implies that it can run indefinitely, most brokers have a limit of 30 or 60 days (or more). I've seen the limit as high as 120 days. By that time, either the broker cancels the order or contacts you (usually by email) to see whether you want to extend it. Ask your broker about his particular policy.

GTC orders are always coupled with condition-related orders (see the next section). For example, say that you think ASAP Corp. stock would make a good addition to your portfolio, but you don't want to buy it at the current price of $48 per share. You've done your homework on the stock, including looking at the stock's price-to-earnings ratio, price-to-book ratio, and so on (see Appendix B for more on ratios), and you say, "Hey, this stock isn't worth $48 a share. I'd only buy it at $36 per share." (It's overpriced or overvalued according to your analysis.) How should you proceed? Your best bet is to ask your broker to do a GTC order at $36. This request means that your broker will buy the shares if and when they hit the $36 mark (unless you cancel the order). Just make sure that your account has the funds available to complete the transaction.

GTC orders are very useful, so you should become familiar with your broker's policy on them. While you're at it, ask whether any fees apply. Many brokers don't charge for GTC orders because if they happen to result in a buy (or sell) order, they generate a normal commission just as any stock transaction does. Other brokers may charge a small fee (but that's rare).

To be successful with GTC orders, you need to know the following:

>> **When you want to buy:** In recent years, people have had a tendency to rush into buying a stock without giving some thought to what they could do to get more for their money. Some investors don't realize that the stock market can be a place for bargain-hunting consumers. If you're ready to buy a quality pair

of socks for $16 in a department store but the sales clerk says that those same socks are going on sale tomorrow for only $8, what do you do — assuming that you're a cost-conscious consumer? Unless you're barefoot, you probably decide to wait. The same point holds true with stocks.

Say that you want to buy SOX, Inc., at $26, but it's currently trading at $30. You think that $30 is too expensive, but you'd be happy to buy the stock at $26 or lower. However, you have no idea whether the stock will move to your desired price today, tomorrow, next week, or even next month (or maybe never). In this case, a GTC order is appropriate.

>> **When you want to sell:** What if you buy some socks at a department store, and you discover that they have holes (darn it!)? Wouldn't you want to get rid of them? Of course you would. If a stock's price starts to unravel, you want to be able to get rid of it as well.

Perhaps you already own SOX at $25 but are concerned that market conditions may drive the price lower. You're not certain which way the stock will move in the coming days and weeks. In this case, a GTC order to sell the stock at a specified price is a suitable strategy. Because the stock price is $25, you may want to place a GTC order to sell it if it falls to $22.50 in order to prevent further losses. Again, in this example, GTC is the time frame, and it accompanies a condition (sell when the stock hits $22.50).

At your command: Condition-related orders

A *condition-related order* (also known as a *conditional order*) is an order that's executed only when a certain condition is met. Conditional orders enhance your ability to buy stocks at a lower price, to sell at a better price, or to minimize potential losses. When stock markets become bearish or uncertain, conditional orders are highly recommended.

A good example of a conditional order is a *limit order*. A limit order may say, "Buy Mojeski Corp. at $45." But if Mojeski Corp. isn't at $45 (this price is the condition), then the order isn't executed. I discuss limit orders, as well as market orders and stop-loss orders, in the following sections.

Market orders

When you buy stock, the simplest type of order is a *market order* — an order to buy or sell a stock at the market's current best available price. Orders don't get any more basic than that. Here's an example: Kowalski, Inc., is available at the market price of $10. When you call your broker and instruct her to buy 100 shares "at the market," the broker implements the order for your account, and you pay $1,000 plus commission.

WARNING

I say "current best available price" because the stock's price is constantly moving, and catching the best price can be a function of the broker's ability to process the stock purchase. For very active stocks, the price change can happen within seconds. It's not unheard of to have three brokers simultaneously place orders for the same stock and get three different prices because of differences in the brokers' capabilities. The difference may be pennies, but it's a difference nonetheless. (Some computers are faster than others.)

The advantage of a market order is that the transaction is processed immediately, and you get your stock without worrying about whether it hits a particular price. For example, if you buy Kowalski, Inc., with a market order, you know that by the end of that phone call (or website visit), you're assured of getting the stock. The disadvantage of a market order is that you can't control the price at which you purchase the stock. Whether you're buying or selling your shares, you may not realize the exact price you expect (especially if you're dealing with a volatile stock).

REMEMBER

Market orders get finalized in the chronological order in which they're placed. Your price may change because the orders ahead of you in line cause the stock price to rise or fall based on the latest news.

Stop-loss orders

A *stop-loss order* (also called a *stop order*) is a condition-related order that instructs the broker to sell a particular stock in your portfolio only when the stock reaches a particular price. It acts like a trigger, and the stop order converts to a market order to sell the stock immediately.

REMEMBER

The stop-loss order isn't designed to take advantage of small, short-term moves in the stock's price. It's meant to help you protect the bulk of your money when the market turns against your stock investment in a sudden manner.

Say that your Kowalski, Inc., stock rises to $20 per share, and you seek to protect your investment against a possible future market decline. A stop-loss order at $18 triggers your broker to sell the stock immediately if it falls to the $18 mark. In this example, if the stock suddenly drops to $17, it still triggers the stop-loss order, but the finalized sale price is $17. In a volatile market, you may not be able to sell at your precise stop-loss price. However, because the order automatically gets converted into a market order, the sale will be done, and you'll be spared further declines in the stock.

The main benefit of a stop-loss order is that it prevents a major loss in a stock that you own. It's a form of discipline that's important in investing to minimize potential losses. Investors can find it agonizing to sell a stock that has fallen. If they don't sell, however, the stock often continues to plummet as investors continue to hold on while hoping for a rebound in the price.

TIP

Most investors set a stop-loss amount at about 10 percent below the market value of the stock. This percentage gives the stock some room to fluctuate, which most stocks tend to do from day to day. If you're extra nervous, consider a tighter stop-loss, such as 5 percent or less.

Keep in mind that this order only triggers the sale, and a particular price isn't guaranteed to be captured because the actual buy or sell occurs immediately after the trigger is activated. If the market at the time of the actual transaction is particularly volatile, then the price realized may be significantly different.

In the following sections, I describe a certain type of stop-loss order (called a trailing stop), and I talk about the use of beta measurement with stop-loss orders.

TRAILING STOPS

Trailing stops are an important technique in wealth preservation for seasoned stock investors and can be one of your key strategies in using stop-loss orders. A *trailing stop* is a stop-loss order that an investor actively manages by moving it up along with the stock's market price. The stop-loss order "trails" the stock price upward. As the stop-loss goes upward, it protects more and more of the stock's value from declining.

Imagine that you bought stock in Peach Inc. (PI) for $30 a share. A trailing stop is in place at, say, 10 percent, and the order is GTC (presume that this broker places a time limit of 90 days for GTC orders). At $30 per share, the trailing stop is $27. If PI goes to $40, your trailing stop automatically rises to $36. If PI continues to rise to $50, your trailing continues along with it to $45. Now say that PI reverses course (for whatever reason) and starts to plummet. The trailing stop stays put at $45 and triggers a sell order if PI reaches the $45 level.

In the preceding example, I use a trailing stop percentage, but trailing stops are also available in dollar amounts. For example, say that PI is at $30, and I put in a trailing stop of $3. If PI rises to $50, my trailing stop will reach $47. If PI then drops from this peak of $50, the trailing stop stays put at $47 and triggers a sell order if PI actually hits $47. You get the picture. Trailing stops can help you sleep at night, especially in these turbulent times.

REMEMBER

William O'Neill, founder and publisher of *Investor's Business Daily*, advocates setting a trailing stop of 8 percent below your purchase price. That's his preference. Some investors who invest in very volatile stocks may put in trailing stops of 20 or 25 percent. Is a stop-loss order desirable or advisable in every situation? No.

It depends on your level of experience, your investment goals, and the market environment. Still, stop-loss orders (trailing or otherwise) are appropriate in many cases, especially if the market seems uncertain (or you are!).

REMEMBER

A trailing stop is a stop-loss order that you actively manage. The stop-loss order is good-til-canceled (GTC), and it constantly trails the stock's price as it moves up. To successfully implement stop-loss orders (including trailing stops), you should

>> **Realize that brokers usually don't place trailing stops for you automatically.** In fact, they won't (or shouldn't) place any type of order without your consent. Deciding on the type of order to place is your responsibility. You can raise, lower, or cancel a trailing stop order at will, but you need to monitor your investment when substantial moves do occur to respond to the movement appropriately.

>> **Change the stop-loss order when the stock price moves significantly.** Hopefully, you won't call your broker every time the stock moves 50 cents. Change the stop-loss order when the stock price moves around 10 percent. For example, if you initially purchase a stock at $90 per share, ask the broker to place the stop-loss order at $81. When the stock moves to $100, cancel the $81 stop-loss order and replace it at $90. When the stock's price moves to $110, change the stop-loss order to $99, and so on.

>> **Understand your broker's policy on GTC orders.** If your broker usually considers a GTC order expired after 30 or 60 days, you should be aware of it. You don't want to risk a sudden drop in your stock's price without the stop-loss order protection. Make a note of your broker's time limit so that you remember to renew the order for additional time.

>> **Monitor your stock.** A trailing stop isn't a "set it and forget it" technique. Monitoring your investment is critical. Of course, if the investment falls, the stop-loss order prevents further loss. Should the stock price rise substantially, remember to adjust your trailing stop accordingly. Keep raising the safety net as the stock continues to rise. Part of monitoring the stock is knowing the beta, which you can read more about in the next section.

BETA MEASUREMENT

To be a successful investor, you need to understand the volatility of the particular stock you invest in. In stock market parlance, this volatility is also called the beta of a stock. *Beta* is a quantitative measure of the volatility of a given stock (mutual funds and portfolios, too) relative to the overall market, usually the S&P 500 index. (For more information on the S&P 500, see Chapter 5.) Beta specifically measures the performance movement of the stock as the S&P moves 1 percent up or down. A beta measurement above 1 is more volatile than the overall market, whereas a beta below 1 is less volatile. Some stocks are relatively stable in terms of price movements; others jump around.

Because beta measures how volatile or unstable the stock's price is, it tends to be uttered in the same breath as "risk" — more volatility indicates more risk. Similarly, less volatility tends to mean less risk. (Chapter 4 offers more details on the topics of risk and volatility.)

TIP

You can find a company's beta at websites that provide a lot of financial information about companies, such as Nasdaq (www.nasdaq.com) or Yahoo! Finance (finance.yahoo.com).

PRACTICING DISCIPLINE WITH STOP-LOSS ORDERS

I have a stack of several years' worth of investment newsletters in which investment experts made all sorts of calls regarding the prospects of a company, industry, or the economy in general. Some made forecasts that were spectacularly on target, but you should see the ones that were spectacularly wrong — ouch! However, even some of the winners suffered because of a lack of discipline. Those spectacular gains disappeared like balloons at a porcupine convention.

At the height of the housing bubble (circa 2007), many real estate and mortgage companies saw record highs in their stock prices. A good example was the Federal National Mortgage Association ("Fannie Mae" with the stock symbol FNMA). FNMA was a public company, but it was technically a government-sponsored entity. Many thought that because it had the backing (real or imagined) of the federal government, it was a safe investment. In 2007, its stock price was around $75. I was very worried about the housing bubble and felt that any stock tied to this dangerous market was at risk. Yet there were still analysts toting the stock with "strong buy" and/or "buy" orders.

Whenever you own a stock (or an exchange-traded fund, known as an ETF; see Chapter 5) that you begin to worry about and aren't sure about selling, consider a stop-loss order. A stop-loss order on FNMA, even at a much lower level, such as $50, would have saved investors a fortune. By the end of 2008, FNMA's stock price fell below $1 per share (you read that right . . . under a buck a share!). In less than 12 months, FNMA fell almost 99 percent.

The beta is useful to know when it comes to stop-loss orders because it gives you a general idea of the stock's trading range. If a stock is currently priced at $50 and it typically trades in the $48 to $52 range, then a trailing stop at $49 doesn't make sense. Your stock would probably be sold the same day you initiated the stop-loss order. If your stock is a volatile growth stock that may swing up and down by 10 percent, you should more logically set your stop-loss at 15 percent below that day's price.

REMEMBER

The stock of a large cap company in a mature industry tends to have a low beta — one close to the overall market. Small and mid cap stocks in new or emerging industries tend to have greater volatility in their day-to-day price fluctuations; hence, they tend to have a high beta. (You can find out more about large, small, and mid cap stocks in Chapter 1; Chapter 4 has more about beta.)

Limit orders

A *limit order* is a very precise condition-related order implying that a limit exists either on the buy or the sell side of the transaction. You want to buy (or sell) only at a specified price. Period. Limit orders work well if you're buying the stock, but they may not be good for you if you're selling the stock. Here's how they work in both instances:

>> **When you're buying:** Just because you like a particular company and you want its stock doesn't mean that you're willing to pay the current market price. Maybe you want to buy Kowalski, Inc., but the current market price of $20 per share isn't acceptable to you. You prefer to buy it at $16 because you think that price reflects its true market value. What do you do? You tell your broker, "Buy Kowalski with a limit order at $16" (or you can enter a limit order at the broker's website). You have to specify whether it's a day order or a GTC order, both of which I discuss earlier in this chapter.

What happens if the stock experiences great volatility? What if it drops to $16.01 and then suddenly drops to $15.95 on the next move? Nothing happens, actually, which you may be dismayed to hear. Because your order was limited to $16, it can be transacted only at $16 — no more and no less. The only way for this particular trade to occur is if the stock rises back to $16. However, if the price keeps dropping, then your limit order isn't transacted and may expire or be canceled.

WARNING

>> **When you're selling:** Limit orders are activated only when a stock hits a specific price. If you buy Kowalski, Inc., at $20 and you worry about a decline in the share price, you may decide to put in a limit order at $18. If you watch the news and hear that Kowalski's price is dropping, you may sigh and say, "I sure am glad I put in that limit order at $18!" However, in a volatile market, the share price may leapfrog over your specified price. It could go from

$18.01 to $17.99 and then continue its descent. Because the stock price never hit $18 on the mark, your stock isn't sold. You may be sitting at home satisfied (mistakenly) that you played it smart, while your stock plummets to $15, $10, or worse! Having a stop-loss order in place is best.

Investors who aren't in a hurry can use a limit order to try to get a better price when they decide to sell. For example, maybe you own a stock whose price is at $50 and you want to sell, but you think that a short-term rally in the stock is imminent. In that case, you can use a limit order such as "Sell the stock at the sell limit order of $55, and keep the order on for 30 days."

When you're buying (or selling) a stock, most brokers interpret the limit order as "buy (or sell) at this specific price or better." For example, presumably, if your limit order is to buy a stock at $10, you'll be just as happy if your broker buys that stock at $9.95. That way, if you don't get exactly $10 because the stock's price was volatile, you'll still get the stock at a lower price. Talk to your broker to be clear on the meaning of the limit order.

The joys of technology: Advanced orders

Brokers have added sophisticated capabilities to the existing repertoire of orders that are available for stock investors. One example is *advanced orders*, which provide investors with a way to use a combination of orders for more sophisticated trades. An example of an advanced order is something like, "Only sell stock B, and if it sells, use the proceeds to buy stock D." You get the idea. My brokerage firm has the following on its website, and I'm sure that more firms will do the same. Inquire with yours and see the benefit of using advanced orders such as the following:

>> **"One order cancels another order":** In this scenario you enter two orders simultaneously with the condition that if one order is executed, the second order is automatically canceled.

>> **"One order triggers another order":** Here you submit an order, and if that order is filled, another order is automatically submitted. Many brokers have different names for these types of orders, so ask them whether they can provide such an order.

Other types of advanced orders and order strategies are available, but you get the picture. Talk to your brokerage firm, and find out what's available in your particular account. Investors need to know that today's technology allows them to have more power and control over the implementation of buying and selling transactions. I love it!

Buying on Margin

Buying on margin means buying securities, such as stocks, with funds you borrow from your broker. Buying stock on margin is similar to buying a house with a mortgage. If you buy a house at a purchase price of $100,000 and put 10 percent down, your equity (the part you own) is $10,000, and you borrow the remaining $90,000 with a mortgage. If the value of the house rises to $120,000 and you sell (for the sake of simplicity, I don't include closing costs in this example), you make a profit of 200 percent. How is that? The $20,000 gain on the property represents a gain of 20 percent on the purchase price of $100,000, but because your real investment is $10,000 (the down payment), your gain works out to 200 percent (a gain of $20,000 on your initial investment of $10,000).

WARNING

Buying on margin is an example of using leverage to maximize your gain when prices rise. *Leverage* is simply using borrowed money when you make an asset purchase to increase your potential profit. This type of leverage is great in a favorable (bull) market, but it works against you in an unfavorable (bear) market. Say that a $100,000 house you purchase with a $90,000 mortgage falls in value to $80,000 (and property values can decrease during economic hard times). Your outstanding debt of $90,000 exceeds the value of the property. Because you owe more than you own, you're left with a negative net worth.

REMEMBER

Leverage is a double-edged sword. Don't forget that you need approval from your brokerage firm before you can buy on margin. To buy on margin, you typically fill out the form provided by that brokerage firm to be approved. Keep in mind that brokers typically require accounts to have a minimum of $2,000 or more before the investor can be approved for margin. Check with your broker because each firm has different requirements.

In the following sections, I describe the potential outcomes of buying on margin, explain how to maintain a balance, and provide some pointers for successfully buying on margin.

Examining marginal outcomes

Suppose you think that the stock for the company Mergatroid, Inc., currently at $40 per share, will go up in value. You want to buy 100 shares, but you have only $2,000. What can you do? If you're intent on buying 100 shares (versus simply buying the 50 shares that you have cash for), you can borrow the additional $2,000 from your broker on margin. If you do that, what are the potential outcomes?

If the stock price goes up

This outcome is the best for you. If Mergatroid goes to $50 per share, your investment is worth $5,000, and your outstanding margin loan is $2,000. If you sell, the total proceeds will pay off the loan and leave you with $3,000. Because your initial investment was $2,000, your profit is a solid 50 percent because your $2,000 principal amount generated a $1,000 profit. (For the sake of this example, I leave out any charges, such as commissions and interest paid on the margin loan.) However, if you pay the entire $4,000 upfront without the margin loan, your $4,000 investment generates a profit of $1,000, or 25 percent. Using margin, you double the return on your money.

REMEMBER

Leverage, when used properly, is very profitable. However, it's still debt, so understand that you must pay it off eventually, regardless of the stock's performance.

If the stock price fails to rise

If the stock goes nowhere, you still have to pay interest on that margin loan. If the stock pays dividends, this money can defray some of the margin loan's cost. In other words, dividends can help you pay off what you borrow from the broker. (Chapter 3 provides an introduction to dividends, and Chapter 9 covers dividend-investing and other income strategies.)

Having the stock neither rise nor fall may seem like a neutral situation, but you pay interest on your margin loan with each passing day. For this reason, margin trading can be a good consideration for conservative investors if the stock pays a high dividend. Many times, a high dividend from 4,000 dollars' worth of stock can equal or exceed the margin interest you have to pay from the $2,000 (50 percent) you borrow from the broker to buy that stock.

WARNING

If the stock price goes down, buying on margin can work against you. What if Mergatroid goes to $38 per share? The market value of 100 shares is then $3,800, but your equity shrinks to only $1,800 because you have to pay your $2,000 margin loan. You're not exactly looking at a disaster at this point, but you'd better be careful, because the margin loan exceeds 50 percent of your stock investment. If it goes any lower, you may get the dreaded *margin call*, when the broker actually contacts you to ask you to restore the ratio between the margin loan and the value of the securities. See the following section for information about appropriate debt to equity ratios.

Maintaining your balance

When you purchase stock on margin, you must maintain a balanced ratio of margin debt to equity of at least 50 percent. If the debt portion exceeds this limit, you're required to restore that ratio by depositing either more stock or more cash into your brokerage account. The additional stock you deposit can be stock that's transferred from another account.

To continue the example from the previous section: If Mergatroid goes to $28 per share, the margin loan portion exceeds 50 percent of the equity value in that stock — in this case, because the market value of your stock is $2,800 but the margin loan is still at $2,000, the margin loan is a worrisome 71 percent of the market value ($2,000 divided by $2,800 equals 71 percent). Expect to get a call from your broker to put more securities or cash into the account to restore the 50 percent balance.

If you can't come up with more stock, other securities, or cash, the next step is to sell stock from the account and use the proceeds to pay off the margin loan. For you, that means realizing a capital loss — you lose money on your investment.

TIP

The Federal Reserve Board governs margin requirements for brokers with Regulation T. Discuss this rule with your broker to understand fully your (and the broker's) risks and obligations. Regulation T dictates margin requirements set by brokers for their customers. For most listed stocks, it's 50 percent.

Striving for success on margin

Margin, as you can see from the previous sections, can escalate your profits on the upside but magnify your losses on the downside. If your stock plummets drastically, you can end up with a margin loan that exceeds the market value of the stock you used the loan to purchase. In 2008, margin debt hit very high levels, and that subsequently resulted in tumbling stock prices. In 2015, total margin debt again hit record highs by midyear, and it contributed to the stock market's down moves during late 2015 and early 2016 as selling pressures forced the sale of stocks tied to margin loans (with margin calls to boot!). In December 2018, one of the worst months in recent memory, excessive exposure of margin debt again exacerbated the losses as many investors were forced to sell and pay back the margin debt. Ugh!

WARNING

If you buy stock on margin, use a disciplined approach. Be extra careful when using leverage, such as a margin loan, because it can backfire. Keep the following points in mind:

>> **Have ample reserves of cash or marginable securities in your account.** Try to keep the margin ratio at 40 percent or less to minimize the chance of a margin call.

>> **If you're a beginner, consider using margin to buy stocks in large companies that have relatively stable prices and pay good dividends.**

Some people buy income stocks that have dividend yields that exceed the margin interest rate, meaning that the stock ends up paying for its own margin loan. Just remember those stop-loss orders, which I discuss earlier in this chapter.

>> **Constantly monitor your stocks.** If the market turns against you, the result will be especially painful if you use margin.

>> **Have a payback plan for your margin debt.** Taking margin loans against your investments means that you're paying interest. Your ultimate goal is to make money, and paying interest eats into your profits.

Going Short and Coming Out Ahead

The vast majority of stock investors are familiar with buying stock, holding onto it for a while, and hoping its value goes up. This kind of thinking is called *going long,* and investors who go long are considered to be *long on stocks.* Going long essentially means that you're bullish and seeking your profits from rising prices. However, astute investors also profit in the market when stock prices fall. *Going short* on a stock (also called *shorting a stock, selling short,* or *doing a short sale*) is a common technique for profiting from a stock price decline. Investors have made big profits during bear markets by going short. A short sale is a bet that a particular stock is going down.

Most people easily understand making money by going long. It boils down to "buy low and sell high." Piece of cake. Going short means making money by selling high and then buying low. Huh? Thinking in reverse isn't a piece of cake. Although thinking of this stock adage in reverse may be challenging, the mechanics of going short are really simple. Consider an example that uses a fictitious company called DOA, Inc. As a stock, DOA ($50 per share) is looking pretty sickly. It has lots of debt and plummeting sales and earnings, and the news is out that DOA's industry will face hard times for the foreseeable future. This situation describes a stock that's an ideal candidate for shorting. The future may be bleak for DOA, but it's promising for savvy investors. The following sections provide the full scoop on going short.

TIP

To go short, you have to be deemed (by your broker) creditworthy — your account needs to be approved for short selling. When you're approved for margin trading, you're probably set to sell short, too. Talk to your broker (or check the broker's website for information) about limitations in your account regarding going short.

REMEMBER

You must understand brokerage rules before you conduct short selling. Your broker must approve you for it (see Chapter 7 for information on working with brokers), and you must meet the minimum collateral requirement, which is typically $2,000 or 50 percent (whichever is higher) of the shorted stock's market value. If the stock generates dividends, those dividends are paid to the stock's owner, not to the person who borrows to go short. Check with your broker for complete details, and review the resources in Appendix A.

WARNING

Because going short on stocks has greater risks than going long, I strongly advise beginning investors to avoid shorting stocks until they become more seasoned.

Setting up a short sale

This section explains how to go short. Say that you believe DOA is the right stock to short — you're pretty sure its price is going to fall. With DOA at $50, you instruct your broker to "go short 100 shares on DOA." (It doesn't have to be 100 shares; I'm just using that as an example.) Here's what happens next:

1. **Your broker borrows 100 shares of DOA stock, either from his own inventory or from another client or broker.**

   That's right. The stock can be borrowed from a client, no permission necessary. The broker guarantees the transaction, and the client/stock owner never has to be informed about it because he never loses legal and beneficial right to the stock. You borrow 100 shares, and you'll return 100 shares when it's time to complete the transaction.

2. **Your broker then sells the stock and puts the money in your account.**

   Your account is credited with $5,000 (100 shares multiplied by $50) in cash — the money gained from selling the borrowed stock. This cash acts like a loan on which you're going to have to pay interest.

3. **You buy the stock back and return it to its rightful owner.**

   When it's time to close the transaction (because either you want to close it or the owner of the shares wants to sell them, so you have to give them back), you must return the number of shares you borrowed (in this case, 100 shares). If you buy back the 100 shares at $40 per share (remember that you shorted this particular stock because you were sure its price was going to fall) and those 100 shares are returned to their owner, you make a $1,000 profit. (To keep the example tidy, I don't include brokerage commissions.)

Oops! Going short when prices grow taller

I bet you guessed that the wonderful profitability of selling short has a flip side. Say that you were wrong about DOA and that the stock price rises from the ashes as it goes from $50 to $87. Now what? You still have to return the 100 shares you borrowed. With the stock's price at $87, that means you have to buy the stock for $8,700 (100 shares at the new, higher price of $87). Ouch! How do you pay for it? Well, you have that original $5,000 in your account from when you initially went short on the stock. But where do you get the other $3,700 ($8,700 less the original $5,000)? You guessed it — your pocket! You have to cough up the difference. If the stock continues to rise, that's a lot of coughing.

WARNING

How much money do you lose if the stock goes to $100 or more? A heck of a lot. As a matter of fact, there's no limit to how much you can lose. That's why going short can be riskier than going long. When going long, the most you can lose is 100 percent of your money. When you go short, however, you can lose more than 100 percent of the money you invest. Yikes!

TIP

Because the potential for loss is unlimited when you short a stock, I suggest that you use a stop order (also called a *buy-stop order*) to minimize the damage. Better yet, make it a good-til-canceled (GTC) order, which I discuss earlier in this chapter. You can set the stop order at a given price, and if the stock hits that price, you buy the stock back so that you can return it to its owner before the price rises even higher. You still lose money, but you limit your losses. Like a stop-loss order, a buy-stop order effectively works to limit your loss.

THE UPTICK RULE

For many years, the stock market had something called the *uptick rule.* This rule stated that you could enter into a short sale only when the stock had just completed an uptick. "Tick" in this case means the actual incremental price movement of the stock you're short-ing. For a $10 stock that was just $9.95 a moment ago, the 5-cent difference represents an uptick. If the $10 stock was just $10.10 a moment before, the 10-cent difference is a downtick. The amount of the tick doesn't matter. So, if you short a stock at the price of $40, the immediate prior price must have been $39.99 or lower. The reason for this rule (a Federal Reserve regulation) is that short selling can aggravate declining stock prices in a rapidly falling market. In practice, going short on a stock whose price is already declining can make the stock price fall even farther. Excessive short selling can make the stock more volatile than it would be otherwise.

In 2007, however, the uptick rule was removed. This action contributed to the increased volatility that investors saw during 2007–2008. Investors had to adapt accordingly. It meant getting used to wider swings in stock price movements on days of heavy activity.

Feeling the squeeze

If you go short on a stock, you have to buy that stock back sooner or later so that you can return it to its owner. What happens when a lot of people are short on a particular stock and its price starts to rise? All those short sellers are scrambling to buy the stock back so that they can close their transactions before they lose too much money. This mass buying quickens the pace of the stock's ascent and puts a squeeze (called a *short squeeze*) on the investors who've been shorting the stock.

In the earlier section "Setting up a short sale," I explain that your broker can borrow stock from another client so that you can go short on it. What happens when that client wants to sell the stock in her account — the stock that you borrowed and which is therefore no longer in her account? When that happens, your broker asks you to return the borrowed stock. That's when you feel the squeeze — you have to buy the stock back at the current price.

WARNING

Going short can be a great maneuver in a declining (bear) market, but it can be brutal if the stock price goes up. If you're a beginner, stay away from short selling until you have enough experience (and money) to risk it.

Chapter **18**

International Stock Investing Opportunities

I am a biased guy — I think that the stock market in the United States is the best out there. But you can't ignore the rest of the world, especially if there are great investment opportunities that could nicely complement your domestic portfolio. That's why this chapter is included — profitable opportunities keep your portfolio's growth humming along.

In this chapter, I focus on the easiest ways for you to invest internationally and notable regions and countries to consider (or avoid) for 2020–2021 and beyond.

Investigating the Basics of International Stock Investing

As with stocks in the United States, you look at an individual international stock with the same lens. You look at the fundamentals — the company's profit, sales, assets, market dominance, and so on. (See Part 3 for more details on picking winning stocks.) But the greatest difference is that company's operating environment. The investing environment may be either hospitable and similar to U.S. stock markets, and therefore a good consideration, or the investing environment may be hostile and too risky to consider. The following sections discuss a convenient way to invest internationally — American Depositary Receipts — and some considerations to make before you dive in.

WARNING

You can invest directly in the shares of a company that operates in, say, Europe or Asia. However, you need to be familiar with the requirements tied to that individual nation or region. Some nations, for example, expect you to report your gains and/or dividends with their tax authority. There may be other requirements to be aware of, so for the purpose of this book (and my own personal views), I don't recommend investing directly, especially if better and more convenient ways exist (they do!).

The easiest way to invest: American Depositary Receipts (ADRs)

The best and most convenient way for investors in the United States to purchase international stocks is through American Depositary Receipts (ADRs). An ADR is a security issued through American brokers where the shares of an international company are purchased and converted into an ADR that can be as easily bought as any regular common stock purchase through your stock brokerage account. (See Chapter 7 for full details on working with a broker.)

A good example of an ADR is Nestle, the global consumer goods giant. You can directly buy shares of the company itself on the Swiss stock exchange, or you can easily buy its ADR shares on Nasdaq as Nestle SA (its symbol is NSRGY). The ADR shares act just like any stock shares would.

As of this writing, there are over 3,000 ADRs trading on U.S. exchanges, so there are plenty to choose from. These ADRs represent major international companies whose stocks are traded across the global financial landscape in a variety of established stock exchanges. Through ADRs, you can easily invest in public companies in Europe, Asia, or other regions of the world. The following sections discuss the major features of ADRs.

REMEMBER

ADRs are great ways to invest in a foreign stock, but you should keep in mind that potential negatives are currency conversion issues and added costs such as conversion fees and potential foreign taxes. Some resources to help you research international investing are at the end of this chapter and in Appendix A.

Convenience

Convenience is probably the top reason for U.S. stock investors to utilize ADRs because you can buy ADR shares as easily as American stock shares (as I explain earlier). Keep in mind that there are usually modest fees attached to the purchase of ADRs, which are part of the standard brokerage commissions charged when you buy or sell shares. Speak to your brokerage firm's customer service about the fee in the specific ADR you're considering; the fee may vary according to the country involved.

Currency conversion

When you invest in foreign stocks directly, currency conversion becomes an issue. If you invest in a Japanese company, for example, they, of course, pay dividends in the yen currency. For American investors, regularly converting that dividend payout from yen to American dollars would be inconvenient to deal with.

Fortunately, the bank that issues the ADR handles this conversion for you. In the example of the Japanese public company, the bank would receive the payout in yen and then convert it to U.S. dollars before making a dividend payout to ADR investors. The same is true for purchasing the shares; the ADR pays for shares in the country's currency, but the ADR shares for you are in American dollars.

Number of shares

Although the ADR may be a ratio of 1-to-1 in terms of common shares (in other words, 100 shares of, say, a German company would be 100 shares in your ADR), sometimes there may be a different ratio due to how the ADR is structured. In some ADRs, the ratio may be 1.5 shares to your ADR share or even 2 or 5 shares or another ratio. This shouldn't be an issue for American investors, but you should be aware of it so you understand how you finally receive the ADR shares in your stock brokerage account.

British Petroleum (BP), for example (as of this writing), has a ratio of 6 shares to be allotted per one ADR share. So if you purchased 20 ADR shares, it would be the equivalent of 120 regular shares (20 × 6). The same ratio would affect the dividend payout; the dividend paid would have the same equivalent.

Taxation

REMEMBER

ADR dividends are, of course, taxable as are U.S. stock dividends, but they can be a little tricky since many countries have a withholding tax on their dividend income (typically 15 percent or 20 percent). You may qualify for a tax credit according to the IRS; full details are in IRS Publication 514. Since countries have different tax laws and different tax rates, check with both your stock brokerage's customer service and your tax advisor for guidance on this both before your make your ADR purchase and when dividends are payable for that given year.

Before you buy: Political considerations

Assessing the company you want to invest in is not that difficult since you generally use the same type of information as you would with domestic companies (see Chapters 6, 8, and 11 for applicable info).

TIP

However, it is critical that you research the country itself. You may not need to visit the country (although that firsthand experience would be helpful), but reading about the country and asking for professional opinions from experienced investors and online investing blogs should be considered a must. Here are some questions to keep in mind:

>> Is the country a friendly trading partner of the United States?

>> Is the country a stable democracy with an English common-law legal system?

>> Does the country have a formal, long-established stock market exchange?

>> Are there mutual funds that extensively trade in that country?

>> Are there extensive information sources (blogs, sites, newsletters) that regularly cover news, data, and views for that country?

The more questions you can get satisfactory answers to and the more information and news available to you, the better your decision-making capabilities for your international stock investing plans. See the resources at this end of this chapter and in Appendix A for more guidance.

An important distinction: Developed markets versus emerging markets

Most countries that you consider for international investing can generally be categorized as either "developed markets" or "developed economies" (such as Germany or Canada) or as "emerging markets," which refers to countries striving to become more developed such as countries in sub-Saharan Africa or Asia.

REMEMBER

The difference in these two categories can be conveniently aligned with the difference between investing and speculating:

» Buying stock (ADRs or otherwise) in a developed, mature economy is investing.

» Buying stock in companies that are in emerging markets is really speculating since emerging markets can produce potentially great gains but come with greater risk and volatility. Since emerging economies do not yet have stable, long-lasting governmental processes and an established common-law framework, there is inherent uncertainty and potential instability that could adversely and negatively affect your investment.

WARNING

I think that for the sake of completeness, I should mention a third category that I label "Keep away." This is a reference to known countries that have a hostile or outright negative environment for anyone's investment dollars. Good examples (as of this writing) include authoritarian socialist/communist countries such as North Korea and Venezuela. Another problematic example to avoid for now is Iran. Of course, governments can change and investing opportunities can improve, but it is better to avoid these venues until those changes do occur.

A good example of positive change is Vietnam. Once a communist country that no sane investor would consider, it collapsed and re-emerged as a more market-based economy and then grew as investment dollars saw it as becoming more investor-friendly. For more information on countries that are considered developed or emerging markets, see the resources at the end of this chapter.

JOHN TEMPLETON'S FOREIGN STOCK GAMBLE

One of the great successes in investing history is the Templeton Fund first started by John Templeton, one of the greatest investors in history. In 1999, *Money* magazine referred to him as the "greatest global stock picker of the century." His investing career started with successfully speculating with penny stocks during the Great Depression, but he gained notoriety with his international stock investing with his fund (which later merged and became part of the Franklin Templeton Funds in 1996).

In the 1950s, he was among the first global investors to buy stocks of Japanese companies in the aftermath of World War II. He felt that Japan's people and institutions were ready to rebound from devastation and to grow. This speculative investment in Japanese companies became a spectacular success, and for decades he successfully managed his international stock investing fund and propelled it to a top-performing, billion-dollar mutual fund.

To find out more about him and his investing exploits (still valuable info for budding international investors today), head over to his foundation's site at www.templeton.org.

International Stock Investing via Exchange-Traded Funds

Although I generally cover exchange-traded funds (ETFs) in Chapter 5, I drill down and cover this specialty — international investing with ETFs — in this section. I think that for beginning investors (and anyone who is nervous about individual stocks), ETFs are a truly great way to invest. All the convenience and features of stock investing with a very generous dose of diversification make ETFs the go-to vehicle for international stock investing.

Global ETFs

Who says that to invest internationally, you have to do so in a specific place or be stuck to a specific country or region? The great thing about a global investing ETF is that it's like investing in the . . . uh . . . globe. A global ETF invests in a cross section of securities that span the globe. It is like the ultimate geographical diversification.

Here are some of the most widely traded/widely held ones (their trading symbols are in parentheses):

>> Schwab International Equity ETF (SCHF)

>> SPDR Global Dow ETF (DGT)

>> iShares Core MSCI Total International Stock ETF (IXUS)

WARNING

ETFs have a fixed portfolio (which can be good), but the problem is that the ETF is stuck with that choice. This is the biggest issue I have with global ETFs. If one part of the world has stocks going up and other parts of the world have stocks going down, you're stuck with counter-vailing values and you don't have the ability to get out of the poorly performing country or region. The global fund tends to be so diversified that you're punished with less growth.

TIP

Given that, I prefer a global mutual fund instead. A global mutual fund is actively managed, and the investment manager can freely shift money away from problem spots (as they emerge) on the globe and allocate more funds to better positions as they are located. Most of the major mutual fund companies have a global mutual fund, such as Fidelity, BlackRock, and Vanguard.

In recent years, the mutual fund companies developed a variant called a *global allocation* fund. This fund seeks diversification across the globe but typically focuses on mature economies such as the United States, Japan, and Western Europe, and it also utilizes several different classes of investments such as stocks (equity), bonds (fixed income), and cash.

Region-specific ETFs

Maybe you have a hunch — a very informed hunch, of course — that a specific region of the world will do very well in the coming months and years. Of course, as many beginning investors, you may find that you are certain about the "big picture" but are too skittish to choose an individual stock. Given that, a region-specific ETF may be the right choice. The following sections describe different regions and their ETFs.

REMEMBER

When you are dealing with international ETFs that are global or regional, see what countries they exclude. There are ETFs, for example, that exclude the United States. This is for those investors who prefer a choice that excludes a specific country due to considerations tied to investing, political, or social preferences.

Africa

TIP

Africa is considered an emerging market, and it can be a tough venue in which to find a single specific stock, but for those investors looking for exposure here due to the continent's potential growth prospects, an ETF is a great way to proceed. A good consideration is the VanEck Vectors Africa Index ETF (AFK).

Asia/Pacific Rim

An ETF covering Asian economies (such as China) and/or the "Pacific Rim" generally invests in stocks of companies in the markets of countries on the Asian landmass. A variety of ETFs have exposure to mainland economies such as China, Russia, and India or economies on the Asian shore such as South Korea, Taiwan, Japan, and the Philippines. This venue may also include the nearby markets of Australia and New Zealand. A good example is iShares Core MSCI Pacific ETF (IPAC).

Europe

Whether you are talking ETFs that have exposure to the entire continent of Europe or individual countries, there are plenty of choices for investors. A good continent-wide ETF is iShares Europe ETF (IEV). To find ETFs for individual countries, head to www.etfdb.com.

WESTERN VERSUS EASTERN EUROPE?

Not that long ago, Western and Eastern Europe were bifurcated — back when the "Iron Curtain" had Europe separated between the free countries (non-communist) and the eastern bloc countries that were dominated by the then-communist Soviet Union. The Soviet Union collapsed in 1989. During the 1990s, Europe became "whole" as a continent; the eastern countries slowly emerged from being dominated and devastated by communism and joined the mainstream European community of nations.

The investment world referred to western countries as "developed" while the eastern countries were referred to as "emerging" since they needed to upgrade and modernize their economies to catch up with Western Europe. The western countries were considered safer and more stable for investing, and there were ETFs that specialized in that half of Europe while different ETFs focused on the growth potential of emerging economies in Eastern Europe.

As of 2020, Eastern Europe has caught up, but there are still mutual funds and ETFs that are labeled as developed and emerging. Germany and France are developed while countries like Poland are still referred to as emerging. Find funds on these categories with the resources at the end of this chapter.

Latin America

ETFs in Latin America focus on established economies in Central and South America. Most typically have exposure to countries such as Brazil, Colombia, Mexico, Chile, and so on. A good example is iShares Latin America 40 ETF (ILF).

North America

For North America, you are basically talking either the United States or Canada so you generally won't find an international ETF that covers this twosome, but no worries. There are plenty (and I mean plenty!) of ETFs covering the United States and its plethora of subsections and sectors.

For the U.S. stock market, an ETF based on the S&P 500 such as the SPDR S&P 500 ETF (SPY) or the Vanguard S&P 500 ETF (VOO) should suffice. For exposure to Canada, the iShares MSCI Canada ETF (EWC) is the most widely held.

Country-specific ETFs

My favorite way to invest in a specific country is (surprise!) a country-specific ETF. Most of the major economies of the world have one or more ETFs that you can choose from. There are over 2,000 country-specific funds! Of course, there aren't 2,000 countries, but there may be many ETFs from different investment firms that simply target the same country. If you are targeting, say, France, then just consider choosing among the top two or three most widely traded ETFs.

TIP

When you get a chance, head over to ETF Database (www.etfdb.com). They have a nifty free tool you can use: their ETF Country Exposure Tool (https://etfdb. com/tool/etf-country-exposure-tool/). You can enter the name of a country, and their tool will show you ETFs with exposure to it. It will rank based on how much exposure there is. Of course, a country ETF offers the most singular exposure to a specific country.

If you enter "South Korea," for example, you will see 298 ETFs (as of this writing). The number-one choice is the Franklin FTSE South Korea ETF. It is a country-specific ETF, and the exposure is 100 percent. Meanwhile, when you look later in that same search, you will find the iShares S&P Asia ETF, which has a 22 percent exposure to South Korea. Hmmm . . . I think I'll check out Croatia.

Creative international ETFs

I want to whet your appetite for investing creatively on the international scene and give you some possibilities to investigate:

>> **Global dividend ETFs:** These funds have a number of global stocks known for solid dividend income.

WARNING

>> **Inverse ETFs:** If you feel that a country will have a declining stock market, perhaps because you see political or economic problems hitting it hard, you can choose an inverse ETF, which rises in value (much like a put option) when that specific country's stock market goes down. Just keep in mind that inverse ETFs (like put options) are a form of speculating — not investing!

>> **International bond ETFs:** These ETFs are income-oriented funds that primarily invest in the bonds of a particular country or region.

Checking Out International Investing Resources

TIP

The bottom line is that international stock investing done with prudence and research offers excellent opportunities for investment income and appreciation, so your best next step is to do some digging and find out more. Here are some places to check out:

>> Franklin Templeton's emerging markets blog (http://emergingmarkets. blog.franklintempleton.com/)

>> MarketWatch's world markets page (www.marketwatch.com/markets)

>> Top Foreign Stocks (www.topforeignstocks.com)

Chapter **19**

Getting a Handle on DPPs, DRPs, and DCA . . . PDQ

W ho says you must buy 100 shares of a stock to invest? And who says that you must buy your stock only from a broker? (There goes that little voice in my head. . . .) Can you buy direct instead? What if you only want to put your toe in the water and buy just one share for starters? Can you do that without paying through the nose for transaction costs, such as commissions?

The answer to these questions is that you can buy stocks directly (without a broker) and save money in the process. That's what this chapter is about. In this chapter, I show you how direct purchase programs (DPPs) and dividend reinvestment plans (DRPs) make a lot of sense for long-term stock investors, and I show how you can do them on your own — no broker necessary. I also show you how to use the method of dollar cost averaging (DCA) to acquire stock, a technique that works especially well with DRPs. All these programs are well-suited for people who like to invest small sums of money and plan on doing so consistently in the same stock (or stocks) over a long period of time.

REMEMBER

Don't invest in a company just because it has a DPP or DRP. DPPs and DRPs are simply a means for getting into a particular stock with very little money. They shouldn't be a substitute for doing diligent research and analysis on a particular stock.

Going Straight to Direct Purchase Programs

If you're going to buy a stock anyway, why not buy it directly from the company and bypass the broker (and commissions) altogether? Several hundred companies now offer *direct purchase programs* (DPPs), also called *direct investment programs* (DIPs), which give investors an opportunity to buy stock directly from these companies. In the following sections, I explain the steps required for investing in a DPP, describe alternatives to DPPs, and warn you of a few minor DPP drawbacks.

REMEMBER

DPPs give investors the opportunity to buy stock with little upfront money (usually enough to cover the purchase of one share) and usually no commissions. Why do companies give investors this opportunity? For their sake, they want to encourage more attention and participation from investors. For your purposes, however, a DPP gives you what you may need most: a low-cost entry into that particular company's dividend reinvestment plan, or DRP (which you can read more about in the later section "Delving into Dividend Reinvestment Plans").

Investing in a DPP

If you have your sights set on a particular company and have only a few bucks to start out, a DPP is probably the best way to make your initial investment. The following steps guide you toward your first stock purchase using a DPP:

1. **Decide what stock you want to invest in (I explain how to do so in Parts 2 and 3), and find the company's contact information.**

   Say that you do your homework and decide to invest in Yumpin Yimminy Corp. (YYC). You can get YYC's contact information through the stock exchange YYC trades on (or at the company's website).

2. **Find out whether the company has a DPP (before it's DOA!).**

   Call YYC's shareholder services department and ask whether it has a DPP. If it does, great; if it doesn't, ask whether it plans to start one. At the very least, it may have a DRP. If you prefer, you can check out the company's website because most corporate websites have plenty of information on their stock purchase programs.

3. **Look into enrolling.**

The company will provide (via email, download, or live at its site) an application along with a *prospectus* — the program document that serves as a brochure and, hopefully, answers your basic questions. Again, the enrollment process is now typically done online from either the company's website or its chosen plan administrator's website.

The processing is typically handled by an organization that the company designates (known as the *plan administrator*). From this point forward, you're in the dividend reinvestment plan. The DPP acts as the entry point to the DRP so that you make future purchases through the DRP.

Finding DPP alternatives

Although many companies offer DPPs (nearly 600 and growing), the full range of companies don't. What if you want to invest in a company directly and it doesn't have a DPP? The following sections present some alternatives.

Buying your first share through a broker to qualify for a DRP

Yes, buying your first share through a broker costs you a commission; however, after you make the purchase, you can contact that company's shareholder services department and ask about its DRP. After you're an existing stockholder, qualifying for the DRP is a piece of cake.

REMEMBER

To qualify for the DRP, you must be on the book of record with the transfer agent. A *book of record* is simply the database the company uses to track every single outstanding share of stock and the stock's owner. The *transfer agent* is the organization responsible for maintaining the database. Whenever stock is bought or sold, the transfer agent must implement the change and update the records. In many cases, you must have the broker issue a stock certificate in your name after you own the stock. Getting a stock certificate is the most common way to get your name on the book of record, hence qualifying you for the DRP.

TIP

Sometimes, simply buying the stock isn't enough to get your name on the book of record. Although you technically and legally own the stock, brokers, for ease of transaction, often keep the stock in your account under what's referred to as a *street name.* (For instance, your name may be Jane Smith, but the street name can be the broker's firm name, such as Jones & Co., simply for administrative purposes.)

Having the stock in a street name really doesn't mean much to you until you want to qualify for the company's DRP. Be sure to address this point with your broker. (Flip to Chapter 7 for more details on brokers.)

Getting started in a DRP directly through a broker

These days, more brokers offer the features of the DRP (like compounding interest) right in the brokerage account itself, which is more convenient than going to the trouble of setting up a DRP with the company directly. This service is most likely a response to the growing number of long-term investors who have fled traditional brokerage accounts for the benefits of direct investing that DPPs and DRPs offer.

WARNING

The main drawback of a broker-run DRP is that it doesn't usually allow you to make stock purchases through optional cash payments without commission charges (a big negative!). See the later section "Building wealth with optional cash payments" for more on this topic.

Purchasing shares via alternate buying services

Organizations have set up services to help small investors buy stock in small quantities. The primary drawback to these middlemen is that you'll probably pay more in transaction costs than you would if you approached the companies directly. Check out the most prominent services, which include the following:

>> Direct Investing (www.directinvesting.com)

>> DRIP Database (www.dripdatabase.com)

>> First Share at www.firstshare.com

>> National Association of Investors Corporation (doing business as BetterInvesting) at www.betterinvesting.org

>> The DRiP Investing Resource Center at www.dripinvesting.org

Recognizing the drawbacks

WARNING

As beneficial as DPPs are, they do have some minor drawbacks (doesn't everything?). Keep the following points in mind when considering DPPs as part of your stock portfolio:

>> Although more and more companies are starting to offer DPPs, relatively few (approximately 600) companies have them.

>> Some DPPs require a high initial amount to invest (as much as $250 or more) or a commitment of monthly investments. In any case, ask the plan administrator about the investing requirements.

>> A growing number of DPPs have some type of service charge. This charge is usually very modest and lower than typical brokerage commissions. Ask about all the incidentals — such as getting into the plan, getting out, and so on — that may trigger a service charge.

Delving into Dividend Reinvestment Plans

Sometimes, *dividend reinvestment plans* (DRPs) are called "DRIPs," which makes me scratch my head. "Reinvestment" is one word, not two, so where does that "I" come from? But I digress. Whether you call them DRIPs or DRPs, they're great for small investors and people who are truly long-term investors in a particular stock. A company may offer a DRP to allow investors to accumulate more shares of its stock without paying commissions. The good news is that over 1,600 companies have DRPs (as of 2019).

A DRP has two primary advantages:

>> **Compounding:** The dividends (cash payments to shareholders) get reinvested and give you the opportunity to buy more stock.

>> **Optional cash payments (OCPs):** Most DRPs give participants the ability to make investments through the plan for the purpose of purchasing more stock, usually with no commissions. The OCP minimum for some DRPs is as little as $25 (or even nothing).

REMEMBER

Here are the requirements to be in a DRP:

>> You must already be a stockholder of that particular stock.

>> The stock must be paying dividends (you had to guess this one!).

In the following sections, I go into more detail on compounding and OCPs, explain the cost advantages of using DRPs, and warn you of a few drawbacks.

REMEMBER

As technology changes and improves, it becomes easier to participate in programs like DRPs because most brokerage firms now make it easier to participate right inside your brokerage account.

Getting a clue about compounding

Dividends are reinvested, offering a form of compounding for the small investor. Dividends buy more shares, in turn generating more dividends. Usually, the dividends don't buy entire shares but fractional ones.

For example, say that you own 20 shares of Fraction Corp. at $10 per share for a total value of $200. Fraction Corp.'s annual dividend is $1, meaning that a quarterly dividend of 25 cents is issued every three months. What happens if this stock is in the DRP? The 20 shares generate a $5 dividend payout in the first quarter (20 shares multiplied by 25 cents), and this amount is applied to the stock purchase as soon as it's credited to the DRP account (buying you half of a share). If you presume for this example that the stock price doesn't change, the DRP has 20.5 total shares valued at $205 (20.5 shares multiplied by $10 per share). The dividend payout isn't enough to buy an entire share, so it buys a fractional share and credits that to the account.

Now say that three months pass and that no other shares have been acquired since your prior dividend payout. Fraction Corp. issues another quarterly dividend for 25 cents per share. Now what?

>> The original 20 shares generate a $5 dividend payout.

>> The 0.5, or half share, in the account generates a 12.5-cent dividend (half the dividend of a full share because it's only half a share).

>> The total dividend payout is $5.125 (rounded to $5.13), and the new total of shares in the account is 21.01 (the former 20.5 shares plus 0.513 share purchased by the dividend payout and rounded off; the 0.513 fraction was gained by the cash from the dividends). Full shares generate full dividends, and fractional shares generate fractional dividends.

REMEMBER

To illustrate my point easily, the preceding example uses a price that doesn't fluctuate. In reality, stock in a DRP acts like any other stock — the share price changes constantly. Every time the DRP makes a stock purchase, whether it's monthly or quarterly, the purchase price will likely be different.

Building wealth with optional cash payments

Most DRPs (unless they're run by a broker) give the participant the opportunity to make *optional cash payments* (OCPs), which are payments you send in to purchase more stock in the DRP. DRPs usually establish a minimum and a maximum payment. The minimum is typically very modest, such as $25 or $50. A few plans even have no minimum. This feature makes it very affordable to regularly invest modest amounts and build up a sizable portfolio of stock in a short period of time, unencumbered by commissions.

DRPs also have a maximum investment limitation, such as specifying that DRP participants can't invest more than $10,000 per year. For most investors, the maximum isn't a problem because few would typically invest that much anyway. However, consult with the plan's administrator because all plans are a little different.

REMEMBER

OCPs are probably the most advantageous aspect of a DRP. If you can invest $25 to $50 per month consistently, year after year, at no (or little) cost, you may find that doing so is a superb way to build wealth.

OCPs work well with dollar cost averaging (DCA). Find out more in the upcoming section "The One-Two Punch: Dollar Cost Averaging and DRPs."

Checking out the cost advantages

In spite of the fact that more and more DRPs are charging service fees, DRPs are still an economical way to invest, especially for small investors. The big savings come from not paying commissions. Although many DPPs and DRPs do have charges, they tend to be relatively small (but keep track of them because the costs can add up).

TIP

Some DRPs actually offer a discount of between 2 and 5 percent (a few are higher) when buying stock through the plan. Others offer special programs and discounts on the company's products and services. Some companies offer the service of debiting your checking account or paycheck to invest in the DRP. One company offered its shareholders significant discounts to its restaurant subsidiary. In any case, ask the plan administrator because any plus is, well, a plus.

Weighing the pros with the cons

When you're in a DRP, you reap all the benefits of stock investing. You get an annual report, and you qualify for stock splits, dividend increases, and so on. But you must be aware of the risks and responsibilities.

WARNING

So before you start to salivate over all the goodies that come with DRPs, be clear-eyed about some of their negative aspects as well. Those negative aspects include the following:

>> **You need to get that first share.** You have to buy that initial share in order to get the DRP started (but you knew that).

» **Even small fees cut into your profits.** More and more DRP administrators have added small fees to cover administrative costs. Find out how much they are and how they're transacted to minimize your DRP costs. The more costs you incur, of course, the more your net profit will be diminished over time.

» **Many DRPs may not have added services that you may need.** For example, you may want to have your DRP in a vehicle such as an Individual Retirement Account (IRA; see Chapter 21). Many investors understand that a DRP is a long-term commitment, so having it in an IRA is an appropriate strategy. Some administrators have the ability to set up your DRP as an IRA, but some don't, so you need to inquire about this.

» **DRPs are designed for long-term investing.** Although getting in and out of the plan is easy, the transactions may take weeks to process because stock purchases and sales are typically done all at once on a certain day of the month (or quarter).

MOVING MONEY OUT OF DRPs TO PAY OFF DEBT

DRPs are a great way to accumulate a large stock holding over an extended period of time. Moreover, think about what you can do with this stock. Say that you accumulate 110 shares of stock, valued at $50 per share, in your DRP. You can, for example, take out $5,000 worth of stock (100 shares at $50 per share) and place those 100 shares in your brokerage account. The remaining 10 shares can stay in your account to keep the DRP and continue with dividend reinvestment to keep your wealth growing. Why remove those shares?

All things being equal, you're better off keeping the stock in the DRP, but what if you have $2,500 in credit card debt and don't have extra cash to pay off that debt? Brokerage accounts still have plenty of advantages, such as, in this example, the use of margin (a topic I discuss in detail in Chapter 17). If your situation merits it, you can borrow up to 50 percent of the $5,000, or $2,500, as a margin loan and use it to pay off that credit card debt. Because you're replacing unsecured debt (credit card debt that may be charging 15 percent, 18 percent, or more) with secured debt, you can save a lot of money (borrowing against stock in a brokerage account is usually cheaper than credit card debt). Another benefit is that the margin loan with your broker doesn't require monthly payments, as do the credit card balances. Additionally, ask your tax consultant about potential tax benefits — investment interest expense is deductible, but consumer credit card debt is not.

>> **You need to read the prospectus.** You may not consider this a negative point, but for some people, reading a prospectus is not unlike giving blood by using leeches. Even if that's your opinion, you need to read the prospectus to avoid any surprises, such as hidden fees or unreasonable terms.

>> **You must understand the tax issues.** There, ya see? I knew I'd ruin it for you. Just know that dividends, whether or not they occur in a DRP, are usually taxable (unless the DRP is in an IRA, which is a different matter). I cover tax issues in detail in Chapter 21.

>> **You need to keep good records.** Keep all your statements together, and use a good spreadsheet program or accounting program if you plan on doing a lot of DRP investing. These records are especially important at tax time, when you have to report any subsequent gains or losses from stock sales. Capital gains taxes can be complicated as you sort out short-term versus long-term capital gains on your investments, but the latest record-keeping technology by plan administrators have made DRP calculations much easier.

The One-Two Punch: Dollar Cost Averaging and DRPs

Dollar cost averaging (DCA) is a splendid technique for buying stock and lowering your cost for doing so. The example in Table 19-1 shows that it's not uncommon for investors to see a total cost that reflects a discount to the market value. DCA works especially well with DRPs and has an excellent track record of helping small investors purchase stocks at a better (lower) average purchase price per share.

TABLE 19-1 **Dollar Cost Averaging (Acme Elevator, Inc.)**

Months	Investment Amount ($)	Purchase Price ($)	Shares Bought	Accumulated Shares
1	25	25	1	1
2	25	20	1.25	2.25
3	25	17.5	1.43	3.68
4	25	15	1.67	5.35
5	25	17.5	1.43	6.78
6	25	20	1.25	8.03
Totals	$150	N/A	8.03	8.03

REMEMBER

DCA is a simple method for acquiring stock. It rests on the idea that you invest a fixed amount of money at regular intervals (monthly, usually) over a long period of time in a particular stock. Because a fixed amount (say, $50 per month) is going into a fluctuating investment, you end up buying less of that stock when it goes up in price and more of it when it goes down in price. Your average cost per share is usually lower than if you were to buy all the shares at once.

DCA is best presented with an example. Say you decide to get into the DRP of the company Acme Elevator, Inc. (AE). On your first day in the DRP, AE's stock is at $25, and the plan allows you to invest a minimum of $25 through its optional cash purchase (OCP) program. You decide to invest $25 per month and assess how well (hopefully) you're doing six months from now. Table 19-1 shows how this technique works.

To assess the wisdom of your decision to invest in the DRP, ask yourself some questions:

>> **How much did you invest over the entire six months?** Your total investment is $150. So far, so good.

>> **What's the first share price for AE, and what's the last share price?** The first share price is $25, but the last share price is $20.

>> **What's the market value of your investment at the end of six months?** You can easily calculate the value of your investment. Just multiply the number of shares you now own (8.03 shares) by the most recent share price ($20). The total value of your investment is $160.60.

>> **What's the average share price you bought at?** The average share price is also easy to calculate. Take the total amount of your purchases ($150) and divide it by the number of shares you acquired (8.03 shares). Your average cost per share is $18.68.

Be sure to take note of the following:

>> Even though the last share price ($20) is lower than the original share price ($25), your total investment's market value is still higher than your purchase amount ($160.60 compared to $150)! How can that be? You can thank dollar cost averaging. Your disciplined approach (using DCA) overcame the fluctuations in the stock price to help you gain more shares at the lower prices of $17.50 and $15.

>> Your average cost per share is only $18.68. The DCA method helped you buy more shares at a lower cost, which ultimately helped you make money when the stock price made a modest rebound.

REMEMBER

DCA not only helps you invest with small sums but also helps you smooth out the volatility in stock prices. These benefits help you make more money in your wealth-building program over the long haul. The bottom line for long-term stock investors is that DCA is a solid investing technique, and DRPs are a great stock investment vehicle for building wealth. Can you visualize that retirement hammock yet?

WARNING

Dollar cost averaging is a fantastic technique in a bull market and an okay technique in a flat or sideways market, but it's really not a good consideration during bear markets because the stock you're buying is going down in price, and the market value can very easily be lower than your total investment. If you plan on holding on to the stock long term, then DCA will help you accumulate more shares during the stock's lower price period during a bear market. Of course, some skittish investors worried about a bear market can simply cease the DCA approach until times improve for the stock (and its industry and the economy).

IN THIS CHAPTER

» Using documents to track insider trading

» Examining insider buying and selling

» Understanding corporate buybacks

» Breaking down stock splits

» Watching Congress closely

Chapter **20**

Corporate and Government Skullduggery: Looking at Insider Activity

I magine that you're boarding a cruise ship, ready to enjoy a hard-earned vacation. As you merrily walk up the plank, you notice that the ship's captain and crew are charging out of the vessel, flailing their arms and screaming at the top of their lungs. Some are even jumping into the water below. Pop quiz: Would you get on that ship? You get double credit if you can also explain why (or why not).

What does this scenario have to do with stock investing? Plenty. The behavior of the people running the boat gives you important clues about the near-term prospects for the boat. Similarly, the actions of company insiders can provide important clues into the near-term prospects for their company.

Company *insiders* are key managers or investors in the company. Insiders include the president of the company, the treasurer, and other managing officers. An insider can also be someone who owns a large stake in the company or someone on the board of directors. In any case, insiders usually have a bird's-eye view of what's going on with the company and a good idea of how well (or how poorly) the company is doing.

In this chapter, I describe different kinds of insider activities, such as insider buying, insider selling, corporate stock buybacks, and stock splits. I also show you how to keep track of these activities with the help of a few resources.

REMEMBER

Keep tabs on what insiders are doing because their buy/sell transactions do have a strong correlation to the near-term movement of their company's stock. However, don't buy or sell stock only because you heard that some insider did. Use the information on insider trading to confirm your own good sense in buying or selling stock. Insider trading sometimes can be a great precursor to a significant move that you can profit from if you know what to look for. Many shrewd investors have made their profits (or avoided losses) by tracking the activity of insiders.

Tracking Insider Trading

Fortunately, we live in an age of disclosure and the internet. Insiders who buy or sell stock must file reports that document their trading activity with the Securities and Exchange Commission (SEC), which makes the documents available to the public. You can view these documents at either a regional SEC office (see `www.sec.gov/page/sec-regional-offices` for locations) or on the SEC's website, which maintains the EDGAR (Electronic Data Gathering, Analysis, and Retrieval) database (`www.sec.gov/edgar.shtml`). Just click "Search for Company Filings." Some of the most useful documents you can view there include the following:

>> **Form 3:** This form is the initial statement that insiders provide. They must file Form 3 within ten days of obtaining insider status. An insider files this report even if he hasn't made a purchase yet; the report establishes the insider's status.

>> **Form 4:** This document shows the insider's activity, such as a change in the insider's position as a stockholder, how many shares the person bought and sold, or other relevant changes. Any activity in a particular month must be reported on Form 4 by the 10th of the following month.

>> **Form 5:** This annual report covers transactions that are small and not required on Form 4, such as minor, internal transfers of stock.

>> **Form 144:** This form serves as the public declaration by an insider of the intention to sell *restricted stock* — stock that the insider was awarded, received from the company as compensation, or bought as a term of employment. Insiders must hold restricted stock for at least one year before they can sell it. After an insider decides to sell, she files Form 144 and then must sell within 90 days or submit a new Form 144. The insider must file the form on or before the stock's sale date. When the sale is finalized, the insider is then required to file Form 4.

For a more comprehensive list of insider forms (among others that are filed by public companies), go to www.sec.gov/info/edgar/forms/edgform.pdf.

TIP

Companies are required to make public the documents that track their trading activity. The SEC's website offers limited access to these documents, but for greater access, check out one of the many websites that report insider trading data, such as www.marketwatch.com and www.bloomberg.com.

TECHNICAL
STUFF

The SEC has enacted the *short-swing profit rule* to protect the investing public. This rule prevents insiders from quickly buying the stock that they just sold at a profit. The insider must wait at least six months before buying it again. The SEC created this rule to prevent insiders from using their privileged knowledge to make an unfair profit quickly, before the investing public can react. The rule also applies if an insider sells stock — he can't sell it at a higher price within a six-month period.

FIGHTING ACCOUNTING FRAUD: THE SARBANES-OXLEY ACT

Very often, a market that reaches a mania stage sees abuse reach extreme conditions as well. Abuse by insiders is a good example. In the stock market mania of 1997–2000, this abuse wasn't limited to just insider buying and selling of stock; it also covered the related abuse of accounting fraud. (Companies like Enron in 2001 and Fannie Mae in 2008 come to mind.) The top management executives at several prominent companies deceived investors about the companies' financial conditions and subsequently were able to increase the perceived value of the companies' stock. The stock could then be sold at a price that was higher than market value.

Congress took notice of these activities and, in 2002, passed the Sarbanes-Oxley Act (SOX). Congress designed this act to protect investors from fraudulent accounting activities by corporations. SOX established a public accounting oversight board and also tightened the rules on corporate financial reporting. To find out more about this act, you can either do a search for it at www.congress.gov or get details from sites such as www.sox-online.com and www.findlaw.com.

Looking at Insider Transactions

The classic phrase "actions speak louder than words" was probably coined for insider trading. Insiders are in the know, and keeping a watchful eye on their transactions — both buying and selling their company's stock — can provide you with very useful investing information. But insider buying and insider selling can be as different as day and night; insider buying is simple, while insider selling can be complicated. In the following sections, I present both sides of insider trading.

Breaking down insider buying

Insider buying is usually an unambiguous signal about how an insider feels about his company. After all, the primary reason that all investors buy stock is that they expect it to do well. If one insider is buying stock, that's generally not a monumental event. But if several or more insiders are buying, those purchases should certainly catch your attention.

Insider buying is generally a positive omen and beneficial for the stock's price. Also, when insiders buy stock, less stock is available to the public. If the investing public meets this decreased supply with increased demand, the stock price rises. Keep these factors in mind when analyzing insider buying:

>> **Identify who's buying the stock.** The CEO is buying 5,000 shares. Is that reason enough for you to jump in? Maybe. After all, the CEO certainly knows how well the company is doing. But what if that CEO is just starting her new position? What if before this purchase she had no stock in the company at all? Maybe the stock is part of her employment package.

REMEMBER

The fact that a new company executive is making her first stock purchase isn't as strong a signal urging you to buy as the fact that a long-time CEO is doubling her holdings. Also, if large numbers of insiders are buying, that sends a stronger signal than if a single insider is buying.

>> **See how much is being bought.** In the preceding example, the CEO bought 5,000 shares, which is a lot of stock no matter how you count it. But is it enough for you to base an investment decision on? Maybe, but a closer look may reveal more. If she already owned 1 million shares at the time of the purchase, then buying 5,000 additional shares wouldn't be such an exciting indicator of a pending stock rise. In this case, 5,000 shares is a small incremental move that doesn't offer much to get excited about.

However, what if this particular insider has owned only 5,000 shares for the past three years and is now buying 1 million shares? Now that should arouse your interest! Usually, a massive purchase tells you that particular insider has strong feelings about the company's prospects and that she's making a huge increase in her share of stock ownership. Still, a purchase of 1 million shares by the CEO isn't as strong a signal as ten insiders buying 100,000 shares each. Again, if only one person is buying, that may or may not be a strong indication of an impending rise. However, if lots of people are buying, consider it a fantastic indication.

REMEMBER

An insider purchase of any kind is a positive sign, but it's always more significant when a greater number of insiders are making purchases. "The more the merrier!" is a good rule for judging insider buying. All these individuals have their own, unique perspectives on the company and its prospects. Mass buying indicates mass optimism for the company's future. If the treasurer, the president, the vice president of sales, and several other key players are putting their wealth on the line and investing it in a company they know intimately, that's a good sign for your stock investment as well.

>> **Notice the timing of the purchase.** The timing of insider stock purchases is important as well. If I tell you that five insiders bought stock at various points last year, you may say, "Hmm." But if I tell you that all five people bought substantial chunks of stock at the same time and right before earnings season, that should make you say, "HMMMMM!"

Picking up tips from insider selling

Insider stock buying is rarely negative — it either bodes well for the stock or is a neutral event at worst. But how about insider selling? When an insider sells his stock, the event can be either neutral or negative. Insider selling is usually a little tougher to figure out than insider buying because insiders may have many different motivations to sell stock that have nothing to do with the company's future prospects. Just because the president of the company is selling 5,000 shares from his personal portfolio doesn't necessarily mean you should sell, too.

Insiders may sell their stock for a couple of reasons: They may think that the company won't be doing well in the near future — a negative sign for you — or they may simply need the money for a variety of personal reasons that have nothing to do with the company's potential. Some typical reasons why insiders may sell stock include the following:

>> **To diversify their holdings:** If an insider's portfolio is heavily weighted with one company's stock, a financial advisor may suggest that she balance her portfolio by selling some of that company's stock and purchasing other securities.

>> **To finance personal emergencies:** Sometimes an insider needs money for medical, legal, or family reasons.

>> **To buy a home or make another major purchase:** An insider may need the money to make a down payment on a home or other real estate purchase, to fund college for a child, or perhaps to buy something outright (such as a car or snazzy vacation) without having to take out a loan.

REMEMBER

How do you find out about the details regarding insider stock selling? Although insiders must report their pertinent stock sales and purchases to the SEC, the information isn't always revealing. As a general rule, consider the following questions when analyzing insider selling:

>> **How many insiders are selling?** If only one insider is selling, that single transaction doesn't give you enough information to act on. However, if many insiders are selling, you should see a red flag. Check out any news or information that's currently available by going to websites such as www.marketwatch.com, www.sec.gov, and finance.yahoo.com (along with other sources in Appendix A).

>> **Are the sales showing a pattern or unusual activity?** If one insider sold some stock last month, that sale alone isn't that significant an event. However, if ten insiders have each made multiple sales in the past few months, those sales are cause for concern. See whether any new developments at the company are potentially negative. If massive insider selling has recently occurred, and you don't know why, consider putting a stop-loss order on your stock immediately. I cover stop-loss orders more fully in Chapter 17.

>> **How much stock is being sold?** If a CEO sells 5,000 shares of stock but still retains 100,000 shares, that's not a big deal. But if the CEO sells all or most of his holdings, that's a possible negative. Check to see whether other company executives have also sold stock.

>> **Do outside events or analyst reports seem coincidental with the sale of the stock?** Sometimes, an influential analyst may issue a report warning about a company's prospects. If the company's management pooh-poohs the report but most of them are bailing out anyway (selling their stock), you may want to do the same. Frequently, when insiders know that damaging information is forthcoming, they sell the stock before it takes a dip.

Similarly, if the company's management issues positive public statements or reports that contradict their own behavior (they're selling their stock holdings), the SEC may investigate to see whether the company is doing anything that may require a penalty (the SEC regularly tracks insider sales).

Considering Corporate Stock Buybacks

When you read the financial pages or watch the financial shows on TV, you sometimes hear that a company is buying its own stock. The announcement may be something like, "SuperBucks Corp. has announced that it will spend $2 billion to buy back its own stock." Why would a company do that, and what does that mean to you if you own the stock or are considering buying it?

When companies buy back their own stock, they're generally indicating that they believe their stock is undervalued and that it has the potential to rise. If a company shows strong fundamentals (for example, good financial condition and increasing sales and earnings; see Chapters 8 and 11 for details) and it's buying more of its own stock, it's worth investigating — it may make a great addition to your portfolio.

REMEMBER

Just because a company announces a stock buyback doesn't always mean that one will happen. The announcement itself is meant to stir interest in the stock and cause the price to rise. The stock buyback may be only an opportunity for insiders to sell stock or it may be needed for executive compensation — recruiting and retaining competent management are positive uses of money.

The following sections present some common reasons a company may buy back its shares from investors, as well as some ideas on the negative effects of stock buybacks.

WARNING

If you see that a company is buying back its stock while most of the insiders are selling their personal shares, that's not a good sign. It may not necessarily be a bad sign, but it's not a positive sign. Play it safe and invest elsewhere.

Understanding why a company buys back shares

You bought this book because you're looking at buying stocks, but individuals aren't alone in the stock-buying universe. No, I don't just mean that mutual funds, pensions, and other entities are buyers; I mean the companies behind the stocks are buyers (and sellers), too. Why would a public company buy stock — especially its own?

Boosting earnings per share

By simply buying back its own shares from stockholders, a company can increase its earnings per share without actually earning extra money (see Chapters 8 and 11 as well as Appendix B for more on earnings per share). Sound like a magician's trick? Well, it is, kind of. A corporate stock buyback is a financial sleight of hand that investors should be aware of.

Here's how it works: Noware Earnings, Inc. (NEI), has 10 million shares outstanding, and it's expected to net earnings of $10 million for the fourth quarter. NEI's earnings per share (EPS) would be $1 per share. So far so good. But what happens if NEI buys 2 million of its own shares? Total shares outstanding shrink to 8 million. The new EPS becomes $1.25 — the stock buyback artificially boosts the earnings per share by 25 percent!

REMEMBER

The important point to keep in mind about stock buybacks is that actual company earnings don't change — no fundamental changes occur in company management or operations — so the increase in EPS can be misleading. But the marketplace can be obsessive about earnings, and because earnings are the lifeblood of any company, an earnings boost, even if it's cosmetic, can also boost the stock price.

If you watch a company's price-to-earnings ratio (see Chapter 8, Chapter 11, and Appendix B), you know that increased earnings usually mean an eventual increase in the stock price. Additionally, a stock buyback affects supply and demand. With less available stock in the market, demand necessarily sends the stock price upward.

REMEMBER

Whenever a company makes a major purchase, such as buying back its own stock, think about how the company is paying for it and whether it seems like a good use of the company's purchasing power. In general, companies buy their stock for the same reasons any investor buys stock — they believe that the stock is a good investment and will appreciate in time. Companies generally pay for a stock buyback in one of two basic ways: funds from operations or borrowed money. Both methods have a downside. For more details, see the later section "Exploring the downside of buybacks."

Beating back a takeover bid

Suppose you read in the financial pages that Company X is doing a hostile takeover of Company Z. A hostile takeover doesn't mean that Company X sends storm troopers armed with mace to Company Z's headquarters to trounce its management. All a *hostile takeover* means is that X wants to buy enough shares of Z's stock to effectively control Z (and Z is unhappy about being owned or controlled by X). Because buying and selling stock happens in a public market or exchange, companies can buy each other's stock. Sometimes, the target company prefers not to be acquired, in which case it may buy back shares of its own stock to give it a measure of protection against unwanted moves by interested companies.

In some cases, the company attempting the takeover already owns some of the target company's stock. In this case, the targeted company may offer to buy those shares back from the aggressor at a premium to thwart the takeover bid. This type of offer is often referred to as *greenmail.*

REMEMBER

Takeover concerns generally prompt interest in the investing public, driving the stock price upward and benefiting current stockholders.

Exploring the downside of buybacks

As beneficial as stock buybacks can be, they have to be paid for, and this expense has consequences. When a company uses funds from operations for the stock buyback, less money is available for other activities, such as upgrading technology, making improvements, or doing research and development. A company faces even greater dangers when it uses debt to finance a stock buyback. If the company uses borrowed funds, not only does it have less borrowing power for other uses, but it also has to pay back the borrowed funds with interest, thus lowering earnings figures.

REMEMBER

In general, any misuse of money, such as using debt to buy back stock, affects a company's ability to grow its sales and earnings — two measures that need to maintain upward mobility to keep stock prices rising.

Say that Noware Earnings, Inc. (NEI), typically pays an annual dividend of 25 cents per share of stock and wants to buy back shares, which are currently at $10 each, with borrowed money with a 9 percent interest rate. If NEI buys back 2 million shares, it won't have to pay out $500,000 in dividends (2 million multiplied by 25 cents). That's money saved. However, NEI has to pay interest on the $20 million it borrowed ($10 per share multiplied by 2 million shares) to buy back the shares. The interest totals $1.8 million (9 percent of $20 million), and the net result from this rudimentary example is that NEI sees an outflow of $1.3 million (the difference between the interest paid out and the dividends savings).

Using debt to finance a stock buyback needs to make economic sense — it needs to strengthen the company's financial position. Perhaps NEI could have used the stock buyback money toward a better purpose, such as modernizing equipment or paying for a new marketing campaign. Because debt interest ultimately decreases earnings, companies must be careful when using debt to buy back their stock.

Stock Splits: Nothing to Go Bananas Over

Frequently, management teams decide to do a stock split. A *stock split* is the exchange of existing shares of stock for new shares from the same company. Stock splits don't increase or decrease the company's capitalization; they just change the number of shares available in the market and the per-share price.

Typically, a company may announce that it's doing a 2-for-1 stock split. For example, a company may have 10 million shares outstanding, with a market price of $40 each. In a 2-for-1 split, the company then has 20 million shares (the share total doubles), but the market price is adjusted to $20 (the share price is halved). Companies do other splits, such as a 3-for-2 or 4-for-1, but 2-for-1 is the most common split.

The following sections present the two basic types of splits: ordinary stock splits and reverse stock splits.

TIP

Qualifying for a stock split is similar to qualifying to receive a dividend — you must be listed as a stockholder as of the date of record. Keep good records regarding your stock splits in case you need to calculate capital gains for tax purposes. (For information on the date of record, see Chapter 6. See Chapter 21 for tax information.)

Ordinary stock splits

An *ordinary stock split* — when the number of stock shares increases — is the kind investors usually hear about. If you own 100 shares of Dublin, Inc., stock (at $60 per share) and the company announces a stock split, what happens? If you own the stock in certificate form (which is very rare now), you receive in the mail a stock certificate for 100 more shares. Now, before you cheer over how your money just doubled, check the stock's new price. Each share is adjusted to a $30 value.

TIP

Not all stock is in certificate form. Stocks held in a brokerage account are recorded in book entry form. Most stock, in fact, is in book entry form. A company issues stock certificates only when necessary or when the investor requests it. If you keep the stock in your brokerage account, check with your broker for the new share total to make sure you're credited with the new number of shares after the stock split.

REMEMBER

An ordinary stock split is primarily a neutral event, so why does a company bother to do it? The most common reason is that management believes the stock is too expensive, so it wants to lower the stock price to make the stock more affordable and, therefore, more attractive to new investors. Studies have shown that stock splits frequently precede a rise in the stock price. Although stock splits are considered a non-event in and of themselves, many stock experts see them as bullish signals because of the interest they generate among the investing public.

Reverse stock splits

A *reverse stock split* usually occurs when a company's management wants to raise the price of its stock. Just as ordinary splits can occur when management believes the price is too expensive, a reverse stock split means the company feels that the stock's price is too cheap. If a stock's price looks too low, that may discourage interest by individual or institutional investors (such as mutual funds). Management wants to drum up more interest in the stock for the benefit of shareholders (some of whom are probably insiders).

The company may also do a reverse split to decrease costs. When you have to send an annual report and other correspondence regularly to all the stockholders, the mailings can get a little pricey, especially if you have lots of investors who own only a few shares each. A reverse split helps consolidate shares and lower overall management costs.

A reverse split can best be explained with an example. TuCheep, Inc. (TCI), is selling at $2 per share on the Nasdaq. At that rock-bottom price, the investing public may ignore it. So TCI announces a 10-for-1 reverse stock split. Now what? If a stockholder had 100 shares at $2 (the old shares), the stockholder now owns 10 shares at $20.

WARNING

Technically, a reverse split is considered a neutral event. However, just as investors may infer positive expectations from an ordinary stock split, they may have negative expectations from a reverse split because a reverse split tends to occur for negative reasons. One definitive negative reason for a reverse split is if the company's stock is threatened to be delisted. If a stock is on a major exchange and the price falls below $1, the stock will face *delisting* (basically getting removed from the exchange). A reverse split may be used to ward off such an event. The bottom line is that a reverse split is ultimately a negative event and investors should avoid the stock.

TECHNICAL STUFF

If, in the event of a stock split, you end up with an odd number of shares, the company doesn't produce a fractional share. Instead, you get a check for the cash equivalent. For example, if you have 51 shares and the company announces a 2-for-1 reverse split, odds are that you'll get 25 shares and a cash payout for the odd share (or fractional share).

Keeping a Close Eye on Congress

The latest sensation in the world of insider trading has been how congresspeople of both parties have reaped fortunes by doing something that's illegal for you and me — but was legal for them! For those folks who've wondered how someone can spend millions to get a "public service" job and then retire a multimillionaire, now you have a clue: congressional insider trading.

Congressmen and women, as you know, pass laws for a variety of matters. They know which companies stand to lose or benefit as a result. They can then invest in the winners and/or avoid (or go short) the losers. (When you *go short* on a stock, you make money by selling high and then buying low; to get a good idea about how short selling works, see Chapter 17.) Many were able to easily reap million-dollar gains because of this privileged perch they stood on.

Some folks in Congress made outrageous profits from shorting strategies during the 2008 crash when they learned of pending financial developments behind closed doors before the public (and most investors) found out. It's maddening that these politicians profited (legally!) from activities that you and I would have ended up in jail for doing.

From the furor in late 2011 over this incredible corruption came a new law passed in early 2012: the Stop Trading on Congressional Knowledge (STOCK) Act (Public Law 112-105). This law was a great start, but it was quietly amended in 2013, and important enforcement provisions were watered down (ugh!). To find out more, you can go to the site for the Office of Government Ethics (www.oge.gov) and discover other sources through your favorite search engine.

TIP

Finding out about corporate insiders and their significant transactions is easier than ever in the digital age, but finding out about government officials' insider trading is still elusive. Given that, it pays to be more vigilant about politicians through the financial and watchdog sites mentioned in this chapter and with some of the resources mentioned in Appendix A.

Chapter **21**

Keeping More of Your Money from the Taxman

After conquering the world of making money with stocks, now you have another hurdle — keeping your hard-earned money! Some people may tell you that taxes are brutal, complicated, and counterproductive. Others may tell you that they're a form of legalized thievery, and still others may say that they're a necessary evil. And then there are the pessimists. In any case, this chapter shows you how to keep more of the fruits from your hard-earned labor.

REMEMBER

Keep in mind that this chapter isn't meant to be comprehensive. For a fuller treatment of personal taxes, you should check with your personal tax advisor and get the publications referenced in this chapter by either visiting the IRS website at www.irs.gov or calling the IRS publications department at 800-829-3676.

However, in this chapter, I cover the most relevant points for stock investors, such as the tax treatment for dividends and capital gains and losses, common tax deductions for investors, some simple tax-reduction strategies, and pointers for retirement investing. And yes, I cover these points through the lens of the recent tax law changes.

TIP

Tax laws can be very hairy and perplexing, and you can easily feel like the mouse going through the maze trying to either find the cheese (a tax refund) or just keep more of the hard-earned cheese you took home. Higher (and more complicated) taxes generally aren't good for stock investors or the economy at large, but fortunately the recent tax laws do have some good news for most investors. But no matter how friendly or unfriendly the tax environment is, you should stay informed through your tax advisor, online tax information sources, and taxpayer advocacy groups like the National Taxpayers Union (www.ntu.org). 'Nuff said.

TIP

An easy place to see the tax reform changes is www.taxchanges.us. It's a service of the IRS's Taxpayer Advocate Service (found at https://taxpayeradvocate.irs.gov/). It shows you the tax changes for 2018, 2019, and subsequent tax years, and it also shows you what changes have occurred either by looking at the actual line items on Form 1040 or by topic or subtopic. It even shows you how to calculate your paycheck's withholdings so you can more closely match the withholdings to the new potential tax rates to avoid under- or over-withholding.

Paying through the Nose: The Tax Treatment of Different Investments

The following sections tell you what you need to know about the tax implications you face when you start investing in stocks. It's good to know in advance the basics on ordinary income, capital gains, and capital losses because they may affect your investing strategy and your long-term wealth-building plans.

Understanding ordinary income and capital gains

Profit you make from your stock investments can be taxed in one of two ways, depending on the type of profit:

>> **Ordinary income:** Your profit can be taxed at the same rate as wages or interest — at your full, regular tax rate. If your tax bracket is 28 percent, for example, that's the rate at which your ordinary income investment profit is taxed. Two types of investment profits get taxed as ordinary income (check out IRS Publication 550, "Investment Income and Expenses," for more information):

  • **Dividends:** When you receive dividends (either in cash or stock), they're taxed as ordinary income. This is true even if those dividends are in a dividend reinvestment plan (see Chapter 19 to find out more about these plans). If, however, the dividends occur in a tax-sheltered plan, such as an IRA or 401(k) plan, then they're exempt from taxes for as long as they're in the plan. (Retirement plans are covered in the later section "Taking Advantage of Tax-Advantaged Retirement Investing.")

Keep in mind that qualified dividends are taxed at a lower rate than nonqualified dividends. A *qualified dividend* is a dividend that receives preferential tax treatment versus other types of dividends, such as unqualified dividends or interest. Typically a dividend is qualified if it is issued by a U.S. corporation (or a foreign corporation listed on U.S. stock exchanges), and the stock is held longer than 60 days. An example of an ordinary dividend that is not qualified is a dividend paid out by a money market fund or a bond-related exchange-traded fund (because the dividend is technically interest).

- **Short-term capital gains:** If you sell stock for a gain and you've owned the stock for one year or less, the gain is considered ordinary income. To calculate the time, you use the *trade date* (or *date of execution*). This is the date on which you executed the order, not the settlement date. (For more on important dates, see Chapter 6.) However, if these gains occur in a tax-sheltered plan, such as a 401(k) or an IRA, no tax is triggered.

>> **Long-term capital gains:** These are usually much better for you than ordinary income or short-term gains as far as taxes are concerned. The tax laws reward patient investors. After you've held the stock for at least a year and a day (what a difference a day makes!), your tax rate on that gain may be lower. (See the next section for more specifics on potential savings.) Get more information on capital gains in IRS Publication 550. Fortunately, you can time stock sales, so always consider pushing back the sale date (if possible) to take advantage of the lesser capital gains tax.

REMEMBER

You can control how you manage the tax burden from your investment profits. Gains are taxable only if a sale actually takes place (in other words, only if the gain is "realized"). If your stock in GazillionBucks, Inc., goes from $5 per share to $87, that $82 appreciation isn't subject to taxation unless you actually sell the stock. Until you sell, that gain is "unrealized." Time your stock sales carefully and hold onto stocks for at least a year and a day (to make the gains long-term) to minimize the amount of taxes you have to pay on them.

TIP

When you buy stock, record the date of purchase and the *cost basis* (the purchase price of the stock plus any ancillary charges, such as commissions). This information is very important come tax time should you decide to sell your stock. The date of purchase (also known as the *date of execution*) helps establish the *holding period* (how long you own the stocks) that determines whether your gains are considered short-term or long-term.

Say you buy 100 shares of GazillionBucks, Inc., at $5 and pay a commission of $8. Your cost basis is $508 (100 shares times $5 plus $8 commission). If you sell the stock at $87 per share and pay a $12 commission, the total sale amount is $8,688 (100 shares times $87 minus $12 commission). If this sale occurs less than a year after the purchase, it's a short-term gain. In the 28 percent tax bracket, the short-term gain of $8,180 ($8,688 − $508) is also taxed at 28 percent. Read the following section to see the tax implications if your gain is a long-term gain.

Any gain (or loss) from a short sale is considered short-term regardless of how long the position is held open. For more information on the mechanics of selling short, check out Chapter 17.

Minimizing the tax on your capital gains

Long-term capital gains are taxed at a more favorable rate than ordinary income. To qualify for long-term capital gains treatment, you must hold the investment for more than one year (in other words, for at least one year and one day).

Recall the example in the preceding section with GazillionBucks, Inc. As a short-term transaction at the 28 percent tax rate, the tax is $2,290 ($8,180 multiplied by 28 percent). After you revive, you say, "Gasp! What a chunk of dough. I better hold off a while longer." You hold onto the stock for more than a year to achieve the status of long-term capital gains. How does that change the tax? For anyone in the 28 percent tax bracket or higher, the long-term capital gains rate of 15 percent applies. In this case, the tax is $1,227 ($8,180 multiplied by 15 percent), resulting in a tax savings to you of $1,063 ($2,290 less $1,227). Okay, it's not a fortune, but it's a substantial difference from the original tax. After all, successful stock investing isn't only about making money; it's about keeping it too.

Capital gains taxes *can* be lower than the tax on ordinary income, but they aren't higher. If, for example, you're in the 15 percent tax bracket for ordinary income and you have a long-term capital gain that would normally bump you up to the 28 percent tax bracket, the gain is taxed at your lower rate of 15 percent instead of a higher capital gains rate. Check with your tax advisor on a regular basis because this rule could change due to new tax laws.

REMEMBER

Don't sell a stock just because it qualifies for long-term capital gains treatment, even if the sale eases your tax burden. If the stock is doing well and meets your investing criteria, hold onto it.

DEBT AND TAXES: ANOTHER ANGLE

If you truly need cash but you don't want to sell your stock because it's doing well, and you want to avoid paying capital gains tax, consider borrowing against it. If the stock is listed (on the New York Stock Exchange, for example) and is in a brokerage account with margin privileges, you can borrow up to 50 percent of the value of marginable securities at favorable rates (listed stocks are marginable securities). The money you borrow is considered a margin loan (see Chapter 17 for details), and the interest you pay is low (compared to credit cards or personal loans) because it's considered a secured loan (your stock acts as collateral). On those rare occasions when I use margin, I usually make sure I use stocks that generate a high dividend. That way, the stocks themselves help pay off the margin loan. In addition, if the proceeds are used for an investment purpose, the margin interest may be tax-deductible. See IRS Publication 550 for more details.

Coping with capital losses

Ever think that having the value of your stocks fall could be a good thing? Perhaps the only real positive regarding losses in your portfolio is that they can reduce your taxes. A *capital loss* means that you lost money on your investments. This amount is generally deductible on your tax return, and you can claim a loss on either long-term or short-term stock holdings. This loss can go against your other income and lower your overall tax.

Say you bought Worth Zilch Co. stock for a total purchase price of $3,500 and sold it later at a sale price of $800. Your tax-deductible capital loss is $2,700.

REMEMBER

The one string attached to deducting investment losses on your tax return is that the most you can report in a single year is $3,000. On the bright side, though, any excess loss isn't really lost — you can carry it forward to the next year. If you have net investment losses of $4,500 in 2019, you can deduct $3,000 in 2019, and carry the remaining $1,500 loss over to 2020, and deduct it on your 2020 tax return. That $1,500 loss may then offset any gains you are looking to realize in 2020.

Before you can deduct losses, you must first use them to offset any capital gains. If you realize long-term capital gains of $7,000 in Stock A and long-term capital losses of $6,000 in Stock B, then you have a net long-term capital gain of $1,000 ($7,000 gain minus the offset of $6,000 loss). Whenever possible, see whether losses in your portfolio can be realized to offset any capital gains to reduce potential tax. IRS Publication 550 includes information for investors on capital gains and losses.

TIP

Here's your optimum strategy: Where possible, keep losses on a short-term basis, and push your gains into long-term capital gains status. If a transaction can't be tax-free, at the very least try to defer the tax to keep your money working for you.

Evaluating gains and losses scenarios

Of course, any investor can come up with hundreds of possible gains and losses scenarios. For example, you may wonder what happens if you sell part of your holdings now as a short-term capital loss and the remainder later as a long-term capital gain. You must look at each sale of stock (or potential sale) methodically to calculate the gain or loss you would realize from it. Figuring out your gain or loss isn't that complicated. Here are some general rules to help you wade through the morass. If you add up all your gains and losses and

>> **The net result is a short-term gain:** It's taxed at your highest tax bracket (as ordinary income).

>> **The net result is a long-term gain:** It's taxed at 15 percent if you're in the 28 percent tax bracket or higher. Check with your tax advisor on changes here that may affect your taxes.

>> **The net result is a loss of $3,000 or less:** It's fully deductible against other income. If you're married filing separately, your deduction limit is $1,500.

>> **The net result is a loss that exceeds $3,000:** You can only deduct up to $3,000 in that year; the remainder goes forward to future years.

Sharing Your Gains with the IRS

Of course, you don't want to pay more taxes than you have to, but as the old cliché goes, "Don't let the tax tail wag the investment dog." You should buy or sell a stock because it makes economic sense first, and consider the tax implications as secondary issues. After all, taxes consume a relatively small portion of your gain. As long as you experience a *net gain* (gain after all transaction costs, including taxes, brokerage fees, and other related fees), consider yourself a successful investor — even if you have to give away some of your gain to taxes.

TIP

Try to make tax planning second nature in your day-to-day activities. No, you don't have to consume yourself with a blizzard of paperwork and tax projections. I simply mean that when you make a stock transaction, keep the receipt and order confirmation and maintain good records. When you're considering a large purchase or sale, pause for a moment, and ask yourself whether this transaction will have positive or negative tax consequences. (Refer to the earlier section "Paying through the Nose: The Tax Treatment of Different Investments" to review various tax scenarios.) Speak to a tax consultant beforehand to discuss the ramifications.

In the following sections, I describe the tax forms you need to fill out, as well as some important rules to follow.

Filling out forms

Most investors report their investment-related activities on their individual tax returns (Form 1040). The reports that you'll likely receive from brokers and other investment sources include the following:

>> **Brokerage and bank statements:** Monthly statements that you receive

>> **Trade confirmations:** Documents to confirm that you bought or sold stock

>> **1099-DIV:** Reporting dividends paid to you

>> **1099-INT:** Reporting interest paid to you

>> **1099-B:** Reporting gross proceeds submitted to you from the sale of investments, such as stocks and mutual funds

REMEMBER

You may receive other, more obscure forms that aren't listed here. You should retain all documents related to your stock investments.

The IRS schedules and forms that most stock investors need to be aware of and/or attach to their Form 1040 include the following:

>> **Schedule B:** To report interest and dividends

>> **Schedule D:** To report capital gains and losses

>> **Form 4952:** Investment Interest Expense Deduction

>> **Publication 17:** Guide to Form 1040

You can get these publications directly from the IRS at 800-829-3676, or you can download them from the website (www.irs.gov). For more information on what records and documentation investors should hang onto, check out IRS Publication 552, "Recordkeeping for Individuals."

TIP

If you plan to do your own taxes, consider using the latest tax software products, which are inexpensive and easy to use. These programs usually have a question-and-answer feature to help you do your taxes step by step, and they include all the necessary forms. Consider getting either TurboTax (www.turbotax.com) or H&R Block at Home (formerly TaxCut; www.hrblock.com/tax-software) at your local software vendor or the companies' websites. Alternatively, you can get free tax preparation software at www.taxact.com.

Playing by the rules

WARNING

Some people get the smart idea of "Hey! Why not sell my losing stock by December 31 to grab the short-term loss and just buy back the stock on January 2 so that I can have my cake and eat it, too?" Not so fast. The IRS puts the kibosh on maneuvers like that with something called the *wash-sale rule.* This rule states that if you sell a stock for a loss and buy it back within 30 days, the loss isn't valid because you didn't make any substantial investment change. The wash-sale rule applies only to losses. The way around the rule is simple: Wait at least 31 days before you buy that identical stock back again.

Some people try to get around the wash-sale rule by doubling up on their stock position with the intention of selling half. Therefore, the IRS makes the 30-day rule cover both sides of the sale date. That way, an investor can't buy the identical stock within 30 days just before the sale and then realize a short-term loss for tax purposes.

Discovering the Softer Side of the IRS: Tax Deductions for Investors

In the course of managing your portfolio of stocks and other investments, you'll probably incur expenses that are tax-deductible. The tax laws allow you to write off certain investment-related expenses as itemized expenses on Schedule A — an attachment to IRS Form 1040. Keep records of your deductions and retain a checklist to remind you which deductions you normally take. IRS Publication 550 ("Investment Income and Expenses") gives you more details.

The following sections explain common tax deductions for investors: investment interest, miscellaneous expenses, and donations to charity. I also list a few items you *can't* deduct.

WARNING

Keep in mind that for 2018, 2019, and beyond, the standard deduction for individuals has increased significantly, so you may not need to itemize on Schedule A since the standard deduction will give you a greater tax benefit. For 2019, the standard deduction for those married filing jointly is $24,400 (in 2018 it was $24,000). Because the 2018 tax act made the standard deduction significantly higher (in 2017 it was only $12,700 for married filing jointly), itemizing (using Schedule A) was less attractive since total itemized deductions needed to be at a higher total than the standard deduction before itemizing made tax sense. The issue for stock investors is that many investment-related deductible expenses are claimed as itemized (Schedule A) expenses, so it will be more difficult to clear the hurdle of the new, higher standard deduction.

Investment interest

If you pay any interest to a stockbroker, such as margin interest or any interest to acquire a taxable financial investment, that's considered investment interest and is usually fully deductible as an itemized expense.

WARNING

Keep in mind that not all interest is deductible. Consumer interest or interest paid for any consumer or personal purpose isn't deductible. For more general information, see the section covering interest in IRS Publication 17.

Miscellaneous expenses

Most investment-related deductions are reported as miscellaneous expenses. Here are some common deductions:

>> Accounting or bookkeeping fees for keeping records of investment income

>> Any expense related to tax service, tax programs, or tax education

>> Computer expense — you can take a depreciation deduction for your computer if you use it 50 percent of the time or more for managing your investments

>> Investment management or investment advisor's fees (fees paid for advice on tax-exempt investments aren't deductible)

>> Legal fees involving stockholder issues

>> Safe-deposit box rental fee or home safe to hold your securities, unless used to hold personal effects or tax-exempt securities

>> Service charges for collecting interest and dividends

» Subscription fees for investment advisory services

» Travel costs to check investments or to confer with advisors regarding income-related investments

REMEMBER

You can deduct only that portion of your miscellaneous expenses that exceeds 2 percent of your adjusted gross income. For more information on deducting miscellaneous expenses, check out IRS Publication 529.

Donations of stock to charity

What happens if you donate stock to your favorite (IRS-approved) charity? Because it's a noncash charitable contribution, you can deduct the market value of the stock.

Say that last year you bought stock for $2,000 and it's worth $4,000 this year. If you donate it this year, you can write off the market value at the time of the contribution. In this case, you have a $4,000 deduction. Use IRS Form 8283, which is an attachment to Schedule A, to report noncash contributions exceeding $500.

TIP

To get more guidance from the IRS on this matter, get Publication 526, "Charitable Contributions."

Items that you can't deduct

WARNING

Just to be complete, here are some items you may think you can deduct, but alas, you can't:

» Financial planning or investment seminars

» Any costs connected with attending stockholder meetings

» Home office expenses for managing your investments

Taking Advantage of Tax-Advantaged Retirement Investing

If you're going to invest for the long term (such as your retirement), you may as well maximize your use of tax-sheltered retirement plans. Many different types of plans are available; I touch on only the most popular ones in the following sections.

Although retirement plans may not seem relevant for investors who buy and sell stocks directly (as opposed to a mutual fund), some plans, called *self-directed retirement accounts*, allow you to invest directly.

IRAs

Individual Retirement Accounts (IRAs) are accounts you can open with a financial institution, such as a bank or a mutual fund company. An IRA is available to almost anyone who has earned income, and it allows you to set aside and invest money to help fund your retirement. Opening an IRA is easy, and virtually any bank or mutual fund can guide you through the process. Two basic types of IRAs are traditional and Roth.

Traditional IRA

The traditional Individual Retirement Account (also called the *deductible IRA*) was first popularized in the early 1980s. In a traditional IRA, you can make a tax-deductible contribution of up to $6,000 in 2020 (some restrictions apply). Individuals age 50 and older can make additional "catch-up" investments of $1,000. For 2020 and beyond, the limits will be indexed to inflation.

The money can then grow in the IRA unfettered by current taxes because the money isn't taxed until you take it out. Because IRAs are designed for retirement purposes, you can start taking money out of your IRA in the year you turn 59½. (Hmm. That must really disappoint those who want their money in the year they turn 58¾.) The withdrawals at that point are taxed as ordinary income. Fortunately (hopefully?), you'll probably be in a lower tax bracket then, so the tax shouldn't be as burdensome.

REMEMBER

Keep in mind that you're required to start taking distributions from your account when you reach age 70½ (that's gotta be a bummer for those who prefer the age of 71⅞). After that point, you may no longer contribute to a traditional IRA. Again, check with your tax advisor to see how this criterion affects you personally.

WARNING

If you take out money from an IRA too early, the amount is included in your taxable income, and you may be zapped with a 10 percent penalty. You can avoid the penalty if you have a good reason. The IRS provides a list of reasons in Publication 590-B, "Distributions from Individual Retirement Arrangements (IRAs)."

To put money into an IRA, you must earn income equal to or greater than the amount you're contributing. *Earned income* is money made either as an employee or a self-employed person. Although traditional IRAs can be great for investors, the toughest part about them is qualifying — they have income limitations and other qualifiers that make them less deductible based on how high your income is. See IRS Publication 590-A, "Contributions to Individual Retirement Arrangements (IRAs)," for more details.

TIP

Wait a minute! If IRAs usually involve mutual funds or bank investments, how does the stock investor take advantage of them? Here's how: Stock investors can open a self-directed IRA with a brokerage firm. This means that you can buy and sell stocks in the account with no taxes on dividends or capital gains. The account is tax-deferred, so you don't have to worry about taxes until you start making withdrawals. Also, many dividend reinvestment plans (DRPs) can be set up as IRAs as well. See Chapter 19 for more about DRPs.

Roth IRA

The Roth IRA is a great retirement plan that I wish had existed a long time ago. Here are some ways to distinguish the Roth IRA from the traditional IRA:

>> The Roth IRA provides no tax deduction for contributions.

>> Money in the Roth IRA grows tax-free and can be withdrawn tax-free when you turn 59½.

>> The Roth IRA is subject to early distribution penalties (although there are exceptions). Distributions have to be qualified to be penalty- and tax-free; in other words, make sure that any distribution is within the guidelines set by the IRS (see Publication 590-B).

The maximum contribution per year for Roth IRAs is the same as for traditional IRAs. You can open a self-directed account with a broker as well. See IRS Publication 590-A for details on qualifying.

401(k) plans

Company-sponsored 401(k) plans (named after the section in the tax code that allows them) are widely used and very popular. In a 401(k) plan, companies set aside money from their employees' paychecks that employees can use to invest for retirement. Generally, in 2020 you can invest as much as $19,500 of your pretax earned income and have it grow tax-deferred. Those over age 50 can contribute up to $6,500 as a "catch-up" contribution.

Usually, the money is put in mutual funds administered through a mutual fund company or an insurance firm. Although most 401(k) plans aren't self-directed, I mention them in this book for good reason.

Because your money is in a mutual fund that may invest in stocks, take an active role in finding out the mutual funds in which you're allowed to invest. Most plans offer several types of stock mutual funds. Use your growing knowledge about stocks to make more informed choices about your 401(k) plan options. For more information on 401(k) and other retirement plans, check out IRS Publication 560.

If you're an employee, you can also find out more about retirement plans from the Department of Labor at www.dol.gov.

REMEMBER

Keep in mind that a mutual fund is only as good as what it invests in. Ask the plan administrator some questions about the funds and the types of stocks the plan invests in. Are the stocks defensive or cyclical? Are they growth stocks or income stocks (paying a high dividend)? Are they large cap or small cap? (See Chapter 1 for more about these types of stocks.) If you don't make an informed choice about the investments in your plan, someone else will (such as the plan administrator), and that someone probably doesn't have the same ideas about your money that you do.

5

The Part of Tens

Want to know a great stock when you see one? Discover the top ten indicators.

When markets are down, this part helps you enact some profitable strategies and tactics.

Stocks are not the only game in town (and they shouldn't be); find some great investments to diversify with.

Get a heads up on powerful trends and meltdowns coming in the next decade (2020–2030), and adjust your stock trading strategies to maximize gains (or minimize losses).

Chapter **22**

Ten Indicators of a Great Stock

In a book like this, the ultimate goal would be to identify the Holy Grail of stock investing — *the* stock — the kind of stock that, if stocks were people, then Apple, Amazon, Procter & Gamble, and Microsoft would be peasants compared to this king. Yeah, that's the kind of stock that would be the Grand Pooh-Bah of your portfolio! Well, hold your horses.

That stock is likely in heaven's stock market right now, and you have to be firmly planted on terra firma. If you have a stock that has all the following features, back up the truck and get as much as you can (and let me know so that I can do the same!).

Seriously, I doubt that you'll find a stock with all ten hallmarks described in this chapter, but a stock with even half of them is a super-solid choice. Get a stock with as many hallmarks as possible and you likely have a winner.

The Company Has Rising Profits

The very essence of a successful company is its ability to make a profit. In fact, profit is the single most important financial element of a company. I can even make the case that profit is the single most important element of a successful economy.

Without profit, a company goes out of business. If a business closes its doors, private jobs vanish. In turn, taxes don't get paid. This means that the government can't function and pay its workers and those who are dependent on public assistance. Sorry for veering away from the company's main hallmark, but understanding the importance of profit is vital.

REMEMBER

Profit is what is left after expenses are deducted from sales. When a company manages its expenses well, profits grow. For info on the numbers measuring a company's success, look at Chapters 6 and 11 as well as Appendix B.

The Company Has Rising Sales

Looking at the total sales of a company is referred to as analyzing the *top-line numbers.* Of course, that's because when you're looking at net income (gross sales minus total expenses), you're looking at the bottom line.

A company (or analysts) can play games with many numbers on an income statement; there are a dozen different ways to look at earnings. Earnings are the heart and soul of a company, but the top line gives you an unmistakable and clear number to look it. The total sales (or gross sales or gross revenue) number for a company is harder to fudge.

TIP

It's easy for an investor — especially a novice investor — to look at sales for a company for a particular year and see whether it's doing better or worse than in the prior year. Reviewing three years of sales gives you a good overall gauge of the company's success.

Granted, some years are bad for everyone, so don't expect a company's sales to go up every year like a rocket. Sometimes success is relative; a company with sales down 5 percent is doing fine if every other company in that industry has sales down much more.

Suffice it to say that when a company's total sales are rising, that's a positive sign. The company can overcome other potential issues (such as paying off debt or sudden expenses) much more easily and can pave the way for long-term success.

Check out Appendix B for ways to look at sales and do your own top-line analysis.

The Company Has Low Liabilities

All things being equal, I would rather have a company with relatively low debt than one with high debt. Too much debt can kill an otherwise good company. Debt can consume you, and as you read this, debt is consuming many countries across the globe.

Because a company with low debt has borrowing power, it can take advantage of opportunities such as taking over a rival or acquiring a company that offers an added technology to help propel current or future profit growth.

Notice that I didn't say a company with no debt. Don't get me wrong — a company with no debt or little in the way of liabilities is a solid company. But in an environment where you can borrow at historically low rates, it pays to take on some debt and use it efficiently. In other words, if a company can borrow at, say, 3 percent and put it to use to yield a profit of 5 percent or more, why not?

REMEMBER

Secondly, notice that I'm talking about liabilities. It isn't always conventional debt that may sink a company. What if that company is simply spending more money than it's bringing in? Liabilities or "total liabilities" takes into account everything that a company is obligated to pay, whether it's a long-term bond (long-term debt), paying workers, or the water bill. Current expenses should be more than covered by current income, but you don't want to accumulate long-term debt, which means a drain on future income.

Also, in some industries, the liabilities can take a form that isn't typically conventional debt or monthly expenses. I read a recent industry report that some very large banks and stock brokerage firms have huge positions in *derivatives*, which are complicated financial instruments that can easily turn into crushing debt that could sink a bank.

In my research, for example, I found one Wall Street broker that had total derivatives of a whopping $35 trillion, even though its net worth on its balance sheet was only $104 billion. There is actually an agency that tracks these numbers (the Office of the Comptroller of the Currency at www.occ.gov), and you should check it out when you're considering investing in these types of financial institutions.

The point is that one of the hallmarks of a successful company is to keep liabilities low and manageable. You find a company's debt in its financial statements (such as the balance sheet). Find out more about debt in Chapter 11.

TIP

To discover some good parameters of acceptable debt, look at the company's financial ratios on debt to assets. Get the scoop about this in Appendix B.

The Stock Is at a Bargain Price

Price and value are two different concepts, and they aren't interchangeable. A low price isn't synonymous with getting a bargain. Just as you want the most for your money when you shop, you want to get the most for your money in stock investing.

You can look at the value of a company in several ways, but the first thing I look at is the price-to-earnings ratio (P/E ratio). It attempts to connect the price of the company's stock to the company's net profits quoted on a per-share basis. For example, if a company has a price of $15 per share, and the earnings are $1 per share, then the P/E ratio is 15.

REMEMBER

Generally speaking, a P/E ratio of 15 or less is a good value, especially if the other numbers work out positively (for example, profits and sales are rising, as I note earlier in this chapter). When the economy is in the dumps and stock prices are down, P/E ratios of 10 or lower are even better. Conversely, if the economy is booming, then higher P/E ratios are acceptable.

I consider myself a value investor, so P/E ratios in the teens or better (lower) make me comfortable. However, someone else might bristle at that and consider P/E ratios of 25 or even 50 acceptable. Then again, at those levels (or higher), you're no longer talking about a bargain. Just keep in mind that stocks with much higher P/Es such as 75, 100, and beyond means that stock investors have high expectations for the company's earnings; if the earnings don't materialize, the risk is that the stock will tumble, so be wary of high P/Es.

WARNING

Too many investors see no problem with buying stocks that have no P/E ratio. These stocks may have the P (price of the stock), but they have no E (earnings). If you invest in a company that has losses instead of earnings, then to me you aren't an investor; you're a speculator.

Investing in a company that is losing money is making a bet, and more importantly, it isn't a bargain at all. (However, when you find a company that is losing money, it could be a good shorting opportunity; see Chapter 17 for details.)

A stock may also be a bargain if its market value is at or below its *book value* (the actual accounting value of net assets for the company). You can find out more about book value in Chapter 11.

Dividends Are Growing

Long-term investing is where the true payoff is for today's investors. But before you start staring at your calendar and dreaming of future profits, take a look at the company's current dividend picture.

Dividends are the long-term investor's best friend. Wouldn't it be great if after a few years of owning that stock, you received total dividends that actually dwarfed what your original investment was? That's more common than you know! I've calculated the history of accumulated dividends for a given stock, and it doesn't take as long as you think to get your original investment amount back (counting cumulated dividends). I know some people who bought dividend-paying stocks during a bear market (when stock prices are very low) and got their original investment back after eight to ten years (depending on the stock and its dividend growth, of course).

Dividend growth also carries with it the potential growth of the stock itself. A consistently rising dividend is a positive sign for the stock price. The investing public sees that a growing dividend is a powerful and tangible sign of the company's current and future financial health.

A company may be able to fudge earnings and other soft or malleable figures, but when a dividend is paid, that's hard proof that the company is succeeding with its net profit. Given that, just review the long-term stock chart (say five years or longer) of a consistent dividend-paying company, and 99 times out of 100, that stock price is zigzagging upward in a similar pattern.

I discuss dividends and dividend-growing stocks in Chapter 9. For exchange-traded funds (ETFs) that have dividend stocks in their portfolios, see Chapter 5. Lastly, check out resources on dividend investing strategies in Appendix A.

The Market Is Growing

In this context, when I say that the market is growing, I mean the market of consumers for a given product. If more and more people are buying widgets (remember those?) and the sales of widgets keep growing, that bodes well for companies that sell (or service) widgets.

Take a look at demographics and market data and use this information to further filter your investing choices. You could run a great company, but if your fortunes are made when a million folks buy from you, and next year that number shrinks to 800,000, and the year after that it shrinks again, what will happen to your fortunes?

Consider this example: If you have a successful company that is selling something to seniors, and the market data tells you that the number of seniors is expanding relentlessly for the foreseeable future, then this rising tide (demographics) will certainly lift that particular boat (your stock). Find out more about market growth using the resources in Appendix A.

The Company Is in a Field with a High Barrier to Entry

If you run a company that offers a product or service that is easy to compete with, building up a strong and viable business will be more difficult for you; you'll need to do something different and better.

Maybe you have a great technology, or a patented system, or superior marketing prowess, or a way to make what you're selling both cheaper and faster than your competition. Maybe you have a strong brand that has endured for decades.

A *high barrier to entry* simply means that companies that compete with you will have a tough time overcoming your advantage. This gives you the power to grow and leave your competition in the dust.

Here's an example: Coca-Cola (KO) positioned and branded itself for decades as the top soda with a secret recipe for its soda. In spite of imitators and competitors, it's still dominant today — more than a century after its founding. The company's soda is still on kitchen tables and in picnic baskets, and its shareholders are still being refreshed with stock splits and dividend increases.

To find resources that can help you discover the advantages and characteristics of stocks with a high barrier to entry, check out Appendix A.

The Company Has a Low Political Profile

Politics: Just the thought of it makes me wince. Political discussions may be great at cocktail parties and perhaps fun to watch as your relatives go at it, but I think that flying below the political radar is a good thing for companies. Why?

We live in times that are politically sensitive (I don't think that is a good thing). All too often, politics affects the fortunes of companies and, by extension, the portfolios of investors. Yes, sometimes politics can favor a company (through backroom deals and such), but politics is a double-edged sword that can ruin a company.

History shows us that companies that are politically targeted either directly or by association (by being in an unpopular industry) can suffer. There was a time that holding tobacco companies in your portfolio was the equivalent of garlic to a vampire.

REMEMBER

All things being equal, I would rather hold a stock in a popular industry or a nondescript industry than one that attracts undue (negative) attention.

The Stock Is Optionable

An *optionable stock* (which has call and put options available on it) means that you have added ways to profit from it (or the ability to minimize potential losses). Options give a stockholder ways to enhance gains or yield added revenue.

Say you do, in fact, find the perfect stock, and you truly load up and buy as many shares as you can lay your hands on, but you don't have any more money to buy another batch of shares.

Fortunately, you notice that the stock is optionable and see that you can speculate by buying a call option that allows you to be bullish on 100 shares with a fraction of the cash needed to actually buy 100 shares. As the stock soars, you're able to take profits by cashing out the call option without having to touch the stock position at all.

Now, with your stock at nosebleed levels, you're getting a little nervous that this stock is possibly at an unsustainable level, so you decide to buy some put options to protect your unrealized gains from your stock. When your stock does experience a correction, you cash out your put with an enviable gain. With the stock down, you decide to take the proceeds from your put option–realized gains and buy more of the stock at favorable prices.

TIP

Options (both the call and the put in this scenario) give you the ability to bank more gains from the same great stock. Just keep in mind that options are a speculative vehicle and can expire. Find out more about options in my book *High-Level Investing For Dummies* (published by Wiley).

The Stock Is Benefiting from Favorable Megatrends

A *megatrend* is a trend that affects an unusually large segment of the marketplace and may have added benefits and/or pitfalls for buyers and sellers of a given set of products and services. A good example of a megatrend is "the aging of America"; the United States has more than 85 million people who are getting ready for retirement as they reach and surpass the age of 65 (although some assume a larger number when they include folks who are over 50). Those companies that provide services and products for senior citizens will have greater opportunities to sell more of what they provide and will then be a good consideration for investors.

REMEMBER

When megatrends are with you, you can even have a mediocre stock but end up with extraordinary gains. In fact, even a "bad stock" will rise sharply if it's swept up in a rally pushed by a powerful megatrend. Of course, a bad stock won't have staying power (the stock will eventually go down if the underlying company is losing money or struggling), so stick to quality stocks to truly optimize the long-term benefits that a megatrend can provide.

The problem is that when a stock has little substance behind it (the company is losing money, growing debt, and so on), its up move will be temporary, and the stock price will tend to reverse in an ugly pullback. Just ask anyone who bought a dot-com stock during 1999 to 2001 (that's right — that guy softly sobbing in the corner). The rising-tide-lifts-all-boats idea is a powerful one, and when you have a great company that will only benefit from this type of scenario, your stock price will go higher and higher.

Find out more about megatrends and other factors in the big picture in Chapters 13 and 15.

Chapter **23**

Ten Ways to Profit in a Bear Market

Bear markets are brutal when they hit. Ask any stock investor who was fully invested in stocks during 1973–1975, 2000–2002, 2008, or the brief-but-brutal month of December 2018. As of January 2020, the market is roaring at new highs, so a bear market may seem like it's hibernating, but it could come without much public notice and devastate unprepared investors. You relieve the pain from the carnage by vigorously pulling your lower lip up and over your forehead to shield your eyes from the ugliness. Fortunately, bear markets tend to be much shorter than bull markets, and if you're properly diversified, you can get through without much damage.

For nimble investors, bear markets can provide opportunities to boost your portfolio and lay the groundwork for more long-term wealth-building. Here are ten ways to make bear markets very bear-able (and profitable).

Find Good Stocks to Buy

In a bear market, the stocks of both good and bad companies tend to go down. But bad stocks tend to stay down (or head into the dustbin of stock history if the underlying companies go bankrupt), while good stocks recover and get back on the growth track. The long-term investor sees a bear market as a good buying opportunity for quality stocks.

REMEMBER

For the investor, the strategy is clear. If the stock of a good, profitable company goes down, that presents a buying opportunity. Translation: Good stuff is on sale! Here's where some basic research yields some diamonds in the rough. When you find companies with good sales and profits and a good outlook (get some guidance from Chapter 8), and then you use some key ratios (such as the price-to-earnings ratio and others covered in Appendix B), you can uncover a great stock at a bargain price (thanks to that bear market).

Many forget that some of the greatest investors in history (such as Warren Buffett and John Templeton) have used bear markets to buy companies when their stocks fell to bargain levels. Why not you?

Hunt for Dividends

A dividend comes from a company's net income, while the stock's price is dictated by buying and selling in the stock market. If the stock's price goes down because of selling, yet the company is strong, still earning a profit, and still paying a dividend, it becomes a good buying opportunity for those seeking dividend income.

Say you have a $50 stock of a great company, and it has a $2.50 annual dividend. That means that you're getting a dividend yield of 5 percent ($2.50 divided by $50 is a percentage yield of 5 percent). Say that it's a brutal bear market, and the stock price falls to $25 per share. In that case, the dividend yield is much higher. If the stock is at $25 and the dividend is at $2.50, the dividend yield is 10 percent because $2.50 is 10 percent of $25.

For more about investing for dividend income, check out Chapter 9.

Unearth Gems with Bond Ratings

As a bear market unfolds, the tough economic environment is like the tide that rolls back from the surf and reveals who still has swim trunks on and who doesn't. A bear market usually occurs in tough economic times, and it reveals who has too much debt to deal with and who is doing a good job of managing their debt.

This is where the bond rating becomes valuable (or is it invaluable?). The *bond rating* is a widely viewed snapshot of a company's creditworthiness. The rating is assigned by an independent bond rating agency (such as Moody's or Standard & Poor's). A rating of AAA is the highest rating available and signifies that the agency believes that the company has achieved the highest level of creditworthiness and is, therefore, the least risky to invest in (in terms of buying its bonds). The ratings of AAA, AA, and A are considered "investment-grade," whereas ratings that are lower (such as in the Bs and Cs or worse) indicate poor creditworthiness (risky). Some consider BBB (or Baa) as investment-grade, too.

TIP

If the economy is in bad shape (recession or worse), and stocks have been battered, and you see a stock whose company has a bond rating of AAA, that may be a good buy! Flip to Chapter 9 for more information about bond ratings.

Rotate Your Sectors

Using exchange-traded funds (ETFs; see Chapter 5) with your stocks can be a good way to add diversification and use a sector rotation approach. Different sectors perform well during different times of the ebb and flow of the economic or business cycle.

When the economy is roaring along and growing, companies that offer big-ticket items such as autos, machinery, high technology, home improvement, and similar large purchases tend to do very well, and so do their stocks (these are referred to as *cyclical stocks*). Sectors that represent cyclical stocks include manufacturing and consumer discretionary. Basically, stocks of companies that sell big-ticket items or "wants" do well when the economy is growing and doing well.

However, when the economy looks like it's sputtering and entering a recession, then it pays to switch to *defensive stocks* tied to human need, such as food and beverages (in the consumer staples sector), utilities, and the like.

For skittish investors, consumer staples and related defensive sectors are the place to be during an economic recession and a bearish stock market. Aggressive investors who like to be contrarians may see battered sectors as a buying opportunity, anticipating that those stocks will rally significantly as the economy returns to a growth path and a new bull market in stocks.

The bottom line is that rotating into sectors that will subsequently benefit from the next expected turn in the economy's ebb and flow has been worth considering for many investors. How about you? See Chapter 13 for the scoop on sectors.

Go Short on Bad Stocks

Bear markets may be tough for good stocks, but they're brutal to bad stocks. When bad stocks go down, they can keep falling and give you an opportunity to profit when they decline further.

When a bad stock (the underlying company is losing money, getting over-indebted, and so on) goes down, the stock often goes into a more severe decline as more and more investors look into it and discover the company's shaky finances. Many folks would short the stock and profit when it continues plunging (I cover the mechanics of how to go short in Chapter 17).

WARNING

Going short is a risky way to bet on a stock going down. If you're wrong and the stock goes up, you have the potential for unlimited losses. A better way to speculate on a stock falling is to buy long-dated put options, which gives you the potential to profit if you're right (that the stock will fall) but limits your losses if you're wrong. I describe put options later in this chapter.

Carefully Use Margin

I typically don't use margin, but if you use it wisely, it's a powerful tool. Using it to acquire dividend-paying stocks after they've corrected can be a great tactic. *Margin* is using borrowed funds from your broker to buy securities (also referred to as a *margin loan*). Keep in mind that when you employ margin, you do add an element of speculation to the mix. Buying 100 shares of a dividend-paying stock with 100 percent of your own money is a great way to invest, but buying the same stock with margin adds risk to the situation. Chapter 17 goes into greater detail about the uses and risks of margin.

WARNING

Notice the phrases "after they've corrected" and "dividend-paying stock." Both phrases are intended to give you a better approach to your margin strategy. You would hate to use margin before the stock corrected or declined because the brokerage firm wants you to have enough "stock collateral," so to speak. Using margin at the wrong time (when the stock is high, and it subsequently falls) can be hazardous, but using margin to buy the stock after a significant fall is much less risky.

Buy a Call Option

A *call option* is a bet that a particular asset (such as a stock or an ETF) will rise in value in the short term. Buying call options is about speculating, not investing. I say this because a call option is a derivative, and it has a finite shelf life; it can expire worthless if you're not careful.

The good part of a call option is that it can be inexpensive to buy and tends to be a very cheap vehicle at the bottom (bear market) of the stock market. This is where your contrarian side can kick in. If the stock price has been hammered but the company is in good shape (solid sales, profits, and so on), betting on a rebound for the company's stock can be profitable.

Say the stock price for DEF, Inc., is at $23 per share. Consider buying a call option with a strike price of $25 that has a long-term expiration such as a year or longer. (In a call option, the *strike price* is the agreed-upon price at which the call buyer has the option but not the obligation to buy the underlying stock or ETF). Doing this means that you're betting the stock will go up and meet or surpass the price of $25. If DEF goes to, say, $28 per share, then your call option could easily go up 100 percent or more in value and net you a tidy profit. Of course, if DEF stays down and doesn't approach $25, then the call option will lose value. If DEF's stock price doesn't go to $25 during the entire time of the life of the call option, then the call option could expire worthless. Fortunately, the option didn't cost that much money, so you probably didn't lose much in the worst-case scenario. Depending on the strike price and the shelf life of the option, an option can cost as little as under $100.

REMEMBER

Options are a form of speculating, not investing. With investing, time is on your side. But with options, time is against you because options have a finite life and can expire worthless. For more on wealth-building strategies with options, consider my book *High-Level Investing For Dummies* (Wiley).

Write a Covered Call Option

When you own a stock, especially an optionable stock, you have the ability to generate extra income from that position. The most obvious way to generate income from the stock (besides dividends) is to write a covered call option.

Writing a *covered call* means that you're selling a call option against a stock you own; in other words, you accept an obligation to sell your stock to the buyer (or holder) of the call that you wrote at a specified price if the stock rises and meets or exceeds the strike price. In exchange, you receive income (referred to as the *option premium*). If the stock doesn't rise to the option's specified price during the life of the option (an option has a diminishing shelf life and an expiration date), then you're able to keep both your stock and the income from doing (writing) the call option.

Writing covered call options is a relatively safe way to boost the yield on your stock position by up to 5 percent, 7 percent, and even more than 10 percent depending on market conditions. Keep in mind, though, that the downside of writing a covered call is that you may be obligated to sell your stock at the option's specified price (referred to as the *strike price*), and you forgo the opportunity to make gains above that specified price. But done right, a covered call option can be a virtually risk-free strategy. Find out more about covered call writing in my book *High-Level Investing For Dummies* (Wiley).

Write a Put Option to Generate Income

Writing a *put option* obligates you (the put writer) to buy 100 shares of a stock (or ETF) at a specific price during the period of time the option is active. If a stock you'd like to buy just fell and you're interested in buying it, consider instead writing a put option on that same stock.

The put option provides you income (called the *premium*) while it obligates you to buy the underlying stock at the option's agreed-upon price (called the *strike price*). But because you want to buy the stock anyway at the option's strike price, it's fine, and you get paid to do it too (the premium).

TIP

Writing put options is a great way to generate income at the bottom of a bear market. The only "risk" is that you may have to buy a stock you like. Cool! For more on writing put options, check out my book *High-Level Investing For Dummies* (Wiley).

Be Patient

REMEMBER

If you're going to retire ten years from now (or more), a bear market shouldn't make you sweat. Good stocks come out of bear markets, and they're usually ready for the subsequent bull market. So don't be so quick to get out of a stock. Just keep monitoring the company for its vital statistics (growing sales and profits and so on), and if the company looks fine, then hang on. Keep collecting your dividends, and hold the stock as it zigzags into the long-term horizon.

Chapter 24

Ten Investments and Strategies That Go Great with Stocks

Y es, I love stocks, and I think some type of stock exposure is good for virtually any portfolio. But you must remember that your total financial portfolio should have other investments and strategies that are not stocks at all. Why?

Diversification means you have other assets besides stocks so you're not 100 percent tied to the whims and machinations of the stock market. All too often, too many investors have too much exposure to the stock market. That's fine, of course, when the stock market is raging upward, but potential down moves are there too. Therefore, you should consider investments and strategies that complement your stock investing pursuits. Check out ten of my favorites in this chapter.

Covered Call Options

Writing a covered call option is a great strategy for generating income from a current stock position (or positions) in your portfolio. A *call option* is a vehicle that gives the call buyer the right (but not the obligation) to buy a particular stock at a given price during a limited time frame (call options expire). The buyer pays what's called the *premium* to the call seller (referred to as the *call writer*). The call writer receives the premium as income but in return is obligated to sell the stock to the buyer at the agreed-upon price (called the *strike price*) if called upon to do so during the life of the option. The call option is typically a speculative vehicle for those who are buying them, but in this case I specifically refer to writing a covered call option.

Covered call writing is a conservative way to make extra cash from just about any listed stock of which you own at least 100 shares. Whether your stock has a dividend or not, this could boost income by 5 percent or more.

To find out more about writing call options on your stock positions, check out *High-Level Investing For Dummies* (authored by yours truly and published by Wiley). There you'll find several chapters detailing the basics of options, along with their advantages and disadvantages. I also discuss writing covered calls in Chapter 9.

Put Options

A *put option* is a bet that a stock or exchange-traded fund (ETF) will fall in price. If you see the fortunes of a company going down, a put option is a great way to make a profit by speculating that the stock will go down. Many use puts to speculate for a profit, while others use put options as a hedging vehicle or a form of "portfolio insurance."

TIP

If you're holding a stock for the long term but you're concerned about it in the short term, then consider using a put option on that stock. You're not hoping the stock goes down; you're merely using a form of protection for your stock-holding. If the stock goes down, the put option will rise in value. What some investors do is then cash out the put option at a profit, and use the proceeds to buy more shares of that stock because the stock's price is lower and possibly a buying opportunity.

For more on put options, see my book *High-Level Investing For Dummies* (Wiley).

Cash

Having some money in the bank or just some cash in your brokerage account comes in handy no matter what's happening with the stock market's gyrations. What's that . . . the stock market is plunging? Whew! Good to have some cash on the sidelines so you can do some bargain-hunting for good value stocks.

REMEMBER

As I write this, interest rates on savings accounts and similar bank vehicles are abysmally low, so cash isn't a great investment. However, cash is an integral part of your overall wealth-building approach for several reasons:

>> Cash you hold on the sidelines (either at your bank or, more conveniently, in your stock brokerage account or money market fund) is necessary when buying opportunities present themselves during the ebbs and flows of the stock market.

>> Cash is necessary for an emergency fund in your overall financial planning picture. Not enough folks have an emergency or "rainy day" fund, which means a hundred different things (big medical expense, job layoff, and so on) could cause them a cash flow problem. If you need money for an unexpected big expense and you don't have it in savings (or your mattress!), where will that money come from? It's a good possibility that you'd have to sell or cash out some investment (such as your stock). See Chapter 2 for more about emergency funds.

>> Cash can be necessary when you are doing an income strategy referred to as writing puts since a put may mean having to buy a stock or ETF. More on writing puts is in Chapter 9.

>> Cash is a good holding during deflationary times. When prices are low or going down, your cash's buying power gets stronger.

EE Savings Bonds

The EE savings bond is issued by the U.S. Treasury and is a great vehicle, especially for small investors (you can buy one for as little as $25). It's a discount bond, meaning that you buy it at below its face value (the purchase price is 50 percent of the face value), and cash it in later to get your purchase price back with interest.

The interest rate paid is equivalent to 100 percent of the average five-year Treasury note rate. If this rate is at 2 percent, then you get 2 percent. To get the full benefit of the rate, you must hold your EE bond for at least five years. If you cash out before five years and after one year (the mandatory minimum holding period), then you get a lower interest rate (equivalent to a savings account rate).

Here are several benefits of an EE bond:

>> The interest rate isn't fixed. Because the rate is pegged to Treasury note interest rates, it will rise (or fall) along with that rate. In the event that interest rates rise (which is a possibility for 2020 and beyond), EE bonds would benefit.

>> The interest you earn on EE bonds is typically higher than a conventional bank account.

>> EE bonds are free from state and local taxes. If you use the bonds for education, much of the interest can be tax-free.

For more details on the EE savings bond, head over to the U.S. Treasury's site on savings bonds (www.savingsbonds.gov).

I Bonds

In the age of low-interest-rate debt investments (such as bonds in general), the I savings bond (the "I" stands for inflation) is a different wrinkle altogether. This is a "sister" to the EE savings bond (see the preceding section), and it's also issued by the U.S. Treasury. The twist here (making it a "twisted sister," I guess) is that the interest rate is tied to the official inflation rate (the *Consumer Price Index*, or CPI). If the CPI goes to 3 percent, then the interest rate on the I bond goes to 3 percent. The interest rate gets adjusted annually.

At the time of this writing, the CPI has been relatively low, and the environment is generally deflationary (a period of low prices), so the I bond's interest rate has been under 1.5 percent.

TIP

I actually like the I bond for the coming years because inflation can easily return because of a variety of factors (increasing money supply and so on), and the I bond can be a solid part of your overall portfolio. For more information on I bonds, head over to www.savingsbonds.gov.

Sector Mutual Funds

I think that sector investing is a great part of your overall wealth-building approach; sometimes it isn't easy to choose a single stock, but you can instead choose a winning sector (or industry). For many investors, a sector mutual fund is a good addition to their portfolios.

A *mutual fund* is a pool of money that's managed by an investment firm (such as Fidelity, Vanguard, or T. Rowe Price); this pool of money is invested in a portfolio of securities (such as stocks or bonds) to reach a particular objective (such as aggressive growth, income, or preservation of capital). The investment firm actively manages the fund by regularly making buy, sell, and hold decisions in the fund's portfolio.

A sector mutual fund limits its portfolio and investment decisions to a particular sector such as utilities, consumer staples, or healthcare. It's your task to choose a winning sector, and the job of choosing the various stocks is left to the investment firm. (Flip to Chapter 13 for details on sectors and industries.)

Motif Investing

Starting with only a few hundred bucks, you can have a theme-based portfolio that can augment your portfolio of individual stocks. *Motif investing* is a relatively new twist on investing (or speculating if you choose a risky motif). It gives you the convenience of investing in a pre-structured portfolio that's designed to do well given a particular expected event, trend, or worldview that will unfold.

If you believe, for example, that interest rates will rise, you can, with a single motif, have a basket of stocks that would optimally benefit from that event. If you believe that inflation will rear its ugly head, then you can consider a motif that intends to benefit from that outcome.

TIP

The major decision on a motif is not necessarily the motif itself but on your particular worldview or expectations going forward. What do you expect in the coming months or years? If there's one positive (or negative) trend that you're fairly certain will unfold, and you're not sure how to profit from it through a single stock or fund, then take a look at motif investing. It may just be your cup of tea . . . or coffee (heck, there may even be a motif on tea and coffee!). Find out more about motif investing at www.motif.com/ (but you could've guessed that!).

Bearish Exchange-Traded Funds

Did you know that there are 77 bearish (also called inverse) ETFs you can play as of 2019? Fortunately, the U.S. stock market had a relatively good year in 2019, but the danger of a sharp correction is possible during 2020–2021. And as you read this in 2020–2021, a possibility of a sharp correction is possible as the stock market recently passed 29,000 (in the Dow Jones Industrial Average), and the tumult of domestic politics and geopolitics still looms due to general economic weakness, unsustainable debt, political upheaval, and global economic and financial difficulties. What should investors do given those possible scenarios?

Investors can do plenty of things, both before and during tumultuous market times. If you're invested in quality stocks, then you shouldn't panic, especially if you have a long-term outlook. But hedging to a small extent can be a good consideration. In other words, why not consider a vehicle that will benefit in the event of a downturn in the stock market?

Exchange-traded funds (ETFs) are a good companion vehicle in your stock portfolio, and their versatility can become part of your overall strategy. If you believe that the stock market is or soon will be in difficult times, then consider a bearish stock market ETF. A bearish (or inverse) stock ETF is designed to go up when stocks go down. If stocks go down 5 percent, then the bearish ETF goes up by a similar inverse percentage (in this case, 5 percent).

TIP

What some investors do with bearish ETFs is cash them out when the market plunges and then take the proceeds to buy more of their favorite stocks (which presumably are cheaper given the market's move down). Tactics such as this mean you keep your portfolio growing for the long term while playing it safe during short-term market difficulties. Flip to Chapter 5 for general information on ETFs.

Dividend Yield Exchange-Traded Funds

The movement of stock prices can certainly be puzzling at times. Because they're subject to buying and selling orders, their movement may not always be logical or predictable, especially in the short term (and I mean especially!). There is, however, one aspect of stocks that is much more logical and predictable: dividends.

Strong, profitable companies that have consistently raised their dividends in the past tend to reliably keep doing so in the future. Many companies have raised their dividends, or at the very least, kept paying them, year-in and year-out through good times and bad. Dividends are paid out from the company's net earnings (or net profit), so dividends also tend to act as a barometer gauging the company's financial health, which basically boils down to profitability.

TIP

Finding good dividend-paying stocks isn't hard; I describe them in Chapter 9. You can also find them with the stock screening tools that I cover in Chapter 16. However, investing in a strong basket of dividend-paying stocks by checking out dividend yield ETFs can be a good idea — especially for those who are too skittish to invest in individual stocks. A dividend yield ETF selects a basket of stocks based on the criteria of dividends — how consistently they're paid and continuously raised. They make it easy to include dividend-payers in your portfolio with a single purchase. I cover ETFs in more detail in Chapter 5.

Consumer Staples Exchange-Traded Funds

REMEMBER

You should consider having investments in your portfolio that are *defensive* in nature — investments tied to those products and services that people will keep buying no matter how good or bad the economy is. Sure, consider that sexy, high-tech gizmo stock if you like, but offset that with stocks of companies that offer food, beverages, water, utilities, and so on. However, sometimes it's not easy to find that one great defensive stock, so why not buy the sector?

The consumer staples sector includes the "old reliables" of stock investing. Consumer staples ETFs may not skyrocket during bull markets (although they'll perform respectably), but they'll forge ahead during bad or uncertain times. Fortunately, the world of ETFs has made it a snap to invest in a basket of stocks that generally mirror a given sector. I discuss ETFs in Chapter 5 and sectors in Chapter 13.

Chapter **25**

Ten Investing Pitfalls and Challenges for 2020–2030

Stock investing doesn't happen in a vacuum. The stock market can face major events that can either help or hurt it — and, of course, affect your stock portfolio. Some events can have a direct impact, while others just provide a glancing blow. But most macro-events have a material effect on stocks.

In this book, I emphasize investing in quality, dividend-paying stocks for the long term, which (in the past) have overcome the occasional crisis or crash. This chapter gives you the scoop on potential challenges that the stock market may face during the next decade.

Trillion-Dollar Pension Shortfalls

The biggest point about stock investing is that it can be a fantastic bulwark in your finances to cement your future financial security. Many people feel the same way about pensions. Most pensions have stocks and stock-related investments (such as mutual funds) in their portfolios. The problem is that many (most?) pensions are underfunded and/or undercapitalized, so the risk of a shortfall (more money leaving pensions during the retirement years versus going in) is a real and present danger.

REMEMBER

Depending on whose research you are reading, the shortfall is a minimum of $1.5 trillion and is likely much, much more (double or triple that figure). So speaking to your pension administrator about the financial health of your pension amount is a necessity. I personally believe that people should do some stock investing outside their pension plans for diversification and focus on income stocks (dividend payers; see Chapter 9).

European Crises

The European Union fostered a bureaucratic setup that is the calm before the storm. A batch of countries there decided to open the floodgates to millions of immigrants, which has caused a massive spike in crime, along with exploding public assistance and national security costs. With soaring violence and related socio-economic problems, this has caused a significant drop in tourism while spiking government costs and debt.

WARNING

Given this, countries such as Sweden and Greece are trending toward financial crisis and major economic difficulties. Stock investors shouldn't wait for a crisis before acting; it's time to reduce your exposure to European stock markets since those stocks will be at great risk. (If you're still interested in international stock investing, check out Chapter 18 for tips.)

The Bond and Debt Bubble

In recent years, interest rates in the United States (and elsewhere) have reached a historic low. Unfortunately, this has helped to fuel a historic bond bubble that dwarfs the bond bubble of 2006–2007 (which led to the 2008–2009 market crash and recession).

Given that, the current bond bubble will be much more problematic since it is much bigger by trillions, and it is a worldwide phenomenon. The question is not if it will pop but when — and what the repercussions will be. What can a stock investor do?

TIP

First, start thinking about what companies and industries will be hit the worst. Companies tied to excessive debt — either having too much or lending too much — will be at greatest risk. Therefore, review your stock choices and start removing debt-laden companies and reducing your exposure to financial stocks such as banks and mortgage companies. To find out more about ratios to help you figure out the debt to worry about, see Chapter 6 and Appendix B.

A Demographic Upheaval

The driving demographic considerations 10–15 years or so ago were baby boomers along with their needs and spending patterns, but that group has been supplanted by — drum roll, please — millennials! Millennials are definitely a different category with very different spending habits and financial concerns. They are less interested in luxuries and walk-in retail spending, while they love their technology and online shopping.

These changes mean new pitfalls and opportunities that stock investors need to pay attention to. Given that, start doing some research online about millennials and their financial habits so that you can adjust your portfolios accordingly. The resources in Appendix A increasingly cover investing habits of millennials. Also, three motifs tied to investing are related to millennials (see Chapter 14 on motif investing).

Federal Deficits and Debt

During 2019, the U.S. federal government's national debt rocketed past the $23 trillion level. Politicians wring their hands about this mind-boggling debt during campaign season but quickly go back to spending mode (increasing the national debt) after election day. This monumental debt has been growing for decades, and many folks and politicians have been lulled to a point of ignoring it or just shrugging it off. However, some rumblings and milestones could take this issue from dormancy to our TV screens in the coming years.

Our total debt now exceeds 100 percent of our gross domestic product (GDP), which means we may be entering a period where carrying this total debt is not sustainable. In addition, much of this debt is held as bonds across the globe and by governments that are not friendly toward the United States, and this debt could easily be re-patriated to the United States. It is uncertain what dangers would arise since other factors could come into play as well (war, trade embargos, and so forth), but these developments could cause major stock market declines and gyrations as investors panic.

REMEMBER

I don't know what our political and economic conditions will be when that happens, but it is probably safe to say that quality companies with good fundamentals offering needed products and services will weather the storm, which means if you stay focused on a company's quality and profitability, you'll get through okay. (If not, make sure you have an adequate supply of soup cans and precious metals.) Check out Part 3 for more on researching company fundamentals and picking stock winners.

A Social Security Reckoning

You have heard for decades about how problematic the multi-trillion-dollar imbalances in Social Security spending have been, but nothing has seemed to materialize in recent years. What gives here? According to both public and private Social Security watchdogs, the full unfunded liabilities for Social Security exceed $50 trillion, and we have entered a period where current outflows (payments to beneficiaries) will exceed the current inflows (social security taxes). I think that if you are on Social Security now, you should be okay, but future beneficiaries may be at risk during 2025–2035 as shortfalls become more problematic.

TIP

Whenever I am doing retirement planning with folks, every chance I get, I plan without imputing Social Security income in the numbers. Why? Because if my client (or you, dear reader) can achieve financial independence without Social Security, then of course any Social Security money you receive is a nice plus! Given that, start loading up on quality dividend-paying stocks as part of your overall wealth-building approach (see Chapter 9), and you'll sleep better.

Terrorism

As I write this book, the world is generally placid in spite of all manners of issues, conflicts, and problems that plague humanity on a daily basis. Unfortunately, a single major terrorist event could easily trigger a stock market panic or be the tipping point that turns a muddled economy into the recessionary zone.

Major terrorist events are never a good thing, of course, but in the singular scope of stock investing, they can cause major damage. In the wake of 9/11 back in 2001, terrorism caused a painful decline that rattled many investors and sent many a stock portfolio plummeting. In the aftermath of a terrorist event, both good and bad stocks do go down, but the good stocks do recover and typically get back on positive track afterward while the bad stocks have their weaknesses exposed and either stay down or suffer a worse fate (such as bankruptcy).

REMEMBER

The lesson is clear: While the world looks rosy, take that opportunity to analyze your stock positions with the help of Parts 2 and 3. Get rid of the weak stocks before they go down — now! Keep the strong ones so your long-term portfolio can continue to zigzag upwards.

A Potential Currency Crisis

I'm telling you, I could easily do a book titled *Economic Collapse For Dummies*, but until then, I will cover all the various types of collapses in pages such as these. And the most common type of collapse is a currency collapse. In the United States, our currency is a global reserve currency that gives it strength versus other currencies since a global reserve currency is necessary for international trade. This provides some insulation from typical currency problems. But that doesn't mean that the world is safe from a crisis coming from lesser currencies.

A currency crisis typically occurs when a currency is overproduced by that nation's central bank. When you overproduce a currency, you tend to diminish the value of each unit. This translates into higher prices for goods and services — inflation! This makes it tougher for consumers as the currency keeps losing value. If the situation is not remedied, the currency will be in crisis, and economic suffering by the public will increase.

At the time I am writing this, the currencies in Venezuela and Argentina are in crisis mode (hyper-inflation!), which is making the citizens suffer big-time in those countries. What would happen if the Euro or the yuan (China's currency) were to become inflated and start to lose its value?

TIP

Fortunately, quality stocks tend to perform well during inflationary times, and dividend payouts tend to match (or exceed) the rate of inflation. A good additional strategy is to consider precious metals and/or precious metals mining stocks, which tend to do very well during inflationary times. Find out more in my book *Precious Metals Investing For Dummies* (published by Wiley). I believe that inflationary times are very possible in the coming years, so get ready now.

A Derivatives Time Bomb

In the past 20–30 years or so, a number of crises were caused when derivatives positions imploded and caused massive losses. Some good examples of this have been the collapses of once-mighty companies such as Enron, AIG, and Bear Stearns. On a grander scale, derivatives played a major role in the housing bubble that popped in 2006–2007 and the 2008 market crash.

The top 25 U.S. banks have total derivatives exposure exceeding $204 trillion, according to the 2Q 2019 bulletin issued by the Office of the Comptroller of the Currency (www.occ.gov). Because many of these trillion-dollar derivatives positions are tied at the hip with debt markets, and debt markets are larger and more unsustainable than ever, it is only a matter of time before the next massive crisis hits. What should you do?

REMEMBER

The main crisis will be with the banking industry, so reduce your exposure to bank and financial stocks. If you have them currently in your portfolio, monitor them and consider trailing stops (covered in Chapter 17).

Socialism

I saved the worst for last. Socialism has caused more economic crises than any other singular economic set of policy ideas. Communism and fascism are just more logical extremes of this dangerous, fallacious ideology. Socialism (entirely or partly) has been the culprit of an extraordinary range of economic crises throughout history and includes the Great Depression, the Great Recession of 2008, and the collapse of the Soviet Union and more recently Venezuela, Zimbabwe, and scores of other ill-fated economies. So what should stock investors know?

Stock investors should be wary when socialists take over an economy (or even an industry), and they should exit positions that are exposed to it. The United States is, fortunately, on balance a free-market capitalist economy, and we can only hope it stays that way, but a recent survey indicated that a plurality of young adults are favorable toward socialism so we can only hope they learn better.

To find out more about economics and socialism, feel free to visit www. ravingcapitalist.com/socialism.

Appendixes

Find my favorite resources to help you succeed with both stocks and exchange-traded funds (ETFs). Get research sites that give you the inside scoop on stocks and market action behind the headlines, as well as resources to help you be ahead of the curve so you aren't surprised by the stock market's gyrations.

Discover the ratios that will help make your choices more successful, along with the key ratios that help you see how profitable (and how solvent) your prospective stocks are.

Appendix A

Resources for Stock Investors

Getting and staying informed are ongoing priorities for stock investors. The lists in this appendix represent some of the best information resources available.

Financial Planning Sources

To find a financial planner to help you with your general financial needs, contact the following organizations.

Certified Financial Planner Board of Standards (CFP Board)
1425 K St. NW, Suite 500
Washington, DC 20005
Phone 800-487-1497
Website www.cfp.net

Get a free copy of the CFP Board's pamphlet *10 Questions to Ask When Choosing a Financial Planner.* Be sure to ask for a financial planner who specializes in investing.

Financial Planning Association (FPA)
1290 Broadway, Suite 1625
Denver, CO 80203
Phone 800-322-4237
Website www.fpanet.org

This is the largest organization of financial planning professionals.

National Association of Personal Financial Advisors (NAPFA)
8700 W. Bryn Mawr Ave., Suite 700N
Chicago, IL 60631
Phone 888-333-6659
Website www.napfa.org

This is the leading organization for fee-based financial planners (in other words, they don't get paid through commissions based on selling insurance/investment products).

The Language of Investing

Investing for Beginners
Website beginnersinvest.about.com

Investopedia
Website www.investopedia.com

Investor Words
Website www.investorwords.com

Standard & Poor's Dictionary of Financial Terms
By Virginia B. Morris and Kenneth M. Morris
Published by Lightbulb Press, Inc.

A nicely laid out A-to-Z publication for investors mystified by financial terms. It explains the important investing terms you come across every day.

Textual Investment Resources

Stock investing success isn't an event; it's a process. The periodicals and magazines listed here (along with their websites) have offered many years of guidance and information for investors, and they're still top-notch. The books provide much wisdom that's either timeless or timely (covering problems and concerns every investor should be aware of now).

Periodicals and magazines

Barron's
Website online.barrons.com

Forbes **magazine**
Website www.forbes.com

Investing.com
Website www.investing.com

Investor's Business Daily
Website www.investors.com

Kiplinger's Personal Finance **magazine**
Website www.kiplinger.com

Money **magazine**
Website www.money.com

Value Line Investment Survey
Website www.valueline.com

The Wall Street Journal
Website www.wsj.com

Books

Common Stocks and Uncommon Profits and Other Writings
By Philip A. Fisher
Published by John Wiley & Sons, Inc.

Elliott Wave Principle: Key to Market Behavior
By A.J. Frost and Robert R. Prechter
Published by New Classics Library

Robert Prechter is one of the leading technicians and has had some very accurate forecasts about the stock market and the general economy.

Forbes Guide to the Markets: Becoming a Savvy Investor
By Marc M. Groz
Published by John Wiley & Sons, Inc.

Fundamental Analysis For Dummies
By Matt Krantz
Published by John Wiley & Sons, Inc.

I had the good fortune to review this book, and it's very worthwhile for serious investors. The author drills down into the financials of a company, which any serious investor needs to know.

How to Pick Stocks Like Warren Buffett: Profiting from the Bargain Hunting Strategies of the World's Greatest Value Investor
By Timothy Vick
Published by McGraw-Hill Professional Publishing

When you're investing, it's good to see what accomplished investors like Warren Buffett do, and this book explains his approach well.

The Intelligent Investor: The Definitive Book on Value Investing
By Benjamin Graham
Published by HarperCollins

This is a classic investing book that was great when it was published and is very relevant in today's tumultuous stock market.

Security Analysis: The Classic 1951 Edition
by Benjamin Graham and David L. Dodd
Published by the McGraw-Hill Companies

This book is a classic, and most investors in this uncertain age should acquaint themselves with the basics.

Standard & Poor's Stock Reports (available in the library reference section)
Website www.standardandpoors.com

Ask your reference librarian about this excellent reference source, which gives one-page summaries on the major companies and has detailed financial reports on all major companies listed on the New York Stock Exchange and Nasdaq.

The Wall Street Journal Guide to Understanding Money & Investing
By Kenneth M. Morris and Virginia B. Morris
Published by Lightbulb Press, Inc.

Special books of interest to stock investors

The Coming Bond Market Collapse: How to Survive the Demise of the U.S. Debt Market
By Michael G. Pento
Published by John Wiley & Sons, Inc.

The global bond market is a huge bubble that will send shockwaves through stock markets and economies; Pento tells you why and what to do.

Crash Proof 2.0: How to Profit from the Economic Collapse
By Peter D. Schiff with John Downes
Published by John Wiley & Sons, Inc.

A great "crash course" on the problems facing our modern economy and how to strategize with your portfolio.

The ETF Book: All You Need to Know About Exchange-Traded Funds
By Richard A. Ferri
Published by John Wiley & Sons, Inc.

Considering the marketplace, ETFs are better choices than stocks for some investors, and this book does a good job of explaining them.

High-Level Investing For Dummies
By Paul Mladjenovic
Published by John Wiley & Sons, Inc.

My shameless plug for another great book. Seriously, this book will indeed take your stock investing to the next level as I cover more strategies and resources on investing and speculating with not only stocks but also ETFs and options so you can find out what it takes to be with history's great investors and speculators.

Hot Commodities: How Anyone Can Invest Profitably in the World's Best Market
By Jim Rogers
Published by Random House

The cornerstone of "human need" investing includes commodities, and Rogers provides great insights in this book.

The Money Bubble
By James Turk and John Rubino
Published by DollarCollapse Press

These are epic times as historic currency bubbles and crises unfold with serious consequences for stocks and other aspects of the financial picture. This book gives you great guidance for enhancing your financial safety.

Why the Federal Reserve Sucks: It Causes Inflation, Recessions, Bubbles and Enriches the One Percent
By Murray Sabrin
Published by Gallatin House, LLC

Investing Websites

How can any serious investor ignore the internet? You can't, and you shouldn't. The following are among the best information sources available.

General investing websites

Bloomberg
www.bloomberg.com

CNN Business
www.cnn.com/business

Financial Sense
www.financialsense.com

Forbes
www.forbes.com

Invest Wisely: Advice From Your Securities Industry Regulators
www.sec.gov/investor/pubs/inws.htm

Investing.com
www.investing.com

MarketWatch
www.marketwatch.com

Money
https://money.com/

Stock investing websites

AllStocks.com
www.allstocks.com

Benzinga
www.benzinga.com

CNBC
www.cnbc.com

Contrarian Investing.com
www.contrarianinvesting.com

DailyStocks
www.dailystocks.com

Morningstar (known for mutual funds but has great research on stocks as well)
www.morningstar.com

Quote.com
www.quote.com

RagingBull
www.ragingbull.com

Standard and Poor's
www.standardandpoors.com

TheStreet
www.thestreet.com

Yahoo! Finance
www.finance.yahoo.com

Stock investing blogs

These blogs offer a wealth of opinions and insights from experts on investing. Peruse them to round out your research (you may even find some articles from me as well).

Best of the Web Blogs: Investing
https://blogs.botw.org/Business/Investing/

Note: The Best of the Web (BOTW) site has an extensive blog directory, and this specific page lists many excellent investing blogs for your review. Many specialize in stocks and related investing matters. There are many excellent financial and stock market blogs that I can't fit in this space, so do a search on BOTW (another source to check is www.blogsearchengine.org).

MarketBeat
www.marketbeat.com

Seeking Alpha
www.seekingalpha.com

StockTwits
www.stocktwits.com

StreetAuthority
www.streetauthority.com

Other blogs that are useful for stock investors

Greg Hunter's USAWatchdog.com
www.usawatchdog.com

HoweStreet
www.howestreet.com

King World News
www.kingworldnews.com

Market Sanity
www.marketsanity.com

Mish's Global Economic Trend Analysis
www.mishtalk.com

SafeHaven
www.safehaven.com

Zero Hedge
www.zerohedge.com

Investor Associations and Organizations

American Association of Individual Investors (AAII)
625 N. Michigan Ave.
Chicago, IL 60611-3110
Phone 800-428-2244
Website www.aaii.com

National Association of Investors Corp. (NAIC)
711 W. 13 Mile Rd., Suite 900
Madison Heights, MI 48071
Phone 877-275-6242
Website www.betterinvesting.org

Stock Exchanges

Chicago Board Options Exchange (CBOE)
Website www.cboe.com

Note: The CBOE is an options exchange, but I include it here because options have been mentioned throughout this book, and the CBOE options learning center has lots of information about how options can enhance your stock investing.

Nasdaq
Website www.nasdaq.com

New York Stock Exchange/Euronext
Website www.nyse.com

OTC Bulletin Board
Website www.otcbb.com

If you decide to research small cap stocks, this is the site to go to for data and research on small, publicly traded companies.

Finding Brokers

The following sections offer sources to help you evaluate brokers and an extensive list of brokers (with telephone numbers and websites) so that you can do your own shopping.

Choosing brokers

Reviews.com
Website www.reviews.com/online-stock-trading

This site provides reviews in many categories, including stock brokerage firms.

Stock Brokers
Website www.stockbrokers.com

Brokers

Ally Financial
Phone 855-880-2559
Website www.ally.com

Charles Schwab & Co.
Phone 800-435-4000
Website www.schwab.com

E*TRADE
Phone 800-387-2331
Website www.etrade.com

Edward Jones
Phone 314-515-3265
Website www.edwardjones.com

Fidelity Brokerage Services
Phone 800-343-3548
Website www.fidelity.com

Merrill Lynch
Phone 800-637-7455
Website www.ml.com

Morgan Stanley
Phone 888-454-3965
Website www.morganstanley.com

Muriel Siebert & Co.
Phone 800-872-0444
Website www.siebertnet.com

TD Ameritrade
Phone 800-454-9272
Website www.tdameritrade.com

thinkorswim
Phone 866-839-1100
Website www.thinkorswim.com

Vanguard Brokerage Services
Phone 877-662-7447
Website https://investor.vanguard.com/home

Wall Street Access
Phone 212-232-5602
Website www.wsaccess.com

Wells Fargo Securities
Phone 866-224-5708
Website www.wellsfargoadvisors.com

Fee-Based Investment Sources

The following are fee-based subscription services. Many of them also offer excellent (and free) email newsletters tracking the stock market and related news.

The Bull & Bear
Website www.thebullandbear.com

The Daily Reckoning (Agora Publishing)
Website www.dailyreckoning.com

Elliott Wave International
Phone 800-336-1618
Website www.elliottwave.com

Hulbert Financial Digest
Website http://hulbertratings.com/

Investing Daily
Website www.investingdaily.com

Mark Skousen
Website www.mskousen.com

The Morgan Report
Website www.themorganreport.com

Profitable Investing
Website https://profitableinvesting.investorplace.com/

Profits Unlimited
Website www.paulmampillyguru.com

The Motley Fool
Website www.fool.com

The Value Line Investment Survey
Phone 800-654-0508
Website www.valueline.com

Wealth Wave
Website www.wealth-wave.com

Weiss Research's Money and Markets
Website www.moneyandmarkets.com

Exchange-Traded Funds

ETF Database
www.etfdb.com

ETF Trends
www.etftrends.com

ETFguide
http://etfguide.com/

Dividend Reinvestment Plans

DRIP Central
Website www.dripcentral.com

DRIP Investor
Website www.dripinvestor.com

First Share
Website www.firstshare.com

Moneypaper's directinvesting.com
Website www.directinvesting.com

Sources for Analysis

The following sources give you the chance to look a little deeper at some critical aspects regarding stock analysis. Whether it's earnings estimates and insider selling or a more insightful look at a particular industry, these sources are among my favorites.

Earnings and earnings estimates

Earnings Whispers
Website www.earningswhispers.com

Thomson Reuters
Website www.thomsonreuters.com

Yahoo's Stock Research Center
Website https://finance.yahoo.com/

Zacks Investment Research
Website www.zacks.com

Sector and industry analysis

D&B Hoovers
Website www.hoovers.com

MarketWatch
Website www.marketwatch.com

Standard & Poor's
Website www.standardandpoors.com

Stock indexes

S&P Dow Jones Indices
Website www.spindices.com/

Investopedia's tutorial on indexes
Website www.investopedia.com/university/indexes

Reuters Markets & Finance News
Website www.reuters.com/finance/markets

Note: If these direct links don't work, do a search for indexes from the site's home page. Also, keep in mind that many of the resources in this appendix offer extensive information on indexes (such as MarketWatch and Yahoo! Finance).

Factors that affect market value

Understanding basic economics is so vital to making your investment decisions that I had to include this section. These great sources have helped me understand the big picture and what ultimately affects the stock market (see Chapter 15 for more details).

Economics and politics

American Institute for Economic Research (AIER)
Website www.aier.org

Note: AIER also has great little booklets for consumers on budgeting, Social Security, avoiding financial problems, and other topics.

Center for Freedom and Prosperity
Website www.freedomandprosperity.org

Credit Bubble Bulletin
www.creditbubblebulletin.blogspot.com

Federal Reserve Board
Website www.federalreserve.gov

Financial Sense
Website www.financialsense.com

Foundation for Economic Education
Website www.fee.org

Grandfather Economic Report
Website http://grandfather-economic-report.com/

Ludwig von Mises Institute
518 W. Magnolia Ave.
Auburn, AL 36832
Phone 334-321-2100
Website www.mises.org

Moody's Analytics
Website www.economy.com

Securities and Exchange Commission (SEC)
Phone 800-732-0330
Websites www.sec.gov and www.investor.gov

The SEC has tremendous resources for investors. In addition to providing information on investing, the SEC also monitors the financial markets for fraud and other abusive activities. For stock investors, it also has EDGAR (the Electronic Data Gathering, Analysis, and Retrieval system), which is a comprehensive, searchable database of public documents that are filed by public companies.

Federal laws

Go to any of these sites to find out about new and proposed laws. The on-site search engines will help you find laws either by their assigned number or a keyword search.

Library of Congress (Thomas legislative search engine)
Website https://congress.gov/

U.S. House of Representatives
Website www.house.gov

U.S. Senate
Website www.senate.gov

Technical analysis

Big Charts (provided by MarketWatch)
Website http://bigcharts.marketwatch.com/

Elliott Wave International
Website www.elliottwave.com

Stock Technical Analysis
Website www.stockta.com

StockCharts.com
Website www.stockcharts.com

Technical Traders
Website www.thetechnicaltraders.com

Insider trading

ProCon
Website www.procon.org

SEC Info
Website www.secinfo.com

Securities and Exchange Commission (SEC)
Website www.sec.gov

StreetInsider
Website www.streetinsider.com

10-K Wizard
Website www.10kwizard.com

Note: This site takes you to Morningstar's Document Research site, which can help you find the filed documents.

Tax Benefits and Obligations

Americans for Tax Reform
Website www.atr.org

Fairmark
Website www.fairmark.com

Fidelity Investments
Website www.401k.com

J.K. Lasser's series of books on taxes
By J.K. Lasser
Published by John Wiley & Sons, Inc.
Website www.jklasser.com

National Taxpayers Union
Website www.ntu.org

TaxMama
Website www.taxmama.com

Fraud

Federal Citizen Information Center
Website www.pueblo.gsa.gov

Investing publications for consumers from the Federal Citizen Information Center catalog are available for free downloading at this website.

Financial Industry Regulatory Authority (FINRA)
1735 K St. NW
Washington, DC 20006
Phone 844-574-3577 or 301-590-6500
Website www.finra.org

This website gives you information and assistance on reporting fraud or other abuse by brokers.

National Consumers League's Fraud Center
Website www.fraud.org

North American Securities Administrators Association
Phone 202-737-0900
Website www.nasaa.org

Securities and Exchange Commission (SEC)
Website www.sec.gov

The government agency that regulates the securities industry.

Securities Industry and Financial Markets Association (SIFMA)
1099 New York Ave. NW, 6th Floor
Washington, DC 20001
Phone 202-962-7300
Website www.sifma.org

Securities Investor Protection Corporation (SIPC)
Website www.sipc.org

SIPC has the role of restoring funds to investors with assets in the hands of bankrupt and otherwise financially troubled brokerage firms (make sure that your brokerage firm is a member of SIPC).

Appendix B

Financial Ratios

Considering how many financial catastrophes have occurred in recent years (and continue to occur in the current headlines), doing your homework regarding the financial health of your stock choices is more important than ever. This appendix should be your go-to section when you find stocks that you're considering for your portfolio. It lists the most common ratios that investors should be aware of and use. A solid company doesn't have to pass all these ratio tests with flying colors, but at a minimum, it should comfortably pass the ones regarding profitability and solvency:

>> **Profitability:** Is the company making money? Is it making more or less than it did in the prior period? Are sales growing? Are profits growing?

You can answer these questions by looking at the following ratios:

- Return on equity
- Return on assets
- Common size ratio (income statement)

>> **Solvency:** Is the company keeping debts and other liabilities under control? Are the company's assets growing? Is the company's net equity (or net worth or stockholders' equity) growing?

You can answer these questions by looking at the following ratios:

- Quick ratio

- Debt to net equity

- Working capital

REMEMBER

While you examine ratios, keep these points in mind:

» Not every company and/or industry is the same. A ratio that seems dubious in one industry may be just fine in another. Investigate and check out the norms in that particular industry. (See Chapter 13 for details on analyzing sectors and industries.)

» A single ratio isn't enough on which to base your investment decision. Look at several ratios covering the major aspects of the company's finances.

» Look at two or more years of the company's numbers to judge whether the most recent ratio is better, worse, or unchanged from the previous years' ratios. Ratios can give you early warning signs regarding the company's prospects. (See Chapter 11 for details on two important documents that list a company's numbers — the balance sheet and the income statement.)

Liquidity Ratios

Liquidity is the ability to quickly turn assets into cash. Liquid assets are simply assets that are easy to convert to cash. Real estate, for example, is certainly an asset, but it's not liquid because converting it to cash can take weeks, months, or even years. Current assets such as checking accounts, savings accounts, marketable securities, accounts receivable, and inventory are much easier to sell or convert to cash in a short period of time.

Paying bills or immediate debt takes liquidity. Liquidity ratios help you understand a company's ability to pay its current liabilities. The most common liquidity ratios are the current ratio and the quick ratio; the numbers to calculate them are located on the balance sheet.

Current ratio

The current ratio is the most commonly used liquidity ratio. It answers the question, "Does the company have enough financial cushion to meet its current bills?" It's calculated as follows:

Current ratio = Total current assets ÷ Total current liabilities

If Schmocky Corp. (SHM) has $60,000 in current assets and $20,000 in current liabilities, the current ratio is 3, meaning the company has $3 of current assets for each dollar of current liabilities. As a general rule, a current ratio of 2 or more is desirable.

WARNING

A current ratio of less than 1 is a red flag that the company may have a cash crunch that could cause financial problems. Although many companies strive to get the current ratio to equal 1, I like to see a higher ratio (in the range of 1–3) to keep a cash cushion should the economy slow down.

Quick ratio

The quick ratio is frequently referred to as the "acid-test" ratio. It's a little more stringent than the current ratio in that you calculate it without inventory. I'll use the current ratio example discussed in the preceding section. What if half of the assets are inventory ($30,000 in this case)? Now what? First, here's the formula for the quick ratio:

Quick ratio = (Current assets – inventory) ÷ Current liabilities

In the example, the quick ratio for SHM is 1.5 ($60,000 minus $30,000 equals $30,000, which is then divided by $20,000). In other words, the company has $1.50 of "quick" liquid assets for each dollar of current liabilities. This amount is okay. *Quick liquid assets* include any money in the bank, marketable securities, and accounts receivable. If quick liquid assets at the very least equal or exceed total current liabilities, that amount is considered adequate.

The acid-test that this ratio reflects is embodied in the question, "Can the company pay its bills when times are tough?" In other words, if the company can't sell its goods (inventory), can it still meet its short-term liabilities? Of course, you must watch the accounts receivable as well. If the economy is entering rough times, you want to make sure that the company's customers are paying invoices on a timely basis.

Operating Ratios

Operating ratios essentially measure a company's efficiency. "How well is the company managing its resources?" is a question commonly answered with operating ratios. If, for example, a company sells products, does it have too much inventory? If it does, that could impair the company's operations. The following sections present common operating ratios.

Return on equity (ROE)

Equity is the amount left from total assets after you account for total liabilities. (This can also be considered a profitability ratio.) The *net equity* (also known as shareholders' equity, stockholders' equity, or net worth) is the bottom line on the company's balance sheet, both geographically and figuratively. It's calculated as

Return on equity (ROE) = Net income ÷ Net equity

The *net income* (from the company's income statement) is simply the total income less total expenses. Net income that isn't spent, distributed in dividends, or used up increases the company's net equity. Looking at net income is a great way to see whether the company's management is doing a good job growing the business. You can check this out by looking at the net equity from both the most recent balance sheet and the one from a year earlier. Ask yourself whether the current net equity is higher or lower than the year before. If it's higher, by what percentage is it higher?

For example, if SHM's net equity is $40,000 and its net income is $10,000, its ROE is a robust 25 percent (net income of $10,000 divided by net equity of $40,000). The higher the ROE, the better. An ROE that exceeds 10 percent (for simplicity's sake) is good, especially in a slow and struggling economy. Use the ROE in conjunction with the ROA ratio in the following section to get a fuller picture of a company's activity.

Return on assets (ROA)

The return on assets (ROA) may seem similar to the ROE in the preceding section, but it actually gives a perspective that completes the picture when coupled with the ROE. The formula for figuring out the ROA is

Return on assets = Net income ÷ Total assets

The ROA reflects the relationship between a company's profit and the assets used to generate that profit. If SHM makes a profit of $10,000 and has total assets of $100,000, the ROA is 10 percent. This percentage should be as high as possible, but it will generally be less than the ROE.

WARNING

Say that a company has an ROE of 25 percent but an ROA of only 5 percent. Is that good? It sounds okay, but a problem exists. An ROA that's much lower than the ROE indicates that the higher ROE may have been generated by something other than total assets — debt! The use of debt can be a leverage to maximize the ROE, but if the ROA doesn't show a similar percentage of efficiency, then the company may have incurred too much debt. In that case, investors should be aware that this situation can cause problems (see the later section "Solvency Ratios"). Better ROA than DOA!

Sales-to-receivables ratio (SR)

The sales-to-receivables ratio (SR) gives investors an indication of a company's ability to manage what customers owe it. This ratio uses data from both the income statement (sales) and the balance sheet (accounts receivable, or AR). The formula is expressed as

Sales-to-receivables ratio = Sales ÷ Receivables

Say that you have the following data for SHM:

Sales in 2019 are $75,000. On 12/31/19, receivables stood at $25,000.

Sales in 2020 are $80,000. On 12/31/20, receivables stood at $50,000.

Based on this data, you can figure out that sales went up 6.7 percent (sales in 2020 are $5,000 higher than 2019, and $5,000 is 6.7 percent of $75,000), but receivables went up 100 percent (the $25,000 in 2019 doubled to $50,000, which is a move up of 100 percent)!

In 2019, the SR was 3 ($75,000 divided by $25,000). However, the SR in 2020 sank to 1.6 ($80,000 divided by $50,000), or was nearly cut in half. Yes, sales did increase, but the company's ability to collect money due from customers fell dramatically. This information is important to notice for one main reason: What good is selling more when you can't get the money? From a cash flow point of view, the company's financial situation deteriorated.

Solvency Ratios

Solvency just means that a company isn't overwhelmed by its liabilities. Insolvency means "Oops! Too late." You get the point. Solvency ratios have never been more important than they are now because the American economy is currently carrying so much debt. Solvency ratios look at the relationship between what a company owns and what it owes. The following sections discuss two of the primary solvency ratios.

Debt-to-net-equity ratio

The debt-to-net-equity ratio answers the question, "How dependent is the company on debt?" In other words, it tells you how much the company owes and how much it owns. You calculate it as follows:

Debt-to-net-equity ratio = Total liabilities ÷ Net equity

If SHM has $100,000 in debt and $50,000 in net equity, the debt-to-net-equity ratio is 2. The company has $2 of debt to every dollar of net equity. In this case, what the company owes is twice the amount of what it owns.

WARNING

Whenever a company's debt-to-net-equity ratio exceeds 1 (as in the example), that isn't good. In fact, the higher the number, the more negative the situation. If the number is too high and the company isn't generating enough income to cover the debt, the business runs the risk of bankruptcy.

Working capital

Technically, working capital isn't a ratio, but it does belong to the list of things that serious investors look at. *Working capital* measures a company's current assets in relation to its current liabilities. It's a simple equation:

Working capital = Total current assets – Total current liabilities

The point is obvious: Does the company have enough to cover the current bills? Actually, you can formulate a useful ratio. If current assets are $25,000 and current liabilities are $25,000, that's a 1-to-1 ratio, which is cutting it close. Current assets should be at least 50 percent higher than current liabilities (say, $1.50 to $1.00) to have enough cushion to pay bills and have some money for other purposes. Preferably, the ratio should be 2 to 1 or higher.

Common Size Ratios

Common size ratios offer simple comparisons. You have common size ratios for both the balance sheet (where you compare total assets) and the income statement (where you compare total sales):

>> **To get a common size ratio from a balance sheet,** the total assets figure is assigned the percentage of 100 percent. Every other item on the balance sheet is represented as a percentage of total assets.

- Total assets equal 100 percent. All other items equal a percentage of the total assets.

For example, if SHM has total assets of $10,000 and debt of $3,000, then debt equals 30 percent (debt divided by total assets, or $3,000 divided by $10,000, which equals 30 percent).

>> **To get a common size ratio from an income statement** (or profit and loss statement), you compare total sales.

- Total sales equal 100 percent. All other items equal a percentage of the total sales.

For example, if SHM has $50,000 in total sales and a net profit of $8,000, then you know that the profit equals 16 percent of total sales ($8,000 divided by $50,000, which equals 16 percent).

REMEMBER

Keep in mind the following points with common size ratios:

>> **Net profit:** What percentage of sales is it? What was it last year? How about the year before? What percentage of increases (or decreases) is the company experiencing?

>> **Expenses:** Are total expenses in line with the previous year? Are any expenses going out of line?

>> **Net equity:** Is this item higher or lower than the year before?

>> **Debt:** Is this item higher or lower than the year before?

REMEMBER

Common size ratios are used to compare the company's financial data not only with prior balance sheets and income statements but also with other companies in the same industry. You want to make sure that the company is not only doing better historically but also as a competitor in the industry.

Valuation Ratios

Understanding the value of a stock is very important for stock investors. The quickest and most efficient way to judge the value of a company is to look at valuation ratios. The type of value that you deal with throughout this book is the *market value* (essentially the price of the company's stock). You hope to buy it at one price and sell it later at a higher price — that's the name of the game. But what's the best way to determine whether what you're paying for now is a bargain or is fair market value? How do you know whether your stock investment is undervalued or overvalued? The valuation ratios in the following sections can help you answer these questions. In fact, they're the same ratios that value investors have used with great success for many years.

Price-to-earnings ratio (P/E)

The price-to-earnings ratio (P/E) can double as a profitability ratio because it's a common barometer of value that many investors and analysts look at. I cover this topic in Chapter 11, but because it's such a critical ratio, I also include it here. The formula is

P/E ratio = Price (per share) ÷ Earnings (per share)

For example, if SHM's stock price per share is $10 and the earnings per share are $1, the P/E ratio is 10 (10 divided by 1).

REMEMBER

The P/E ratio answers the question, "Am I paying too much for the company's earnings?" Value investors find this number to be very important. Here are some points to remember:

>> Generally, the lower the P/E ratio, the better (from a financial strength point of view). Frequently, a low P/E ratio indicates that the stock is undervalued, especially if the company's sales are growing and the industry is also growing. But you may occasionally encounter a situation where the stock price is falling faster than the company's earnings, which would also generate a low P/E. And if the company has too much debt and the industry is struggling, then a low P/E may indicate that the company is in trouble. Use the P/E as part of your analysis along with other factors (such as debt, for instance) to get a more complete picture.

>> A company with a P/E ratio significantly higher than its industry average is a red flag that its stock price is too high (or that it's growing faster than its competitors). If the industry's P/E ratio is typically in the range of 10–12 and you're evaluating a stock whose P/E ratio is around 20, then you may want to consider avoiding it. A company's P/E ratio not only needs to be taken in context with its industry peers but also based on its year-over-year performance.

>> Don't invest in a company with no P/E ratio (it has a stock price, but the company experienced losses). Such a stock may be good for a speculator's portfolio but not for your retirement account.

>> Any stock with a P/E ratio higher than 40 should be considered a speculation and not an investment. Frequently, a high P/E ratio indicates that the stock is overvalued.

TIP

When you buy a company, you're really buying its power to make money. In essence, you're buying its earnings (net profit). Paying for a stock that's priced at 10 to 20 times earnings is a conservative strategy that has served investors well for nearly a century. Make sure that the company is priced fairly, and use the P/E ratio in conjunction with other measures of value (such as the ratios in this appendix).

Price-to-sales ratio (PSR)

The price-to-sales ratio (PSR) helps to answer the question, "Am I paying too much for the company's stock based on the company's sales?" This is a useful valuation ratio that I recommend using as a companion tool with the company's P/E ratio (see the preceding section). You calculate it as follows:

PSR = Stock price (per share) ÷ Total sales (per share)

This ratio can be quoted on a per-share basis or on an aggregate basis. For example, if a company's market value (or market capitalization) is $1 billion and annual sales are also $1 billion, the PSR is 1. If the market value in this example is $2 billion and annual sales are $1 billion, then the PSR is 2. Or, if the share price is $76 and the total sales per share are $38, the PSR is 2 — you arrive at the same ratio whether you calculate on a per-share or aggregate basis. For investors trying to make sure that they're not paying too much for the stock, the general rule is that the lower the PSR, the better. Stocks with a PSR of 2 or lower are considered very undervalued, but typically look for under 3 or 4.

WARNING

Be very hesitant about buying a stock with a PSR greater than 5. If you buy a stock with a PSR of 5, you're paying $5 for each dollar of sales — not exactly a bargain.

Price-to-book ratio (PBR)

No, this doesn't have anything to do with beer, although I am enjoying a cold Pabst Blue Ribbon as I write this! The price-to-book ratio (PBR) compares a company's market value to its accounting (or book) value. The book value refers to the company's net equity (assets minus liabilities). The company's market value is usually dictated by external factors such as supply and demand in the stock market. The book value is indicative of the company's internal operations. Value investors see the PBR as another way of valuing the company to determine whether they're paying too much for the stock. The formula is

Price-to-book ratio (PBR) = Market value ÷ Book value

An alternative method is to calculate the ratio on a per-share basis, which yields the same ratio. If the company's stock price is $20 and the book value (per share) is $15, then the PBR is 1.33. In other words, the company's market value is 33 percent higher than its book value. Investors seeking an undervalued stock like to see the market value as close as possible to (or even better, below) the book value.

REMEMBER

Keep in mind that the PBR may vary depending on the industry and other factors. Also, judging a company solely on book value may be misleading because many companies have assets that aren't adequately reflected in the book value. Software companies are a good example. Intellectual properties, such as copyrights and trademarks, are very valuable yet aren't fully covered in book value. Just bear in mind that generally, the lower the market value is in relation to the book value, the better for you (especially if the company has strong earnings, and the outlook for the industry is positive). Don't let the PBR be a "showstopper" because there are many excellent companies where the PBR could be 5 (or more) to 1. Let the PBR confirm your choice when other ratios in this appendix look good.

Index

Numbers

52-week high/low, 80–81
401(k) plans, 25, 292–293

A

account executive, 91
accounting, 71–76
  overview, 71
  principles of, 72–73
accounting fraud, 271
accounting value, 147
accounts receivable, 156
accumulate recommendation, 98
actively managed funds, 60
ADRs. *See* American Depositary Receipts
advanced orders, 238
aggressive investing, 39–40, 56
Ally, 94
Amazon (AMZN), 185
American Depositary Receipts (ADRs), 197, 248–250
  currency conversion, 249
  taxation, 249–250
American Stock Exchange (Amex), 70
annual growth rate, 17
annual report, 164–169
  company identity data, 168
  company's offerings, 166–167
  CPA opinion letter, 168
  financial statements, 167
  letter from chairman of board, 165–166
  management issues, 168
  stock data, 168
  summary of past financial figures, 168
appreciating assets, 21–22
appreciation, 36–37
artificial intelligence, 185
ascending triangle pattern, 140
asset allocation motifs, 198
assets

allocation, 58
  on balance sheet, 16–18
  calculating net worth with, 72
automobiles, 18, 188
avoid recommendation, 98

B

baby boomers, 321
bailouts, 203
balance sheet, 150–153
  analyzing, 150–152
  in annual report, 167
  common size ratio from, 350
  judging financial strength of company, 152–153
  overview, 72, 148
  preparing, 14–22
    emergency fund, 15
    liabilities, 18–20
    liquidity, 16–18
    net worth, 21
    overview, 21–22
Bank for International Settlements, 167
bankruptcy, 42, 322
bar charts, 137
Barron's, 95
BDCs (business development companies), 123–124
bear markets, 29, 149
  defined, 13
  profiting in, 305–310
    bond ratings, 306–307
    call options, 309
    covered call options, 309–310
    dividends, 306
    finding good stocks, 305–306
    margin loans, 308
    patience, 310
    put options, 310
    sector rotation, 307
    short selling, 308

K

Kiplinger's Personal Finance, 95

L

lagging indicators, 141
large caps
  conservative investing and, 39
  defined, 11
Last10K.com, 170
laws, 211
leading economic indicators (LEI), 78, 141, 210
leverage, 239–240
liabilities
  analyzing, 152
  on balance sheet, 18–20
  calculating net worth with, 72
  stocks from companies with low, 299
limit orders, 193, 232, 237–238
line charts, 137
liquidity, 16–18
liquidity ratios, 346–347
listing fees, 70
loans, 18
long-term assets, 16
long-term goals, 28
long-term investing, 35–36, 130
long-term trends, 135
low-yield investments, 22

M

macro effect, 201
margin, buying on, 239–242
  guidelines, 241–242
  maintaining balance, 240–241
  marginal outcomes, 239–240
  overview, 239
margin accounts, 96–97
margin debt, 46
margin interest charges, 90
margin loans
  in bear markets, 308
  general discussion of, 22
  paying debt with, 264, 285

marijuana investing, 180–181, 185–186
market capitalization
  calculating, 146
  for investing goals, 32–33
  overview, 10–11
market makers, 99
market orders, 232–233
market perform recommendation, 98
market risk, 47–48
market value, 146–147, 351
MarketInOut, 222
MarketWatch, 54, 77, 118, 181, 207, 216
mega caps, 11
megatrends
  defined, 104
  as indicator of great stocks, 304
Merck, 106
metals, precious, 186–187, 323
MFs (mutual funds)
  comparing ETFs and, 60–62
  REITs and, 122–123
  sector mutual funds, 315
micro caps, 10, 190
Microsoft, 105
mid caps, 10
millennials, 321
Mises Institute, 207
Mish's Global Economic Trend Analysis, 207
monetary inflation, 210
money market fund, 50
Moody's Analytics, 207
Moody's Handbook of Common Stocks, 172
Morgan Stanley, 92
mortgages, 18
motif investing, 196–199, 315
  categories, 198–199
  examples of, 196–197
  features of, 198
  risks of, 199
moving averages, 222
mutual funds (MFs)
  comparing ETFs and, 60–62
  REITs and, 122–123
  sector mutual funds, 315

N

nano caps, 10

Nasdaq, 70, 194, 216

Nasdaq Composite, 66

National Association of Investors Corporation, 260

National Taxpayers Union, 79, 282

National Unemployment Report, 209

near-term trends, 134

negative interest rates, 45

Nestle, 248

net assets. *See* shareholders' equity

Net change, on stock tables, 84

net equity, 348

net gain, 286

net income, 72, 155, 348

net worth, 152

   calculating, 21, 72

   defined, 14

neutral recommendation, 98

New York Stock Exchange (NYSE), 70

newsletter recommendations, 109

niches, 105–106

nominal rate, 44

nonrecurring items, 157

nonsystemic effects, 204–205

NYSE (New York Stock Exchange), 70

NYSE American, 70

O

OCPs (optional cash payments), 262–263

Office of Government Ethics, 280

Office of the Comptroller of the Currency, 299, 323

O'Neill, William, 234

Online Gaming motif, 196

online references

   10K reports, 170

   access to annual reports, 164

   Ally, 94

   analysis, stock, 339–343

   balance sheets and income statements, 150

   Bank for International Settlements, 167

   BDCs, 124

   blogs, stock investing, 334–335

   Bloomberg, 20, 77, 118

   brokers, 94, 336–337

   Bureau of Labor Statistics, 209

   cheat sheet for this book, 4

   CIA World Fact Book, 66

   Conference Board, 210

   Congress, 79

   Department of Labor, 293

   dividend reinvestment plans, 339

   economic data, 207, 211

   ETFs, 64, 338–339

   fee-based investment sources, 337–338

   Fidelity, 94

   financial planning sources, 327–328

   Financial Times, 66

   FINRA, 90–91

   fraud, 343–344

   general investing websites, 77, 332–333

   How the Market Works, 55

   indexes, 65

   industries, 181

   insider forms, 271

   international investing, 255–256

   investor associations and organizations, 335

   Investor's Business Daily, 77

   language of investing, 328

   MarketWatch, 54, 77, 118

   megatrends, 182

   money market funds, 21

   motif investing, 315

   Nasdaq, 71

   National Taxpayers Union, 79

   New York Stock Exchange (NYSE), 71

   Office of Government Ethics, 280

   periodicals and magazines, 329

   Sarbanes-Oxley Act (SOX), 271

   savings bonds, 314

   screening tools, 158, 216, 222, 224

   SEC, 90–91

   sectors, 181

   SIPC, 90–91

   small cap stocks, 194

   socialism and economics, 324

   stock exchanges, 335

profit
  on income statement, 156–157
  stocks from companies with rising, 297–298
profit and loss statement. *See* income statement
prospectus, 259, 265
proxy statement, 169
PSR (price-to-sales ratio)
  overview, 353
  for potential stock investment, 160–161
  on screening tools, 221
Public Law 112-105, 280
public officials, 79
Public Register's Annual Report Service, 164
Publication 17, 287
purchasing power risk, 48
put options, 64, 310, 312

Q

qualified dividends, 283
quick liquid assets, 347
quick ratio, 347

R

R&D (research and development), 106, 121, 154
ratios, 157–161, 345–354
  during bear markets, 306
  common size, 350–351
  liquidity, 346–347
  operating, 347–349
  overview, 149, 345–346
  price-to-earnings (P/E) ratio, 158–160
    checking value of companies with, 300
    general discussion of, 50–51, 52
    on screening tools, 220
    on stock tables, 84
  price-to-sales ratio (PSR), 160–161
  solvency, 349–350
  valuation, 351–354
real estate, 16, 46
real estate investment trusts (REITs), 122–123
reallocating, 23, 52
recessionary GDP, 209
recessions, 209

recommendations from brokers, 98–100
  asking questions, 99–100
  overview, 98
region-specific ETFs, 253–254
registered rep, 91
Regulation T, 241
REITs (real estate investment trusts), 122–123
Relative Strength Index (RSI), 141–142, 222
research and development (R&D), 106, 121, 154
resistance, 135–136
restricted stock, 271
retirement
  dividend-paying ETFs, 63
  income stocks, 111, 113
  investing, 290–293
    401(k) plans, 292–293
    Individual Retirement Accounts (IRAs), 291–292
  megatrend of aging, 182
  Social Security spending, 322
return, risk versus, 57–58
return on assets (ROA), 348
return on equity (ROE), 107–108, 348
return on investment (ROI), 221–222
reverse head and shoulders, 139
reverse stock splits, 279
Rising Food Prices motif, 196
risk, 41–58. *See also* beta; volatility
  general discussion of, 8
  minimizing, 54–56
    diversification, 55–56
    gaining knowledge, 54
    personal financial security, 55
    simulated stock investing, 54–55
  of motif investing, 199
  overview, 41–42
  return versus, 57–58
  types of, 42–52
    emotional risk, 50–51
    financial risk, 42–43
    inflation risk, 48
    interest rate risk, 44–47
    market risk, 47–48
    personal risk, 49–50
    political and governmental risk, 49
    tax risk, 48

About the Author

Paul Mladjenovic is a Certified Financial Planner (CFP), national speaker, educator, author, and consultant. Since 1981, he has specialized in investing, financial planning, and home business issues. During those nearly four decades, he has helped hundreds of thousands of students and readers build wealth through his nationwide seminars, workshops, conferences, and coaching program. Paul has been a CFP since June 1985 (over 35 years).

Besides this book (this edition and all prior editions), Paul has written *High-Level Investing For Dummies, Micro-Entrepreneurship For Dummies, Zero-Cost Marketing, Precious Metals Investing For Dummies,* and *The Job Hunter's Encyclopedia.* In 2019, he co-authored *Affiliate Marketing For Dummies.* His national (and online) seminars include "The $50 Wealth-Builder," "Ultra-Investing with Options," and the "Home Business Goldmine," among others. The full details on his (downloadable) financial and business startup audio seminars can be found at www.RavingCapitalist.com. A page at this site (www.RavingCapitalist.com/stocks) provides resources and views to help readers navigate today's uncertain markets and gives them a venue for questions. His online courses can also be found at educational venues such as Udemy.com, Skillshare.com, Freeu.com, and MtAiryLearningTree.org.

Since 2000, Paul has built a reputation as an accurate economics and market forecaster. His long record includes accurate forecasts of the housing bubble, the energy crisis, the great recession, the rise of precious metals, and much more. He has been interviewed or referenced by numerous media sources, such as Comcast, CNN, MarketWatch, Bloomberg, OANN, Fox Business, *Futures* magazine, Kitco, GoldSeek.com, Investopedia, Minyanville.com, FinancialSense.com, PreciousMetalsInvesting.com, and other media venues.

You can view Paul's profile at www.linkedin.com/in/paulmladjenovic/ and follow him at www.twitter.com/paulmlad, and you can also check out the author's page at www.amazon.com/author/paulmladjenovic. I invite readers to email questions or inquiries directly to paul@mladjenovic.com or at the bio page at www.RavingCapitalist.com.

Author's Acknowledgments

First and foremost, I offer my appreciation and gratitude to the wonderful folks at Wiley. It has been a pleasure to work with such a top-notch organization that works so hard to create products that offer readers tremendous value and information. I wish all of you continued success! Wiley has some notables whom I want to single out.

Michelle Hacker, my project manager, is the sensational pro who guided me throughout. I truly appreciate her professional guidance (and patience!), which helped me get through this sixth edition. Thank you for being fantastic!

A very special thanks to Georgette Beatty, my development editor, who is a magnificent professional whom I have had the pleasure and honor of working with on several books. I thank you for being so good to me and with me!

Christy Pingleton, I thank this great copy editor for taking my mush of words and turning them into worthy messages.

The technical editor, James Taibleson, was very detailed and spot on with his suggestions and constructive comments — it is no wonder he is a fantastic financial advisor and educator!

With deep and joyful gratitude, I thank Tracy Boggier, my superb acquisitions editor. Thank you so much for being my champion at Wiley and shepherding yet another *For Dummies* guide for me to author, and I can't express enough appreciation for all that you do. *For Dummies* books are great, and they appear on your bookshelf only through the planning and professional efforts of publishing pros like Tracy.

I am grateful to my book agents Sheree Bykofsky and Janet Rosen, two of the best pros on the planet! Their guidance and assistance made this book (and many others) arrive in the Wiley universe, and I appreciate all that they do.

Fran, Lipa Zyenska, thank you and my boys, Adam and Joshua, with all my heart for your support and being my number one fans throughout the writing of this book. I am grateful to have you by my side always! I thank God for you, and I love you beyond words!

Lastly, I want to acknowledge you, the reader. Over the years, you've made the *For Dummies* series the popular and indispensable books they are today. Thank you, and I wish you continued success!

Publisher's Acknowledgments

Senior Acquisitions Editor: Tracy Boggier
Project Manager: Michelle Hacker
Development Editor: Georgette Beatty
Copy Editor: Christine Pingleton
Technical Editor: James A. Taibleson

Production Editor: Magesh Elangovan
Cover Image: © JVE001/Shutterstock

Take dummies with you everywhere you go!

Whether you are excited about e-books, want more from the web, must have your mobile apps, or are swept up in social media, dummies makes everything easier.

Find us online!

dummies.com

dummies
A Wiley Brand

Leverage the power

Dummies is the global leader in the reference category and one of the most trusted and highly regarded brands in the world. No longer just focused on books, customers now have access to the dummies content they need in the format they want. Together we'll craft a solution that engages your customers, stands out from the competition, and helps you meet your goals.

Advertising & Sponsorships

Connect with an engaged audience on a powerful multimedia site, and position your message alongside expert how-to content. Dummies.com is a one-stop shop for free, online information and know-how curated by a team of experts.

- Targeted ads
- Video
- Email Marketing
- Microsites
- Sweepstakes sponsorship

20 MILLION PAGE VIEWS EVERY SINGLE MONTH

15 MILLION UNIQUE VISITORS PER MONTH

43% OF ALL VISITORS ACCESS THE SITE VIA THEIR MOBILE DEVICES

700,000 NEWSLETTER SUBSCRIPTIONS TO THE INBOXES OF

300,000 UNIQUE INDIVIDUALS EVERY WEEK

# of dummies

Custom Publishing

Reach a global audience in any language by creating a solution that will differentiate you from competitors, amplify your message, and encourage customers to make a buying decision.

- Apps
- Books
- eBooks
- Video
- Audio
- Webinars

Brand Licensing & Content

Leverage the strength of the world's most popular reference brand to reach new audiences and channels of distribution.

For more information, visit dummies.com/biz

PERSONAL ENRICHMENT

Staying Sharp	**Facebook**	**Guitar**	**Investing**	**Beekeeping**	**Digital Photography**
9781119187790	9781119179030	9781119293354	9781119293347	9781119310068	9781119235606
USA $26.00	USA $21.99	USA $24.99	USA $22.99	USA $22.99	USA $24.99
CAN $31.99	CAN $25.99	CAN $29.99	CAN $27.99	CAN $27.99	CAN $29.99
UK £19.99	UK £16.99	UK £17.99	UK £16.99	UK £16.99	UK £17.99

Meditation	**Pregnancy**	**Samsung Galaxy S7**	**iPhone**	**Crocheting**	**Nutrition**
9781119251163	9781119235491	9781119279952	9781119283133	9781119287117	9781119130246
USA $24.99	USA $26.99	USA $24.99	USA $24.99	USA $24.99	USA $22.99
CAN $29.99	CAN $31.99	CAN $29.99	CAN $29.99	CAN $29.99	CAN $27.99
UK £17.99	UK £19.99	UK £17.99	UK £17.99	UK £16.99	UK £16.99

PROFESSIONAL DEVELOPMENT

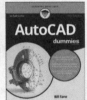

Windows 10	**AutoCAD**	**Excel 2016**	**QuickBooks 2017**	**macOS Sierra**	**LinkedIn**	**Windows 10 ALL-IN-ONE**
9781119311041	9781119255796	9781119293439	9781119281467	9781119280651	9781119251132	9781119310563
USA $24.99	USA $39.99	USA $26.99	USA $26.99	USA $29.99	USA $24.99	USA $34.00
CAN $29.99	CAN $47.99	CAN $31.99	CAN $31.99	CAN $35.99	CAN $29.99	CAN $41.99
UK £17.99	UK £27.99	UK £19.99	UK £19.99	UK £21.99	UK £17.99	UK £24.99

SharePoint 2016	**Fundamental Analysis**	**Networking**	**Office 2016**	**Office 365**	**Salesforce.com**	**Coding**
9781119181705	9781119263593	9781119257769	9781119293477	9781119265313	9781119239314	9781119293323
USA $29.99	USA $26.99	USA $29.99	USA $26.99	USA $24.99	USA $29.99	USA $29.99
CAN $35.99	CAN $31.99	CAN $35.99	CAN $31.99	CAN $29.99	CAN $35.99	CAN $35.99
UK £21.99	UK £19.99	UK £21.99	UK £19.99	UK £17.99	UK £21.99	UK £21.99

dummies.com

dummies
A Wiley Brand

Learning Made Easy

ACADEMIC

9781119293576
USA $19.99
CAN $23.99
UK £15.99

9781119293637
USA $19.99
CAN $23.99
UK £15.99

9781119293491
USA $19.99
CAN $23.99
UK £15.99

9781119293460
USA $19.99
CAN $23.99
UK £15.99

9781119293590
USA $19.99
CAN $23.99
UK £15.99

9781119215844
USA $26.99
CAN $31.99
UK £19.99

9781119293378
USA $22.99
CAN $27.99
UK £16.99

9781119293521
USA $19.99
CAN $23.99
UK £15.99

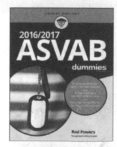

9781119239178
USA $18.99
CAN $22.99
UK £14.99

9781119263883
USA $26.99
CAN $31.99
UK £19.99

Available Everywhere Books Are Sold

dummies.com

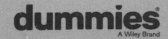
dummies®
A Wiley Brand

Small books for big imaginations

GETTING STARTED WITH Coding
Get Creative with Code!
Camille McCue, PhD

9781119177173
USA $9.99
CAN $9.99
UK £8.99

MODDING Minecraft™
Build Your Own Minecraft Mods!
Sarah Guthals, PhD
Stephen Foster, PhD
Lindsay Handley, PhD

9781119177272
USA $9.99
CAN $9.99
UK £8.99

MAKING YouTube® VIDEOS
Star in Your Own Video!
Nick Willoughby

9781119177241
USA $9.99
CAN $9.99
UK £8.99

DESIGNING Digital Games
Create Games with Scratch™!
Derek Breen

9781119177210
USA $9.99
CAN $9.99
UK £8.99

GETTING STARTED WITH Raspberry Pi®
Program Your Raspberry Pi!
Richard Wentk

9781119262657
USA $9.99
CAN $9.99
UK £6.99

WRITING Computer Code
Learn the Language of Computers!
Chris Minnick and Eva Holland

9781119177302
USA $9.99
CAN $9.99
UK £8.99

4/2021

$26.99

LONGWOOD PUBLIC LIBRARY
800 Middle Country Road
Middle Island, NY 11953
(631) 924-6400
longwoodlibrary.org

LIBRARY HOURS

Monday-Friday	9:30 a.m. - 9:00 p.m.
Saturday	9:30 a.m. - 5:00 p.m.
Sunday (Sept-June)	1:00 p.m. - 5:00 p.m.

dummies.co

dummies
A Wiley B...